BURNING
HERESIES

SAINTE DEN STOC

WITHDRAWN FROM DÚN LAOGHAIRE-RATHDOWN
COUNTY LIBRARY STOCK

BURNING
HERESIES

A MEMOIR
OF A LIFE
IN CONFLICT
1979–2020

KEVIN MYERS

MERRION
PRESS

First published in 2020 by
Merrion Press
10 George's Street
Newbridge
Co. Kildare
Ireland
www.merrionpress.ie

© Kevin Myers, 2020

9781785372612 (Paper)
9781785372629 (Kindle)
9781785372636 (Epub)

A CIP catalogue record for this book is
available from the British Library.

All rights reserved. No part of this publication may be reproduced,
stored in a retrieval system, or transmitted, in any form or by any
means (electronic, mechanical, photocopying, recording or
otherwise), without the prior written permission of both
the copyright owner and the publisher of this book.

Typeset in Adobe Garamond Pro 11.5/15 pt

Merrion Press is a member of Publishing Ireland.

'It is an heretic that makes the fire, not she which burns in it.'

– Paulina, *The Winter's Tale*
William Shakespeare

Acknowledgements

TO THOSE WHO stood loyally by me when the mob rampaged – foremost of all, the Jewish people of Ireland, and then, of course, my lovely Rachel, the Myers, Teevan and Nolan families, the Chaps, John Wilson, few journalists save Mary, Mary Ellen, Ruth, Lionel, Niamh, Eoghan and Ben, a smaller group of friends than I would have believed possible, my agent, Jonathan Williams, and all at Merrion Press.

Prologue

EACH TUESDAY, I would email ideas back and forth with my page editor from the *Sunday Times* Ireland edition. On this particular Tuesday, both the last of July 2017 and of my career as a newspaper columnist, I told him that either of two related subjects would be my preferred choice for the following Sunday. One was the absurdity of one wing of the Irish Defence Forces, the Army, being warned to prepare for terrorist attacks while another, the Naval Service, was promiscuously ferrying thousands of unscreened migrants from the Libyan coast to Italy. The second option was the story of Ashers bakery in Belfast rejecting a request to ice a wedding cake with 'Support Gay Marriage'. Either would have slotted neatly into the broader subject of the culture wars that have made rational discussion on so many subjects virtually impossible.

My page editor then strongly urged me to write about the gender pay row in the BBC: 'So what about this gender pay row.' He then cited the random example of a fictional woman who 'wants to work less hours than her male counterparts, slope off to have babies whenevs, and yet be paid exactly the same. Gwan.' I argued that the case had no relevance in Ireland, pointing out that two RTÉ presenters, Marian Finucane and Miriam O'Callaghan, were amongst the station's highest earners and, anyway, the story 'will be quite old by Sunday'. We then had a phone conversation on the subject. I pointed out that my brief was to write on Irish matters, not British ones, and I again reiterated my reluctance to cover the story. However, he did not relent and, in what was the greatest blunder of my life, I finally capitulated, and with catastrophic stupidity not merely agreed to go along with his wishes but did so in a disastrously jaunty vein. The column that resulted was, as I have consistently admitted since, hastily written and poorly thought-out, covering too many subjects with too many vague generalisations – or, by the standards of modern journalism, a pretty average piece.

I observed: 'The HR department – what used to be called "personnel" until people came to be considered as a metabolising, respiring form of mineral-ore – will probably tell you that men usually work harder, get sick less frequently and seldom get pregnant.'

The purpose of that tongue-in-cheek conclusion was to establish a wry tone for the piece throughout: namely, this is neither a Shakespearean sonnet nor the Gettysburg Address. Nonetheless, my generalisations were not plucked out of the ether. According to the British Office of National Statistics, women take about 42 per cent more sick leave than men, and the *British Medical Journal* had recently reported that Finnish women aged between forty and sixty took on average 46 per cent more short-term sick-leave than men. However, my observation was not meant to be a mathematical, QED assessment, but an impressionistic one, which might have different explanations. Comparable observations about men could equally have been made, but without the ferocious accusations of gender-hatred that were to follow.

I also observed that men *tended* to be more ambitious than women, but without providing any evidence, or indeed meaning that to be a compliment. In fact, I had researched this also, and knew that the CEOs of 95.2 per cent of the Fortune 500 companies (or 476 of them) were male. And is there a more depressing insight into male behaviour than that testosterone trinity of corporate ego, corporate drive and corporate jets (effectively spelling 'absentee-fathers') which such figures reveal? Then moving on to the BBC row itself, I mused that such male ambition perhaps explained how 'the deeply irritating jackanapes-on-steroids', Jeremy Vine, was earning a berserk £750,000 a year, adding that he must have one hell of an agent.

I continued: 'So, have the BBC's top women found a revolutionary new kind of negotiator that likes to start high and chisel downwards?

Is this amazing unter-agent dedicated to the concept of seeking ever-lower salaries for his/her clients, so earning a smaller commission for him/herself? And if such unter-agents actually exist, who is idiotic enough to employ them? The BBC's women presenters, apparently. I note that two of the best-paid women presenters in the BBC – Claudia Winkleman and Vanessa Feltz – with whose (no doubt) sterling work I am tragically unacquainted – are Jewish. Good for them. Jews are not generally noted for their insistence on selling their talent for the lowest possible price, which is the most useful measure there is of inveterate, lost-with-all-hands stupidity. I wonder: who are their agents? If they're the same ones who negotiated the pay for the women on the lower scales, then maybe the latter have found their true value in the marketplace.'

These words were intended as a compliment for the women's chutzpah, as well as a statement of the importance of agents. It did not occur to me that I might be playing into some objectionable Jewish stereotype. And I most certainly was not indulging in any anti-Semitism, because not merely is anti-Semitism the most ignoble of all the base prejudices, it is also utterly stupid. 22 per cent of all Nobel prizes have gone to Jews, though this group constitutes just 0.2 per cent of the world's population. There are no more exacting examinations of individual scruple and intellectual integrity than those set by the Nobel committees – and I already knew that amongst the greatest beneficiaries to humanity in the twentieth century were three Jewish scientists: Ernst Chain had effectively invented penicillin as an antibiotic (not Alexander Fleming, as myth proclaims), while Jonas Salk and Albert Sabin had separately created the two anti-polio vaccines which had eliminated that accursed disease from the face of the earth, as well as from my childhood. All three had disavowed any profits from their discoveries. Moreover, I was aware that Rabbi Julia Neuberger would be alongside me in a panel discussion at a conference in Cork that same Sunday, and such was my inability to detect what *others* might regard as offensive Jewish stereotypes that I even assumed she and I could share a little joke about my column. I filed my copy at 4.34 p.m. on Thursday, twenty hours before the usual deadline, headlining it 'Nice and early'.

One hour and forty minutes later, at 6.14 p.m., I received an email asking me how I knew the two women were Jewish, and what was my source.

I replied 'Wikipedia.'

So, clearly, my references to Winkleman and Feltz had not slipped under the editorial radar. Copy is read by five people: two editors in Dublin, and a contents editor, a lawyer and a subeditor in London. They had over forty-eight hours to assess my column before publication, and I got no more phone calls about it. I certainly had no hand in the creation of an inaccurate and needlessly provocative headline, 'Sorry, ladies – equal pay has to be earned,' which reflected neither the terminology of my article nor its central argument, which was not about earnings but negotiations.

The newspaper came online at 12.01 a.m. on 31 July 2017 and shortly thereafter the first attacks on it came from London, where someone had accessed my column, read it, and swiftly denounced it. The instantaneity of this suggests that some people had been tipped off from within *The Sunday Times*. Either way, the tweets started about my 'deeply offensive, misogynistic, anti-Semitic article'. Other tweeters duly responded, denouncing the Jew-hating, woman-despising creature Kevin Myers. Moods never moderate in such exchanges, their intensifying frenzies being untutored by fact and untroubled by truth.

At 9 a.m. in my hotel room in west Cork, still unaware of the internet horror show, I received a phone call from my page editor, who told me I was in trouble. I was astonished: for what? If anything, I assumed it was for my disrespectful remarks about Jeremy Vine. Soon, even though North Korea had fired a missile over Guam the night before, I was the lead news story on the BBC, and my 'anti-Semitism' was a 'fact'. Instead of standing up to the mob, the then editor of *The Sunday Times*, Martin Ivens, took down my column and issued a statement apologising for it. Around noon, I received a text asking me to phone the administrative manager of *The Sunday Times* in London. I did. He asked me no questions, sought no explanations, offered no due process, but curtly told me I was being sacked. Ivens never once spoke to me.

The newspaper then publicly announced that I would *never* work for it again, as if I had just been exposed as an undercover neo-Nazi agent, thereby rendering me a journalistic pariah all over the world – an unprecedented sentence in the history of the media in my lifetime. Matters grew rapidly worse as the online lies about me swiftly and malevolently mutated, next turning me into a Holocaust denier. Over the following fortnight, amid an inferno of falsehood, misrepresentation and internet lies, my career, my good name and my position in public life in Ireland were incinerated beyond recovery in the most merciless pyre of recent journalistic history.

This was not an accident. The Holocaust-denial allegations came mostly from a loosely connected cumulation of *Guardian*-connected journalists, one of whom is closely affiliated with the Irish Republican movement. On page 279 you may read more about how this despicable defamation proved to be even more successful than its instigators could possibly have hoped, but in the meantime, if you wish to discover something about the man whom these evil lies cast into reputational ruin across the English-speaking world, from Manchester to Miami and Melbourne – which I know, because I got emails from all three places – then please turn the page.

One

FLEET STREET, DUBLIN, noon, February 1979, and the dank grey sleet was enfolding me like a winding sheet of the dead as I scurried towards my first day of work at *The Irish Times*. I was dressed casually: jeans, open shirt, padded anorak. This was the house style of the *Irish Times* journalists not covering the Dáil or the courts. That, as much as anything else, says something about the newspaper and its workforce: a caste apart. Their rivals, from *The Irish Press* and the *Irish Independent*, as befits the journalistic wings of the two main political parties, Fianna Fáil and Fine Gael, tended to be attired in baggy-kneed suits, rather like country dads attending their children's first communions. *The Irish Times'* Protestant genes, still evident in the remaining Normans and Godfreys in the workforce, had mutated into a semi-Californian denim.

Litter lay everywhere. Lightning strikes had paralysed different arms of the public service: street sweepers one day, postal workers the next, then telephone operators, followed by binmen. That noontide, the brand-new, Irish-made Bombardier buses were sitting incontinently outside the *Irish Times* offices on Dublin's Fleet Street, their fuel pipes dripping diesel like shot-gunned oil barrels while their drivers kept revving their engines to maintain the pressure in their already-leaking hydraulic systems. Nothing, including me, seemed to function in this Ireland where I was about to embark on my new life. I was unaware that I was probably suffering from Post-Traumatic Stress Disorder (PTSD) after my years in Belfast. Some half-dozen people had been killed beside me, and I had seen too many others soon after death had claimed them. I was to remain clasped in the tentacles of PTSD for years to come – and perhaps still am. But I also knew that, from childhood, I was imbued an almost irresistible tendency to immerse myself in the soup.

The delightful imp of a man on security, Paddy Williams, had already been told of my arrival and he waved me through. I walked up to the newsroom on the second floor. Inside, it was like a London smog from the 1950s, with a sickly margarine-coloured luminescence seeping from light fittings overhead, the plastic casings of which were speckled with the blackened exoskeletons of hundreds of dead flies. The newsroom walls were painted in the nameless municipal hue of a Victorian mortuary, somewhere between pond algae and tortoise droppings. A few journalists were already working at large old communal desks, the fabric surfaces of which were peeling away in green, gum-lined strips. Cigarette smoke coiled up from plastic ashtrays everywhere, as if to repel malarial mosquitos. Huge mechanical typewriters were scattered between these little censers, but, as I was soon to discover, most of these were broken, and there was no known system for replacing them. They were abandoned where they lay, like battlefield casualties after a failed cavalry charge in Paraguay.

I went over to the news desk, and introduced myself to the news editor, Gerry Mulvey, a tiny, balding and aged creature, who looked as if he had been left out all night. He then introduced me to the human opposite, the newsroom secretary Seong Loh, who was young, Chinese and beautiful, shimmering with improbable glamour amid such funereal hues. I already knew most of the deputy news editors, including Nigel Brown and Pat Smiley, the human bladderwrack left by the receding tide of the Protestant demographic.

As I was soon to learn, the news desk staff did most of their work in the morning. A two-hour lunch break in Bowes pub usually followed, from which they would emerge carrying one another like the few bedraggled survivors of the Retreat from Kabul. Meanwhile, Seong held the fort at the news desk and the soberer citizens of the features and arts pages toiled within their tiny, airless offices opposite. One of these was Conor Brady, like me, a graduate of University College Dublin, but, unlike me, a man of singular purpose and unalloyed ambition. Other cubicles housed arts, with Brian Fallon and Fergus Linehan, and another deputy editor, Donal Foley, whom I already knew. As with so many journalists of the time, myself included, he belonged to the vapid, candy-mint tendency within the Irish media, whose green and pink stripes combined a soft Irish republicanism with an insincere and solipsistic socialism. Foley was also the author of a Saturday column, 'Man Bites Dog', subtitled 'A satirical column'. The explanation was often necessary.

The editor, Douglas Gageby, shared his office with Bruce Williamson, an alcoholic who – as I would learn – would spend the day furtively sipping on naggins of gin from his desk drawer, Ken Gray, another Protestant, and Denis Kennedy, a pugnaciously honest Ulsterman as straight on the page as the equator. A fifth eminence, Major Thomas McDowell, dwelt elsewhere, in offices that I would never once visit during all my decades at *The Irish Times*. Basically, three men – two Protestants (McDowell, Gageby) and a Catholic (Foley) – had supervised the transformation of the old *Irish Times* from a Protestant, unionist newspaper into one for the rising Catholic middle classes. This new market did not merely seek a change from the Civil War diet of the party-political rivals, the *Independent* and the *Press*; it also wanted a newspaper that would tell the unvarnished truth, and the erroneous belief amongst Catholics that Protestants were fundamentally more honest was the alchemy behind the newspaper's new-found success.

Gerry Mulvey – it being well before 3 p.m., the gnome was still sober – explained the system to me. Copy would be typed on one of the huge, upright typewriters – if you could find one that worked – and the top sheet would be sent to the subeditors, who would exercise their ineffable charm on it, or, as Gerry drily observed, would separate the nutritious wheat from the worthless chaff and throw away the former. I thought he was jesting. He wasn't. One carbon copy would go to the news editor's desk, and the second would be taken by copy boys into the editor's office. Under no circumstances was I *ever* to distribute these carbon copies myself. That would violate the Gutenbergian guild rules that still dominated the print industry and, if detected by a shop steward, would instantly shut down the newspaper, with the culprit being chained and dragged away to the stocks to be pelted with raw urchins.

I was shown to a desk in the farthest and most unilluminated corner of the newsroom and given some press statements to summarise. It was easy, and I soon delivered my copy to the news desk.

'Finished already?' said Gerry. 'You're a quick worker. I'll keep an eye on you.'

'Have you anything else for me?'

'Not at the moment. Relax. Read something.'

He then slid off to the pub. It was always my practice to carry a paperback novel – today it was Patrick O'Brian's *Desolation Island*. I began to read it.

'Gageby,' said a voice. I looked up, startled. The newspaper's editor was greeting me.

I half-rose, mumbling 'Kevin Myers,' and offering a hand.

He ignored it.

'What are you doing?'

'Reading.'

'Who's that? Patrick O'Brian? Never heard of him. Listen. We're not paying you to read *novels*. Have you no work to do?'

'No. 'fraid not.'

'Well find some,' he growled, his eyes glinting like sparks from struck flints, the sulphurous tang of his anger lingering in my nostrils as he walked away. So my professional life under Douglas Gageby began and it didn't get much better in the years to come. (I know that others will not like my picture of Gageby, but it is *my* picture.)

When my shift ended that evening, I returned to my freezing flat in Mountjoy Square, thinking that the success of my first day's work would be a prelude to more such shifts. I was in a bad way financially. The previous summer, I had taken the ferry to England to visit my mother, but, arriving late at Dún Laoghaire, I had to abandon my car in a side street. Most of my genes are my father's: face, build and general ineptitude. But in two regards I resemble her, having neither a sense of direction, nor any inhibition about talking to strangers. I fell into a deck-rail conversation with an elderly man originally from Carlow, but now, coincidentally, living in Leicester. He had been revisiting his homeplace to bury his brother.

I offered my condolences, and then asked how he liked Leicester.

'It's not a bad place. The cricket's good.'

'Why did you leave Ireland?'

'No choice. Ireland was no place for Protestants like us after 1922. We'd both served in the Great War. Which made us a sort of target. He went up north to Antrim, and I went to England. So many of our people were murdered or their homes were burnt in retaliation for policies and events over which we had no control.'

Incredibly, I rejected his claims, believing that only Northern Protestants were capable of such sectarian atrocities.

'You'd know better than me, I suppose,' he said in his soft Carlow tones. Decades of living abroad had not changed his accent. 'So why do you think we left? Why do you think my brother chose to be buried in Carlow rather than Antrim? My home is Carlow. My people are Carlow. I dream of Mount Leinster still. I like Leicestershire, but I love Carlow. Carlow just didn't love us.'

The understated passion behind this declaration silenced me.

'We would have settled for Home Rule under the likes of Colonel Murphy.'

'Colonel Murphy? Who was he?'

'An officer my brother and I served under in the Leinsters. The Murphys of Ballinamona.'

'Murphy? That's usually a Catholic name.'

'It is. Which is my point.' (I had naively assumed that back then there were no Irish Catholic officers in the British Army.)

A tear stood in his eye as the Wicklow Hills slid beneath the churning wake. I turned away. When we parted, it was for all time. Yet our oddly similar paths, back and forth, had been created by the strange bipolar magnetism of a beguiling-repellent island from which the Myers family had fled/been rejected before I was born. Only a series of accidents resulting from my father's death fifteen years before had brought me back to it, and now I was returning for the annual Myers family reunion in Leicester. Next day, we were having afternoon tea beneath the apple tree when the man painting the guttering at the front came racing round the side of the house.

'Ah say, could ya call the fire brigade? Yer 'ouse is on fire.'

This fool's blowtorch had flared under the bottom of the roof tiles, igniting the roof insulation. Anything that had not been destroyed by fire upstairs was ruined by the firemen's water. I spent the rest of the summer with my mother, as builders rebuilt. I had been given a £2,000 down payment from the house sale in Belfast; I gave her half the money and returned to Ireland. At Dún Laoghaire, I found my Triumph 2000, still on its side street, but now a wheelless hulk on bricks, leaving me carless and nearly cashless.

That had been the previous autumn. So, a fortnight after that first shift, not having heard from *The Irish Times*, I popped down to the newspaper's unofficial headquarters: Bowes pub. I pushed open the door and was assailed by the welcoming smells of stale stout, cloves, lemon, warm whiskey and the ancestral incense of burnt tobacco, infused into the walls and smeared on the light fittings in H-Block hues. It was an atmosphere that is as gone now as the breath of the Pharaohs, but at this stage in world history the toxic smoke from the burning leaves of *Nicotiana Tabacum* was what mankind breathed whenever taking alcohol in public.

A votary of this suicide cult was now propped up on a high stool by the counter. It was Bruce Williamson, assistant editor of *The Irish Times*, looking slightly under 600, with grizzled stubble pushing through the greyness of a ghastly hangover. A cigarette trembled in his hand, before it fell from his sad, fatly unretentive fingers as he conferred with a footbath of gin.

I moved down the bar, to where Gerry Mulvey was sinking a pint – no, actually, the pint was sinking him.

'Douglas doesn't like you,' Gerry said, when I asked about work prospects. 'He caught you reading.'

'But you said I could.'

'There's another casual he's asked me to bring in instead of you. A Northern lad. Would you like a drink to drown your sorrows?'

There's no such thing as alcoholic singularity in a Dublin pub. Instead, I headed for the National Library, where I had been going through the 49,400 names on the Memorial Records of the Irishmen killed in the Great War. It had quickly become clear that the number of Irish casualties had been inflated by its main compiler, the unionist Eva Bernard, presumably to create the impression that Britain owed more to Ireland's loyalty than London was disposed to feel. Whenever the sheer onerousness of analysing all those names, with regiments, decorations, places of birth, residence and enlistment became unbearable, I would browse through the pertinent regimental histories. Now I put in a requisition docket for Frederick Ernest Whitton's *History of the Prince of Wales's Leinster Regiment*.

I sat at a numbered desk with a green-shaded reading light, waiting for one of the porters – who by this time knew me well – to attend to the docket. He duly arrived.

'Your books,' he whispered with confidential menace, 'about these *traitors*. Tell me this. Why do you never order some books about real Irishmen, real heroes, true patriots, the men of 1916, rather than these blackguards, shoneens and wastrels?'

He glared before stalking away, his back straight, his patriotic duty done. Though perhaps decades old, Whitton's volume still had uncut pages, indicating that I was the first person ever to consult it. I carefully separated the bound sheets and began to read this account of Irish nationalists serving the Crown. Finally, I came to the officer whom Whitton acclaimed as the regiment's war hero, Lieutenant Colonel Alfred Durham Murphy, the very fellow mentioned by my Carlow friend. He had won the Distinguished Service Order and the Military Cross, but had not been awarded the Victoria Cross for which he had been recommended. At the time of his death in 1917, this half-colonel was just *twenty-seven*. Younger than me.

I worked for the rest of the day, and then popped into a supermarket to restock my kitchen, and now, too overburdened to walk, joined a bus queue, where I stood for an hour amid the litter that covered the streets like sun-bleached seaweed after an Atlantic storm. Word came that the bus drivers were on strike. *Fuck it, I'll get a taxi.* For another hour, I stood at the cab rank, my arms clinging to the supermarket paper bags, before hearing that the taxi drivers were also on strike. I started walking home. Of course, it began to rain. My paper bags dissolved, and, one by one, all of my shopping – including my precious bottle of wine – fell to the ground. I rescued a couple of eggs and returned to my flat at 15 Mountjoy Square, above the Family Planning clinic. Its ill-fitting windows meant that it resembled Portrush seafront during the January gales. Naturally, my recently bought second-hand Superser gas heater wouldn't light. I fried the two eggs, ate them with a blanket wrapped around me and wondered: here I was, dear sweet Jesus Christ almighty, older than Lieutenant Colonel Alfred Durham Murphy DSO MC – how on earth had I been reduced to this?

My lot, my flat, my landlord and this part of Dublin were all emblematic of the fate of Ireland. I was living in a dilapidated Georgian square that resembled Berlin in 1945, with about half the houses missing, above a clinic which promiscuously dispensed condoms in a country where the unrestricted sale of condoms was illegal. How? Because they were not actually *sold*. Customers were given the condoms without charge and were *invited* to make a voluntary contribution to the welfare of the clinic. Within this penile colony, the state had declared its moral authority over its citizens' genitalia, but had then declined to assert it, thus allowing its less abject subjects to assert their gonadical independence.

Yet the state still exercised its power over the minds of the Irish people through rigorous censorship – the British feminist publication *Spare Rib*, for example, was regularly banned because it gave contraceptive advice. No wonder people felt such contempt for government generally, a contempt they expressed in wildcat strikes, both for good causes or no cause at all – it was usually hard to tell the difference. The postal strike meant no mail. With the banks also on strike, cheques were scribbled with a Weimarian frenzy, almost regardless of the financial *Götterdämmerung* that would one day follow. And of course there was rubbish everywhere.

In my Great War project, I had written to every single Irish newspaper, all sixty-five of them, asking for veterans to contact me, but now, because of a postal strike, any replies were stranded in sorting offices like litter in rock pools at low tide. One evening, I cycled up along the Liffey, looking for Edwin Lutyens' Memorial Park at Islandbridge, created to commemorate the Irish dead of the Great War, but no one I asked knew what I was talking about. I could have been asking for directions to the Great Pyramid of Giza. In one of the greatest cultural and moral scandals of its short history, independent Ireland had closed ranks in amnesiac solidarity against any memory of the 49,400 names the park had been built to honour; although by this time I already knew that the true number of Irish dead was probably thousands below that figure. Nonetheless, even though this was by far the largest number of Irishmen killed in a single war, all public recollection of it had perished.

'Th'ould war memorial?' one rheumatic Methuselah volunteered. 'Sure that's long gone. It's the Corpo tiphead these days.'

The circling gulls now made it easy to spot. Dublin Corporation had turned the memorial park into a vast rubbish dump, alongside which an itinerant encampment, as it would have been called in those days, had sprung up. Corporation lorries were reversing into the dump and unloading the city's detritus with a feverish incontinence that suggested that another strike was imminent. Traveller children were scavenging over the tons of waste like famished Sherpas upon a Nepalese mountainside, and piebald ponies browsed through the long grasses that had grown up around the felled lapidary candles. The poor, the thick and the ignorant had scrawled their illiterate graffiti upon the lithic Lutyens uprights – a suitable adumbration upon those who had cast this, probably the finest war memorial park in Europe, into abject ruin. Not only had Dublin forgotten these dead soldiers; it was prepared to shit on their memory.

The palpably evident had within a generation become palpably disposable as an entire political class turned 1916 into Year Zero. The survivors of the insurrection of that year – the architects of the new state – had over time woven a monochrome history from which any uncomfortable obtrusions were eliminated. There was one official view of Ireland and its history, enforced by politicians, teachers, editors and library porters alike, and as the lorries emptied their bowels onto the memorials to the dead, I swore that I should not rest until this cosmic injustice had been undone.

But, of course, this was a state that moved through epicycles of wrongdoing, as electorates were given unsustainable bribes that had to be revoked, with taxes raised to repay the banks that had made the bribes possible. Emigration was back, once again proclaiming the failure of

Ireland's political classes. It seemed that the circumstances of the state's birth, in an orgy of needless violence, had both ushered in a dysfunctional political order, and placed a curse on its existence thereafter. Yet, bad as things already were, moral control over the state's key policies was about to pass into the hands of two minority cliques: the IRA and the Catholic hierarchy.

Two

THE FIRST REPORTS on the radio news that morning were of an explosion in County Sligo. The subsequent disclosures came in hourly instalments of intravenous poison. Lord Louis Mountbatten, near-octogenarian scion of the house of Saxe-Coburg-Gotha, along with a party of old people and children in a dinghy, had been slaughtered by an IRA bomb in Mullaghmore Bay. Soon afterwards, a landmine destroyed a British Army Land Rover on a Border patrol at Narrow Water, County Down, killing everyone on board. Soldiers deployed in a recovery operation were themselves the target of a second bomb. In all, eighteen men were slaughtered, two of them blown into the sort of molecular extinction that merits sealed coffins, stone ballast and widows weeping beside untenanted marble. In the confusion that followed, with panic-stricken soldiers firing across the Border, a servant from Buckingham Palace, who happened to be holidaying in the Republic, was shot dead.

The IRA had intentionally killed twenty-two people; the British Army had accidentally killed one. The next day's midday news-magazine on RTÉ radio led with the latter, and a searching investigation into this latest British atrocity. Irish society was an aeon away from grappling with the depravity of the IRA campaign, but the Taoiseach, Jack Lynch, a decent if querulous creature, assented to a secret British request to allow hot-pursuit overflights in Border areas (though the demand was meaningless: terrorists seldom behaved in such a congenial Wild West, splashing-across-the-Rio Grande manner). The underlying truth was stark: despite ten full years of civil unrest and terrorist warfare in the North, the Defence Forces still did not have a proper air component – neither troop-carrying helicopters nor any aircraft capable of engaging terrorists on the ground. Word of this agreement soon leaked out, and Lynch's backbenchers rose in revolt – not at the IRA's use of the Republic's territory to murder nearly two dozen people, but at the possible intrusion into Irish airspace of British Army helicopters. Jack Lynch resigned. Two men would contest the leadership: the renegade leader of the republican faction in Fianna Fáil, the mysteriously wealthy Charles Haughey, and his rival since his schooldays, George Colley.

Meanwhile, the lunacy characteristic of a semi-collapsing state intensified. Dublin Corporation street sweepers had gone on strike because a clerk had been ordered to end his practice of bringing his dog to work and tying it to his desk. I had not heard from *The Irish Times* for a while, but an outbreak of flu called for desperate measures, so they asked me to cover this dispute. Outside the Corporation headquarters, I met the trade union organiser Eric Fleming, a member of the Communist Party and a chum from my lefty days a decade before.

'What's going on?' I asked.

'Fuckin' madness is what's going on,' he snarled. 'I've got to get these stupid cunts back to work tomorrow and *also* make sure Dublin Corporation doesn't fuckin' pay them for today.'

'*What?* Jesus, Eric, why would a trade union organiser try to stop them getting money?'

'Why? Because they're out of fuckin' control. The last time they went on strike, they refused to return to work without full fuckin' back payment, *includin' lost overtime,* for the whole fuckin' time they were on strike. The Corpo folded and gave them every fuckin' penny, includin' the fuckin' overtime. And of course, while they were on strike, they spent the whole time in the fuckin' boozer. Lookit, they're at again.'

He nodded across the road, where the pub was filled with a raucous and carousing crowd.

'They your men?'

'Oh, by fuck they are. And if they get away with it again, they'll spend the rest of their fuckin' lives in the bleedin' pub, bein' paid be the fuckin' Corpo to get fuckin' langers. And all because of that fuckin' mutt.'

There, tied to some railings, was the guilty dog.

So here, in this madness, we had a communist but dutiful trade union official desperately trying to get strikers back to work, while the public-service employers were apparently eager to pay them for drinking in the pub. I wrote a colour piece for the newspaper, talking about the 'caninisation' of Irish life, with a mutt on a lead outside the Corporation offices and a Colley outside the Taoiseach's office. All references to the pub were cut by subeditors, as was my pun about caninisation.

The next morning, the surviving remnants of my piece were quoted approvingly by Gay Byrne on his radio programme. Gageby's commercial instincts would normally have been delighted by such exposure, but kind words about me must have been purest gall and wormwood to him. Either way, publicity being publicity, I was called in for another shift that afternoon. In the evening, as the subs arrived, one of them sidled up to me.

'You this Kevin Myers?'

'Yes.'

'I'm just telling you, for your own sake. This isn't a unionist paper any longer: it's a union one.'

'Was it you who cut the stuff about the pub?'

'Point one. The rule here is you never know who subbed your copy, so don't ask. And point two, don't ever knock the working classes again, all right?'

It was icily polite, but frostily emphatic – and the really stupid thing about that exchange was that I agreed with him. Being 'anti-working class' was now taboo according to the journalistic penal code, and not long before I had picketed Ireland's first-ever McDonald's because of its refusal to negotiate with trade unions. In my usual middle-class, dim-witted, left-wing way, I accepted that 'working class' was synonymous with 'trade unions', never wondering why it was that the majority of both staff and customers in McDonald's on O'Connell Street were themselves of the class I had chosen to revere. Anyway, that evening, the (now happily Myersless) picket around McDonald's had led to an affray, and

I was told to get a comment from the franchise owner, Mike Mehegan, who had probably gone out to the US as Mick and come back Mike. What I did was harangue him.

'You fweelance, eh?' he finally said in the Noo Yawk accent that was apparently available at JFK duty free for anyone returning to Ireland after a week's visit to the US. 'Cos you do sure sound like one, knowing everyting without asking no questions. Okay, so listen here, my fwend, and listen good, and hey, take notes: you ain't got a goddman cloo about economic weality. You get that? Good. See yah.'

The accent might have been somewhat bogus, but the observation was spot on. Both episodes go to the core of journalism. Information that was vital to understanding what was going on – in the earlier story, Dublin Corporation's practice of rewarding workers for going on strike – was cut by a subeditor, presumably for political reasons. The fact that the decision-making of the strikers had been corrupted by alcohol was deleted, no doubt on sound legal grounds: otherwise, every single striker could sue the paper. It was my decision not to report the fact that the trade union leader representing the workers was a communist who was doing his best to end the strike, and that he had called the workers 'stupid cunts'. What remained was an entertaining piece of folderol, immune to external analysis, not just then, but for all time. And, of course, coverage of the McDonald's dispute – as became evident over the years to follow – proved to be a standard modus operandi of journalists like myself: approach a story from a modishly lefty angle, ensuring that your questions elicit the answers that will produce the desired outcome. The facts that you garner in this way will not be inaccurate. You then fuse the results of your biased questions, your biased opinions, and your biased observations, and the outcome – the term 'synthetic' really does apply here – is your pseudo-objective report. Moreover, if the result made fun of the US or capitalism – McDonald's was perfect for both – or, later, Israel or middle-class, white, heterosexual males, you would be applauded for being radical and daring. However, if a report made fun of the left, or the 'working classes', or feminism or the trade-union movement, or, in later years, the Palestine Liberation Organisation or environmentalism, you would become an object of professional scorn expressed, in ascending order, with a moue of disdain, a small passing jeer, or finally, *Are you serious?* The most common, most effective and least visible acts of press censorship are those performed by journalists themselves to propitiate their peers.

My mother came over for the visit of Pope John Paul II that autumn and I took her to the mass at the Phoenix Park. On one level, it was an enchanting day – one million people in apparent harmony – but the hypocrisy that underlay so much of Irish life was personified by 'The Singing Priest', Father Michael Cleary, who welcomed the Pope at one of the venues, complete with beard and guitar. I had interviewed this delightful creature in his parochial house some nine years before.

'You're a fine-looking young fella,' he kept interjecting in his bogus Dublin working-class accent. 'I bet you're a great man for the ride, wha'? Riding rings about yourself! Helping yourself to the birds, left right and centre, heh?'

Even then, only Neanderthals referred to young women as 'birds', which he of course pronounced 'boards'. I dealt with his otiose intrusions with a straight bat, till his housekeeper came in with tea and biscuits. As she left, he folded his right hand into the crook of his left elbow in the standard continental representation of 'fuck', and then winked lubriciously. He knew that I could never report his violation both of his own vow of celibacy and the rules of common decency. Now this odious, strumming shyster, whose secrets could not have been unknown to the hierarchy, was the public face of the Irish Catholic Church.

The next day I was asked to write a report on the aftermath of the mass in the Phoenix Park: as they departed, the one million people left a paper trail that would have been visible from the moon. In the park, a Mercedes, its boot door open, was cruising along the lines of Portaloos, while the owner's children scampered back and forth, stealing the spare rolls of lavatory paper and throwing them into the car boot. Such was the moral elevation that resulted from the Pope's visit.

Back in the newsroom, Gageby was noisily in charge. 'Only upbeat stories, only upbeat stories,' he boomed proudly. I typed out a colour piece based on a pun about 'larseny' in the park and left it at the news desk. Gageby picked it up, scanned it, glared at me with twin laser beams and then so emphatically spiked it that he narrowly avoided gaining Ireland's first Protestant stigmata.

Another more telling event passed almost unnoticed that autumn: the 'liberal' film censor Frank Hall banned Monty Python's *Life of Brian* for contradicting the teachings of the Catholic Church. The following January, following complaints of blasphemy, the distributor was obliged to withdraw the LP record of the film's soundtrack. Other stories painted a still bleaker picture. An opinion poll showed that, *despite the Narrow Water and Mullaghmore massacres*, one-fifth of the population of the Republic supported the IRA campaign, and two-fifths backed the IRA's aims – the forcible incorporation of more than one million unwilling Northern protestants into a united Ireland. The Special Criminal Court – truly living up to the more adjectival interpretation of its name – had just released the terrorist Dessie O'Hare, even though he had been positively identified as the gunman who had shot and critically wounded a British soldier, Lieutenant Gary Cass, on the steps of St Patrick's Church, Trim, *on his wedding day*. O'Hare went on to murder at least twenty-seven people after this shamelessly shameful acquittal, including Margaret Hearst beside her sleeping three-year-old daughter in a caravan in south Armagh.

The following January (1980), I got a scoop: Dublin Corporation had announced that it was taking emergency measures to clear the thousands of tons of litter that had accumulated in west Dublin. I rang the press office, which admitted that the Corporation was now openly – as opposed to *covertly* – using Islandbridge Park as an emergency tip-head. In my indignant 800-word story, I explained the history of the park and the significance of the Corporation's decision. A sub deleted all references to Islandbridge and a 100-word filler appeared. Similarly buried was the news that the Taoiseach, Charles Haughey, had sent an Army officer to represent him at the funeral of a senior IRA officer, John Joe Sheehy, in Tralee, County Kerry, during which members of the Provisional IRA fired a volley of graveside shots. The scandal of a uniformed officer of the Army of the Republic being forced to stand idly by while terrorist-usurpers of that noble title had publicly discharged firearms, only four months after the most terrible day in decades, earned no editorial disapproval from *The*

Irish Times. I can only assume the incident escaped Gageby's attention: his attachment to the Army was unconditional, yet there was no larger outcry about this scandal, almost as if we now expected the worst from Haughey, and he seldom let us down.

In relation to my larger task, I interviewed a clergyman and former artilleryman, Claude Chavasse, originally from Castletownshend, County Cork, where he had lived with his aunts, the writers Somerville and Ross. He was very much of the landed gentry class, with an accent to match, but he detested the very concept of 'Anglo-Irish'.

'We are Irish, to the backbone. Only those detestable Sinn Féiners use the term "Anglo" about us. Cads, the lot of them.'

The story he told contradicted the received version of Irish history, effectively reaffirming the larger narrative of my Carlow friend. He had gone to enlist with the British Army in 1915, along with his cousin Nevill Coghill – later the Chaucerian scholar whom I had always assumed was English. No, he was Irish, which was Claude's point: the term 'Anglo-Irish' invariably involved the acquisition of its subject by the prefix and a rejection by the suffix. Claude spoke of the attacks on Protestants in west Cork, and the departure of thousands between 1921 and 1924. 'I had to get away too for a while – ex-serviceman, well-connected Protestant and all that, even though we loved Ireland just as much as – no, *more!* – than those unspeakable, vile republican bounders. We stayed, through thick and thin – you know that Emily Lawless poem about Catholic exiles? – *Yet still their love comes home to me.* Well, it applied to us Protestants too.'

His cousin Vice-Admiral Boyle Somerville had returned to Ireland and was murdered for that love by the republican 'hero' Tom Barry, who shot him after he answered a knock on the door. 'They were dangerous times for us. Very. I was rector at Teampall na mBocht during the coronation of George VI. We all gathered in the church behind locked doors to hear the BBC commentary on the wireless, and we had sturdy young lads with shotguns manning the boreens to make sure we weren't attacked.'

Gageby agreed to my proposal that I do a series on the long ordeals of the Church of Ireland. My first interview was with Henry McAdoo, a senior churchman in Dublin, since deceased, who warned me of the dangers ahead. 'I can tell you the truth of what happened to the Church, but only off the record. We survive by not putting our heads above the parapet. That is our strategy: social camouflage, pretending to be what we are not. Most of us are still unionist. I am, but I'd never admit it.'

My four-part series turned out to be disastrous, not least because Claude Chavasse – in great distress – rang to say his family were appalled that he had talked to me and that I couldn't use most of what he'd said. My series was filleted by the removal of that backbone, along with all the connective tissue, and Henry McAdoo's admissions had been off the record. I didn't compensate for the many last-minute deletions, and some of my judgements were a little trite. Nonetheless, before publication, Gageby dropped me a note thanking me for 'an elegantly written series', whereas Bruce Williamson, who had inexplicably taken a great shine to me, demurred. He had just emerged from a drying-out clinic to which he had been sent by Douglas.

'Rather shallow, dear boy, and inclined towards the cliché. *The Great War as a shutter on a golden Edwardian era,* et cetera. Otherwise, quite well-written. But you'll ruffle a few feathers, so 'ware the storm, lad, 'ware the storm!'

''Ware the storm' was right. The articles caused uproar among Protestant readers, who thought they were ill-informed – correct – and that I was attacking the Church of Ireland – incorrect. The Protestant clergy detested my series and let Gageby know it, causing his congratulatory note to vanish from his memory, rather like a non-aggression pact the moment that tanks smash through the customs posts.

Somehow my name had caught the attention of an RTÉ producer, who asked me to write and present a programme about the law courts. I agreed. The tv crew and I were allowed very limited access to the bar library and we got a ghastly interview with the chief justice, Tom O'Higgins, all bewigged, bemused and bewildered. It was then that I met Mella Carroll, Ireland's first woman senior counsel, and a barrister of great intellect and distinction.

My financial worries were finally relieved by the arrival of my money from Belfast, a year late, during which time my solicitor had been earning its interest. Inflation, at 20 per cent, had devoured much of its real value, but the £7,000 was still enough for a deposit on a house in Ranelagh.

However, I chanced to meet a genial stockbroker, to whom I confided my intentions. He shook his head.

'Listen, old fellow, this is absolutely the wrong time to get into the property market. House values are going to go pop any day now. Thing to do is to invest in equities, sound as a bell, and I can set you right on that. Then you can get the hell out of the bloody things when the property market's settled, and Bob's your uncle. Give me a ring next week, and we'll see what we can do for you.'

Delighted at my great good fortune in finding my financial white knight and making a new friend, with singular folly I obliged.

Yet it is a letter I wrote that autumn to the then leader of Fine Gael, Garret FitzGerald, rather than my aberrant financial decisions that is more deserving of a place in any story of my life. Having been present for yet another sparsely attended Remembrance Sunday service, I wrote to Garret, remonstrating about the absence of any political representatives at the service. He replied:

The point which you make about the St Patrick's Cathedral Service is one which had not struck me – which itself is, I suppose, a commentary on our society! We did in Government make what turned out to be a very half-hearted attempt to substitute for the separate commemorations which now exist for different groups of Irishmen a single day of commemoration but this effort came to nothing.

It is fair to add that I am not aware of ever having received an invitation to the Remembrance Service. Perhaps it would be a good thing if all parties were invited to be represented there and I shall see what I can do about that.

I believe out of that letter grew the plant that was to be the National Day of Commemoration and its kindred memorial the same weekend, the British Legion service for the Irish dead of two world wars at Islandbridge Memorial Park. I can therefore claim part-ownership of both events, as well as the park itself, which makes the state's later behaviour to me utterly inexcusable – but that disgrace still lay decades ahead.

Three

ON WESTLAND ROW on my way to the National Library, I had noticed a crew of road-workers jackhammering up a newly laid stretch of tarmac that had been a trench only the week before. I stopped and asked what was going on, and the reply sounded like the instructions for gathering frogspawn with a blunt knife. The next day, I was called in to do a shift at the paper. Having swiftly got through the supplied scripts, I wrote an unsolicited, tongue-in-cheek story about Westland Row, and handed it to Gerry. He read it in silence, then laughed out loud, before catching my eye and nodding approvingly. Next day, it was in the much-cherished bottom-of-the-front-page slot, even getting a favourable mention on the radio. From then on, the *Irish Times* bookings became more regular. A couple of months on, another stroll through Westland Row revealed that trench matters there had actually worsened, so I did a second piece about it, to renewed general acclaim.

'I never thought of Westland Row as Troy,' opined Bruce, amid an approving cloud of cigarette smoke, 'but by Jove, it has certainly moved your muse.'

My letters to local newspapers looking for veterans had finally produced a meagre harvest. Two veterans had died since replying. Others told me of their families' concerns for their own safety should it become known that they had served with the British army. Yet others agreed to meet me, but their memories were vague, or even useless. However, one veteran, Michael Tierney, of Monkstown, was outstanding. A former

Irish National Volunteer, he had followed John Redmond's call to enlist to support the rights of small nations.

'I was intended for the 7th battalion, which contained a cadet company for future officers, but I got the flu when my batch was due to leave for the front. So I was put into the 2nd battalion instead – and right glad I was, because what the 7th did was shameful, shameful.'

By this time, I had read through Whitton's history of the Leinsters, and had no idea what Tierney was talking about. I pressed him for details, but he refused to give any, declaring that it was the darkest episode in the history of the regiment, and instead talked about his days with the 2nd battalion.

'Finest battalion in the British Army bar none.'

'So you knew Alfred Durham Murphy?'

He looked at me in astonishment. 'You've heard of Colonel Murphy?'

His face went grey, and he broke into uncontrolled sobbing for several minutes. Finally, he composed himself and spoke.

'He would have been the future of Ireland. A soldier, a patriot, a nationalist. His death was the greatest blow I have ever suffered in my life, and I include there the death of my wife. We loved him. We all did. Finest Irishman who ever lived.'

Then he broke down again.

Later, he spoke of the years that followed, as each November veterans of the Leinsters gathered for a memorial mass to honour Lieutenant Colonel Alfred Durham Murphy DSO MC of Ballinamona House, near Cashel, County Tipperary. That loyalty, that honour, that passionate love of Ireland: these were the untold stories of Irish history that I felt must be told.

A vacancy arose in the newsroom. The consensus was that I should get the job, with Gageby the sole dissenter – and indeed, whenever he saw me in the newsroom he would scowl like a bride gazing into the mirror on her wedding day and seeing a boil emerging between her eyebrows. However, he was too big a man to block my appointment for personal reasons, and so, after an interview with Ken Gray, during which neither one of us said very much, as we whiled away the required amount of time by furtively studying our watches, I was appointed to the staff of *The Irish Times*. Not long afterwards, my television programme *The Law Courts* was broadcast. None of the clips showing me were included, though my script and my voiceover were retained.

That November 1980 I presented the fruits of my research into Ireland's Memorial Records in a 3,000-word article for the newspaper. It was treated with incredulity. Almost no one was aware that so many Irishmen had been killed in the Great War, or that hundreds of thousands of Irish soldiers had served. (Time would show that the actual figure for the Irish dead, including many thousands overlooked by the records, was approximately 40,000.) I also wrote of German atrocities in Belgium that had aroused the wrath of nationalist Ireland – the sacking of Louvain in particular – and this too was not merely a revelation but a provocation to some. One pugnacious subeditor, a tribally verdant Glasgow-born, Celtic-supporting Ulsterman, came up to me, almost tapping me on the chest. 'That stuff about German atrocities is just British propaganda, *British fucking propaganda*. There were no German atrocities. I always knew you were a Brit at heart. Now you've proved it!'

The newspaper's daily social column, 'An Irishman's Diary', had been unfilled since the death of its former author, Seamus Kelly, eighteen months earlier. Kelly was legendary for his alcoholic belligerence and beetle-browed irascibility: the very space that the diary occupied seemed infused with choler and the heady fumes of the still. The general feeling was that whoever followed him on a full-time basis must do so in every cantankerous regard. Until a replacement was found, the column was passed around the newsroom. Gerry Mulvey asked me whether I was interested in doing a diary or two. Well, I certainly didn't want to be a daily columnist – that seemed far too daunting a prospect, both journalistically and hepatically – but I didn't mind writing one occasionally. So I did a couple of Irishman's Diaries, and though they now seem to be burdened with the whimsy of depleted uranium, they were warmly received.

'It is a rare gift that brings a smile to my sour old puss,' wheezed Bruce. 'You have it, my boy, you have it. Guard it well.'

Around this time, the outstanding Conor O'Clery was appointed news editor and Gerry Mulvey was given a secluded desk behind which to slumber his way to pensionhood. O'Clery told Gageby that someone would have to be appointed to write the 'Diary' full-time, and he wanted me to do it.

'Very well,' Gageby rumbled (or so I was told). 'Let it be Myers. But I'm making no announcement. I don't want him, and I want him and our readers to know that.'

'Douglas – all staff appointments are announced in the paper.'

'Ha! Not this one.'

Such an unprecedented departure from tradition and good manners did not prevent Gageby from telling me what he wanted – a light, chatty column, full of names.

'People like seeing their names in newspapers. It's what sells. And I'm not in the least interested in your opinions. Just keep it light and make yourself invisible. And remember: names, loads of names.'

I can revisit my early efforts now with the deep unease of a time traveller watching his first woebegone attempts at adolescent bra-removal. The past is not so much another country as a different civilisation on a different planet, where, mysteriously, the same words have different meanings. Yet for all the bemusement and embarrassment they cause me now, my columns appeared to be popular, and I was acquiring a reputation for an unpredictable, tongue-in-cheek style. One morning I had champagne with Joan Collins, followed by lunch with the England international footballer Kevin Keegan. Collins was charmingly brittle, having turned flagrant insincerity into a brilliant social art: she smoked non-stop, guzzled champagne with no appreciable effect, and repeatedly called me 'darling', her glowing dark eyes searching for the parrot on my shoulder, that is, looking for someone more interesting to talk to. Kevin Keegan grinned like a denture model and, having had a certain baptismal advantage when it came to recalling my name, addressed me by it before every full stop. My column self-mockingly described their delight at meeting me.

The IRA hunger strikes, a moral and needless catastrophe, were underway. On specific instructions from Gageby, I did not write about them, though I was unsure what could be usefully said, when the obdurately stupid policies of the British government were colliding with the papist neo-paganism of the republicans: the Iron Lady versus the Iron Age. The strikes, the appalling deaths, and the cynical prolongation of the campaign by the republican leadership after the British had effectively capitulated to their demands constitute one of the greatest tragedies of Irish history.

Meanwhile, my journalism and my own personal development was surely limited by my drinking, which was often on the scale of a motorway navvy on a Friday night. Drinking in Bowes was part of our nightly routine. I would sink pints through to the early hours, before swaying majestically into the *Irish Times* canteen, the haunt and home of the many unwashed and elderly eccentrics who used to roost in the various nooks of the D'Olier Street buildings like flea-infested bats.

For much of my time at *The Irish Times* the canteen was run by Joan O'Brien, a cheerful and welcoming soul, who embodied the courteous culture that marked the newspaper, which was, despite its many failings, a happy place. This was evident from the moment visitors arrived at security, which was run by Paddy Williams – the charming, ever-smiling imp whom you have already met. His colleague Harry Saunders miraculously managed to be fatly haggard. He devoured raw onions like apples in accordance with an anti-oxidant regime that he said would guarantee centennial longevity. The ever-loyal operators sat invisibly at the switch, Máirín McGrath, Marie-Therese Tighe and Carol Hayden, and at night their place was taken by Ambrose Kenny, who whiled away the many quiet moments by noisily swishing his false teeth back and forth over his gums. Such fine, if anonymous, people made *The Irish Times* possible, just as much as its better-known names.

The most outrageously eccentric of us all was Hoddy, or George Hodnett, the paper's jazz critic, probably the dirtiest individual I have ever met: a Bombay street beggar was a freshly showered, coiffed and perfumed Vidal Sassoon in comparison – and I say this with some certainty, having met all three. Hoddy had once been discreetly famous for composing the ballad 'Monto', so authentic-sounding that people still believe it was a Dublin street song. Now in his late sixties, Hoddy was a complete stranger to hygiene, apparently not having had a bath since the Middle Cretaceous. A phone used by him would stink for hours afterwards. Whenever he came in from the rain, the hum of ancient lanolin, encrusted dirt and the colonies of bacteria rioting in the nooks and crannies of his person would cause the entire newsroom to wheel around in appalled enquiry. But nobody ever showed any discourtesy to Hoddy, for that would violate the *Irish Times* code. An incredulous janitor from the Whitla Hall in Belfast once rang Gageby to declare: 'Some fellow says he's your jazz critic and wants to sleep here on the floor tonight.'

'Let him,' carolled Gageby. 'It'll mean a break for the poor devil on night-town here!'

'Night-town' was the hated watch, from 9 p.m. till 4 a.m., detested not merely because of the hours and the horrors of having to rearrange the paper if a major story broke, but also because it meant conversation with Hoddy. He had bedding of a kind in the corner of the newsroom, a badger's sett composed of ancient newspapers announcing the Relief of Mafeking or lamenting the death of the Queen Empress. Before he laid himself down for the night, he would treat night-town to his mad opinions at point-blank range. Finally, he would curl up on his paper bedding, coiled around the vast hernia in his groin that usually resembled an elephantine erection. The tolerance shown to Hoddy was admirable, though rather less so if you were on night-town.

Gageby's identity was created by the Army, in which he had been perhaps the only Northern Protestant volunteer during the war (he had been born in Dublin but raised in Belfast). He was a passionate patriot, proud of Ireland, proud of its history, and, rightly, most proud of the Defence Forces. He was very brave. One evening, the news desk got an urgent warning call from Paddy Williams: Tom, a former member of staff and a diagnosed paranoid schizophrenic who had been confined to a mental hospital, had just burst past security with an axe, and was running upstairs. Next moment, an angry presence burst through the newsroom doors like a bull erupting from its cage and catching sight of a sword-bearing matador prodding his first-born. The news desk paled and quavered, hands to mouths: I, having spent years in Belfast, and knowing precisely what to do when bravery was desperately needed, in a microsecond slid under my desk. Through a crack, I watched as Tom considered his options, put down his axe, lifted a desk typewriter, weighing not less than 20 kilos – many women journalists needed assistance to lift them – and hurled it in a straight trajectory through the window directly behind me – *CRASH!* – and down into Fleet Street. A second later, it exploded on the happily unpeopled pavement below – *BANG!*

Seconds later another typewriter was in flight, this time shattering against the wall over my head. So much for typewriters – when would he resort to the axe?

But then I heard Gageby's gruff, kindly voice: 'Now, Tom, what are you doing to our precious typewriters? These poor people have to work on them. What'll they do when you've smashed them all up? Come on inside to my office and you can tell me what your problem is. And leave the axe there, if you please. You know I don't allow weapons in the editor's office.'

Tom meekly followed an affably cardiganed Gageby into his sanctuary and I gallantly stole homewards.

Gageby's capacity for anger matched his bravery. One night, the National Union of Journalists decided to block copy from *The Times* of London during what was an epoch-making dispute between management and print unions at Wapping in London's docklands. Gageby stalked out of his office, his face as dark and glowering as an Oklahoma sky just before a twister turns Tulsa into matchwood. He glared at the quivering subeditors. 'I am the fucking editor of this fucking newspaper, and if any one of you even dares to tell me what should *not* go into it, I'll simply resign, and leave the whole fucking caboodle to you fucking shower.'

This was met with an awed and terror-struck silence. The next morning the newspaper duly appeared, complete with copy from Wapping. Moreover, Gageby expected everyone to do their job, regardless. After early-morning deliveries of the paper were halted because of heavy snowfalls, he had the entire despatch team lined up by noon, all of them palely quivering outside his office, as one by one they offered their own explanations, while the editorial door shook from the rages within. Temperamentally, Gageby was still a Soldier of the Republic for whom there was no excuse for not doing your duty. Journalism's great gain was the Army's even greater loss.

Four

DESPITE GAGEBY'S ADMONITIONS, I took up certain causes, the most consistent of which was the Irish in the Great War. This led to me appearing on Gay Byrne's radio show, on which I also spoke about the appalling state of Islandbridge. Soon afterwards, I was contacted by Campbell Heather, formerly of the Irish Guards. Would I show him and an unnamed friend around the park? Two days later, we met. Campbell's friend turned out to be Sir John Gorman, a Northern Catholic and former senior RUC officer who had won a spectacular Military Cross with the Irish Guards in Normandy by ramming his Sherman tank into a German Tiger.

I guided them round the park. Gulls and urchins were delving into the tons of rubbish and we were studied by shaggy, nonchalantly chewing piebald ponies. Sir John grew so angry that he abandoned his usually impeccable public-school manners. 'This is a fucking scandal, and no longer just something for you journalist chappies. This is a violation of an understanding between the two governments and is a matter for the Northern Ireland Office to pursue.'

He and Campbell were thereafter largely responsible for the political initiatives that resulted in the park being restored, but I certainly played a formative role in their common resolve. Yet, for the most part, my columns – consistent with the abject traditions of the 'Diary' – consisted of saying nice things about existing institutions. I knew that Údarás na Gaeltachta, whose primary purpose was to provide jobs for Irish speakers, was an inherently stupid and profoundly hypocritical organisation. Management in imported companies would never be speaking Irish, nor indeed would most of the workforce, but back then I never said as much, for Údarás lavished hospitality on journalists. So too did Shannon Development, both to protect its own little bailiwick alongside the larger Industrial Development Authority and to maintain the Shannon Airport stopover. This was another of a long series of prostrations to the political and cultural power of an economically backward West, which absurdly required that all Dublin–New York jumbo jets land there, involving costly, time-consuming 120-mile hops in both directions.

One issue that did exercise me was the refusal of Jacob's Biscuits to supply cream crackers for sale as own brands for Irish supermarkets, which had to import them instead. The complexity of marketing was beyond me: I merely wanted to sound off on a cause that seemed patriotic. Attempts by the Jacob's PR woman, Frankie Byrne, to end my campaign foundered on my pre-existing loathing of her. In my first year in UCD, I would listen to a radio programme sponsored by Jacob's and presented by her, then masquerading as a professional agony aunt. One woman in her late thirties had written that she had been engaged for *ten years*, and recently her fiancé had tried to touch her 'in my chest area'? What should she do?

'Well now, Mary,' whispered Frankie. She always began her advice with an intimately husky vocative. 'It's clear to me that this fellow is up to no good: he's after one thing and one thing only, and the sooner you get rid of him, the better.'

What? After *ten years*, the poor fellow was merely trying to touch her breasts? What ruin had Byrne's wretched advice visited on those innocent lives? Now, a decade later, I was encountering Byrne again. That she might have been right about the biscuits – as she surely was – never entered my precious little head as I penned my furiously fatuous pieces about the unpatriotic iniquity of Jacob's.

Another issue also troubled me. My time in Belfast had made me alert to the hazards of fire. After noticing that a fire door was padlocked, I reported this to a manager. He said that, in case of fire, designated keyholders would unlock the doors – a clearly absurd policy. I contacted company head office, who directed me to Dublin Fire Brigade. The officer there replied that they didn't discuss fire safety with the press, at which point, instead of pursuing the matter as I should have, I allowed the greatest momentum known to mankind to supervene: inertia.

Meanwhile, my columns about the Great War had prompted Gay Byrne to invite me on to *The Late Late Show*. The Saturday morning of the show, I was awoken at seven by a phone call from Conor O'Clery, who told me to go immediately to the Stardust nightclub in Coolock, where there had been a terrible fire. My taxi driver was grey-faced and silent: he had spent the night driving terror-stricken families to various hospitals. When we arrived at the Stardust, knowing my mission, he refused to accept any payment. I approached the smouldering ruins with stomach-sinking reluctance. Yes, here once more were the last lingering molecules of barbecued human flesh, which I thought I had left behind me in Belfast, though they sometimes returned to curse my dreams. I entered the dark interior, which was steeped with the sinister, caramel fragrance of just-doused burnt timbers, and crept along a corridor. I finally reached the fire doors: yes, still padlocked. In the half-light, I could see that the surrounding walls were daubed with the broken, bloodstained claw marks of youngsters inscribing the last wordless messages of their lives. Though their bodies were gone, here were their final frantic hieroglyphs in browning haemoglobin. I have seen the aftermath of a fair amount of death in my time, but this memory retains a curious tenacity.

In all, forty-eight young people had perished, and more than 200 were injured in the Stardust fire. RTÉ cancelled that night's *Late Late*, of course. But for me, the real question was whether I, through an energetic pursuit of the issue of the widespread fire hazards in Dublin, could have prevented the Stardust disaster? Probably not, for Irish society in those days simply didn't respond to threats to the powerless. The Noyeks fire in Dublin, in which eight working-class people had perished nine years earlier, had not caused the necessary revulsion for the political classes to impose and maintain serious fire regulations.

However, the Stardust catastrophe was too great to ignore, and a long enquiry followed, which finally showed that yes, indeed, all these young people had died in a fire. What a sensational discovery. Not untypically, the many barristers involved were paid vast sums, long before the survivors received a penny in compensation. Occasionally, one might see victims on the streets of Dublin, their faces melted into wax pancakes, with perpetually bared teeth, nostrils like buttonless buttonholes and glaring, lidless, lashless eyes.

When, some time later, I finally appeared on *The Late Late Show* to discuss the forgotten Irish and the Great War, the hostility in the studio was palpable. Some of the audience booed me, and one woman shrieked that John Redmond had tried to introduce conscription: her outburst – a complete untruth – was applauded. Such was the simmering anger that I was later advised not to enter the general hospitality area, where guests and the public usually mingled. My cause had a long, long way to go indeed.

Press receptions, half-a-dozen a night, were a staple and a curse of journalistic life, for they were simply a way of hacks getting free drink with the usually insincere promise of some publicity. Of course, everyone knew the result of mixing youngish people with ceaseless gin and tonics and the occasional slice of lemon. Officially Ireland was still a Catholic country, but humans here behaved just as they did anywhere else. However, all that booze hose-piped at you without question or cost hour after hour, night after night, became the main allure. At the end of the night, you might, if you were lucky, get off with someone, most probably to share a drunken coma with. How one negotiated the next day, upon waking up at noon with a naked but possibly still unsullied and probably very appalled stranger, who might now be seeing you properly for the very first time, was a not infrequent challenge.

The media circuit included the Witches' Coven, a gang of old crones whose gossip went from charitable ill-will, pausing to linger lovingly over the m-words – malicious, malevolent, malignant and malign – before hastening on to intravenous polonium. They were invited to everything, because *not* inviting them would be a disaster for any PR consultant. Aloof from that gang, though of the same age, was the broadcaster Monica Carr, a resolutely virginal sexagenarian who could regularly be seen on the outskirts of the gin-and-tonic melees, steel-swathed in armour-plated corsets and perhaps occasionally inhaling the chaster vapours of a small sherry.

One evening, I was one of the hundred or so guests attending a seafood company's dinner at a hotel in Wexford. Sitting opposite me was Monica. Despite her age – vast to my mind – she was wearing an astonishing low-cut dress that revealed that she was the owner of sumptuously large breasts, which she proudly bore as if a flood was expected any moment and lifebelts were being worn on the chest that season. I found my eyes being irresistibly drawn to this astonishing display, and it was only with great difficulty that I could persuade them to scan the seafood platter below me, which they briefly did before mutinously resuming their avid study.

Most diners then moved to the bar, whereas Monica retired, and I remained transfixed, downing drink to cool my fevers. Finally, I went to reception and asked for her room number. The receptionist gave it to me. Without even phoning in advance, I went up and knocked on her door. She opened it. She was wearing a nightgown. She smiled enquiringly.

'May I come in?'

She stepped back and gestured me in. I shut the door behind me.

'I'm just out of my bath,' she said. 'How can I help you?'

'Frankly, I was admiring your breasts downstairs, and was wondering if I could see the rest of them.'

She blinked in surprise, thought for a moment, then replied: 'Of course.'

She opened the top of her dressing gown to reveal God's own creation, hand-made in heaven on the usually forgotten eighth day, when he was fully refreshed and at his very best. Lost in speechless admiration, I studied them for several moments.

'May I kiss them?' I finally asked, in a low, supplicant growl.

'It would be fierce bad manners not to,' she replied, as if the etiquette for this kind of thing had been taught in her Wicklow finishing school.

I dutifully immersed myself.

'You really should try the rest,' she murmured, as her nightgown fell to the floor. 'You won't be disappointed.'

She was sixty-four, twice my age, and I duly feasted as bidden. After two hours of glorious mamillary revels, I crawled brokenly from her room. The next morning at breakfast, she winked at me with a conspiratorial lubricity over the coffee, then smiled privately into her cup.

Sometime later, I learnt that the television programme *The Law Courts*, which I had written and presented, had won the Jacob's Award for best television documentary, and although the producer would receive the award – as I might have, had not all sight of me been deleted – I was invited to the awards ceremony at Jurys Hotel. The hostess for the event was Frankie Byrne.

'I know you have no time for me,' she said when I arrived, 'but you understand nothing about biscuits.'

'And you understand nothing about love or sex,' I replied with a leaden sanctimony that fully deserved the bolt of lightning that I didn't get. The hospitality of most press dinners in Dublin at that time was predicated on the born-again notion of baptism, namely total immersion – not in water, but its hydroxide cousin, alcohol, and this awards ceremony was no exception. At 2 a.m., I found myself alone in a corner talking to Frankie Byrne. She was about twenty-eight years older than I was.

'Why do you hate me, Kevin?' she slurred. (Everything that follows is slurred: I'm just not going to keep reminding you.)

'I don't hate you – but I do hate your attitude to sex.'

'What do you know about my attitude to sex?'

I reminded her of the advice she had given to that unfortunate young woman all those years before.

'Ha! Great memory. But you're wrong – I love sex. And let me remind you, Mr Englishman, this is Ireland. I have to give Catholic advice like that, or otherwise I'm out of work.'

'Jacob's is Protestant.' (*Prahteshtantt* …)

'But the people we sell our fucking biscuits to aren't. I can't tell my audience that I *love* sex. What happens then! I get the sack! But I always loved sex! Since school! I know a little secret about you, so let me tell you a little secret to even things up. My friend Sharon took me into a toilet and showed me how to do it. Changed my life. You like older women, don't you?'

'Do I? Where'd you get that idea?'

'Monica Carr said you did it with her.'

'Did she?'

'You can do it with me, if you like.'

'Frankie, believe me, I couldn't get it up even if all Charlie's Angels got into bed with me.'

''s all right. I don't need you. I've got a real man waiting for me. A married man who would ride rings around you.'

'You don't say. Who is he?'

'Not saying, But he's famous. Ver ver famous.'

Then she slid off the chair.

I duly proceeded homeward by the mysterious transportational machinery known only to drunks, which whisks you from a place of debauchery to your own bed, where you wake up the next morning with no idea how you got there. A couple of days later, I received a phone call from Frankie Byrne.

'You're not going to print what I told you, are you?'

'What? The sex stuff? Don't be mad. Why would I do that?'

'You hate me because I said my man would ride rings around you.'

'That night anyone could. We were both drunk. It's fine.'

I never heard from her again. It was only many years later that I discovered the man who would ride rings around me was the film censor, Frank Hall – he who had banned *The Life of Brian* because it 'contradicted the teachings of the church'. Moreover, as broadcaster, he had twice won Jacob's Awards, and the chair of the panel that made the awards was none other than his long-term mistress, Frankie Byrne.

Five

I MANAGED TO INTERVIEW Jack Moyney, the Irish Guards VC, shortly before he died. He was a cantankerous old geezer and deeply suspicious of me, a feeling I allayed with a generous donation of £5 to the Jack Moyney Appreciation Society. He relaxed with me only when he thought my tape recorder was turned off.

'Do you know what I really think of de Valera? A fucking bastard who should have got one between the eyes, same as that other bastard Collins. I'd have been happy to oblige. And as for that evil bollocks Breen …'

He glared at me with unwavering eyes which had seen death close up on the Somme and at Passchendaele – in neither place did he feel as much fear as he had back in Ireland.

'There was no way of knowing who was going to get you, or where or when. 'Twas only thanks to me being a VC that I was spared.'

I didn't press him on that, not knowing at the time that former soldiers were common targets for unemployed IRA men who wanted to kill someone – *anyone* – for Ireland, but finding the police and Army inconsiderately difficult targets, settled for these lesser, unarmed substitutes. Many soldier-veterans had become indigent outcasts in the fervently nationalist atmosphere that was sweeping post-war Ireland. Their fate, moreover, was to be excluded from all subsequent history books, though newspapers of the time bore almost daily headlines, 'Another Ex-Soldier Shot'. As we talked, word got around the neighbourhood that a sympathetic journalist was present, and a dozen men filtered in like late arrivals at the back of the church for mass. They were part of a secret Ireland that no one ever spoke about: pro-British Irish nationalists.

I had started an office fling with Grania Willis, the equestrian correspondent for *The Irish Times* and editor of our sister publication, *The Irish Horse World*. Soon she moved into Mountjoy Square as a temporary measure until she found her own place, but the arrangement acquired a power of its own, though without any expectation on either side of pelvic fidelity, and when I finally left Mountjoy Square, I did so with her as a companion.

I had moved my custom to Frank Lavery's pub next door to Bowes, and though its decor was comparatively seedy, Frank was a gentleman and soon it became the main drinking hole of *The Irish Times*. Val Lamb, Grania's boss, was a regular in Lavery's; he was a small, round, blond, pot-bellied cherub whose capacity for drinking matched his appetite for a good time. Each night he would drive home, criminally over the limit, happily not hitting anyone, and was never caught, as he surely deserved to be. On a similar alcoholic trajectory was our boxing correspondent Seán Kilfeather, a prematurely bald closet homosexual who strangely resembled Jean Genet. His many inner angers would swiftly be goaded by drink into dangerous, but usually unsuccessful, belligerence. He often arrived at work looking as if he should have been writing a professional report of what had happened to him the previous night, his eyes blackened and swollen, his oft-broken nose bent to one side yet again.

Dick Walsh was our political correspondent, a tiny bearded leprechaun, charming, wry and bitter. A repository of Kerry folklore, Dick seldom got drunk in public, but eyed people with guarded mischief over his whiskey. He detested capitalism, and in future years nothing would arouse his columnar ire so much as Ryanair's success. But, bizarrely, he never seriously examined Charles Haughey's vast wealth – the only subject worth examining in the Ireland of the time, yet one that Ireland's national newspapers studiously ignored.

Gageby and Foley's great contribution to Irish journalism was in their encouragement and promotion of women journalists, and accordingly most of the stars of *The Irish Times* were female. Nell McCafferty, the legendary lesbian feminist, had left by the time I arrived. Her scorching reports from the District Courts had transformed the administration of justice in Ireland. Maeve Binchy was to become world-famous, but I seldom saw her. Olivia O'Leary was both stylish, shrewd and fearless: I believe she was the first journalist ever to use the word 'cunt' in the newspaper. The education correspondent, Christina Murphy, knew more on her subject than did the Secretary of the Department of Education. Caroline Walsh was a one-woman literary powerhouse. Eileen Battersby (who joined the paper after me and who would die in a car crash, with so much still to give, while these memoirs were being finished) became the finest literary journalist on these islands. The best all-round colour writer in the newspaper was Maeve Kennedy: funny, sharp and endlessly inventive, her departure for *The Guardian* in later years would be a heavy loss for us.

It was through Grania that I was invited to Brigadier Fowler's annual point-to-point in Meath. Most of his guests were well-born country Protestants, and he welcomed them by herding them through a car wash of gin, after which they spent the afternoon wandering from car boot to car boot, inhaling alcohol like trapped submariners taking turns to breathe oxygen. Horses variously cantered. As twilight fell, through my own personal haze, I watched car-boot social clusters break up as people headed vaguely for their own vehicles. Here and there, stragglers buckled and fell, as if communist snipers were stalking through the gloaming and potting members of the gentry. Soon, sensibly shod little human tussocks of tweed lay everywhere on the grass, around which homeward-drivers – often with a hand over one eye to prevent double vision – would attempt to steer their cars, the odd squishing or cracking sound suggesting that they did not always do so accurately.

The Brig, as he was called, had won a DSO and Bar in the Second World War and an MC in the First, and his larger world – Protestant, Big House, Undiscussed Service for the Crown – rather overlapped with my historical projects. (His splendid daughter Jessica Harrington would later become one of Ireland's finest national hunt trainers.) When his house was burgled and the medals stolen, the gardaí kept the theft completely secret lest disclosures prompt some patriotic incendiarism rather than a return of the gallantry awards, which were never recovered. In those days, an entire sector of Irish society lived secret lives, usually emerging for Remembrance Sunday at St Patrick's Cathedral, where the few surviving veterans would totter up to greet me. Naturally, they assumed that their trials and their courage had been forgotten by all but me. Gageby was not pleased by my regular columnar returns to the trenches but would usually confine his dissatisfaction to that bridal glare of his. One day, Ken Gray approached my desk, clearing his throat apologetically.

'Douglas was wondering if you'd finally leave the Great War stuff alone. He feels it's not really right for the column, which is meant to be light and chatty and social. With names. He mentioned names. Several times. He feels you're giving a tone to the paper that really isn't right.'

'You mean West Brit?'

'Sort of, yes.'

'Ken, I promise not to refer to the Great War ever again' – a small smile of relief played around the edges of his mouth – 'but only when the government of this Republic publicly acknowledges our dead of the Great War.'

He looked at me briefly. 'Good man,' he murmured, patting my shoulder.

But of course, the Taoiseach, Charles Haughey, would as soon acknowledge our war dead as seek readmission to the United Kingdom. As Minister for Finance, he had funded the formation of the Provisional IRA, while his brother Jock had driven round the North, with guns and wads of money to distribute to IRA units. Charles Haughey's absurd acquittal on arms charges was the prelude to a long fightback from the political wilderness. Through the serendipity that the thoroughly evil often attract, the triumphant conclusion of this had been brought about by the terrorist atrocities at Mullaghmore and Narrow Water, perpetrated by the very IRA he had helped to form. And though by this time Haughey had no control or influence over the IRA or its many barbarities, there had been an almost condign symmetry in the way he finally came to power.

In office, Haughey sought to impose his own vision of Ireland on the state and its monuments. The first casualty of this was Ireland's only major seventeenth-century building, the recently and magnificently restored Royal Hospital Kilmainham, originally a resting place for old soldiers of the Crown. This £10 million project – a perfect miracle of careful craftsmanship and architectural integrity – had been the most extravagant piece of reconstruction in Ireland since the post-war rebuilding of Dublin in the 1920s. The hospital's neglect since then had reflected its role as a perceived symbol of imperial oppression. The restoration had reversed those decades of neglect, but no sooner was it complete than it was destroyed anew. Under the deranged guidance of his cultural guru, Anthony Cronin, Haughey ordered that this ancient jewel be turned into a modern art gallery. The meticulously restored door-opes were blocked up to create hanging space, artificial ceilings were suspended from the recently restored original ones and the eighteenth-century barrack rooms were demolished. Though this was both an architectural tragedy and a cultural travesty, its new role suited Haughey's perceptions of himself as a modernising Gaelic warrior-king and sponsor of the arts. His understanding of economics was of the Argentinian school, that is, Perónist. When the Talbot car plant in his constituency closed, he ordered that the entire workforce be re-employed as civil servants. By employing such brilliant strategies across the nation, unemployment could be abolished, the Irish language restored and the island united once again.

Yet despite all this nonsense, Haughey had few supporters more enthusiastic than Douglas Gageby. From the party-faithful pages of *The Irish Press*, one could expect little better, but from Gageby, the Protestant editor of the last public Protestant voice in Ireland – even if its Canterbury tones were now rather muted, such acquiescence seemed extraordinary. It certainly rankled greatly with Protestant readers, who often shared their indignation with me in the erroneous assumption that I too was a Protestant. Initially I assumed that Gageby's policies were strategic: under the influence of his political columnist, the Haughey-worshipping John Healy, he was aligning the newspaper with mainstream politics in Ireland. But, as we shall see, there was rather more to it than that.

Gageby knew of my loathing of Haughey, and I was in no doubt whatever about my editor's dislike of me. Naturally, my predilection for immersing myself in the soup would invariably cause me to say things that could not possibly benefit me. Well past my deadline one evening, I was hammering at my keyboard when Gageby approached me and cleared his throat.

'Come over the road,' he said. 'Have a jar.'

'Not now, Douglas. I'm way behind. Later perhaps.'

He blinked, straightened his shoulders and walked away, with the disbelieving air of a sacked Bismarck stepping down the gangplank. On another occasion, presumably in a deranged attempt at ingratiation, I asked Gageby if his name was a toponymic from the Danelaw part of England, as suggested by the -*by* suffix. I may as well have asked him if he sodomised his wife on Sundays.

'England? England?' he snarled, glaring orbs bursting incredulously from his face. 'There's nothing remotely English about me. Gageby is a Norman name. And it was the Normans who made Ireland, not the fucking English.'

One day, after Paddy Williams and I had carried a very angry wheelchair-visitor up the steps from the pavement to security, I wrote a memo to the newspaper's management pointing out that we had published many editorials demanding that the government do more for disabled people, while we lived in a building which was effectively wheelchair-proof.

Some two hours later, Gageby erupted from his office, this time waving my memo like the Ems Telegram, his eyes livid with anger.

'Are you saying to our MD that I'm a hypocrite?' he rasped. 'That I'm a liar, a charlatan?'

'No, Douglas, not at all,' I whispered. 'That was not the—'

'So what the fuck is the meaning of this?' he asked, waving the incriminating piece of paper.

'I think it speaks for itself.'

'It does indeed. Says I'm a fucking hypocrite.'

'That was not my intention.'

He turned and walked away, the incense of anger fumigating the entire newsroom. And, indeed, it was not my intention to cast any reflection upon him, for management of the building was not his responsibility.

Nonetheless, I had a point: from that day to when *The Irish Times* left Fleet Street over twenty years later, it remained as wheelchair-proof as the Maginot Line.

The British *Flight* magazine would send a weekly copy to *The Irish Times* for publicity purposes, and the news desk, knowing my adolescent interest in aircraft, would pass it on to me. The regular browsing that resulted was to have a wholly unwelcome impact on my life. However, before this could happen, one further magic ingredient was required: General Galtieri, Argentina's dictator, and his invasion of the Falkland Islands.

Before Galtieri's act of insanity, I would have been unable to find these islands on a map or confidently state the language spoken by their inhabitants. I did, however, know that the Argentinian regime consisted of a quasi-fascist gang of torturers whose conquest of the islands could not be countenanced, even though a military response might be a cataclysmic folly. Yet, mysteriously, within days of the invasion, I heard some fellow journalists refer knowingly to 'Las Malvinas', seeming to have suddenly acquired a mastery of the territorial disputes. I thought – and still think – that there is hardly a more startling example of man's, or perhaps *men's*, irredeemable stupidity than this contest over such inhospitable (if congenially alliterative) garrisons of gale, gull and gannet. Thanks to *Flight* magazine, I knew something about the respective military forces, and I tentatively suggested to our features editor, the immensely clever Paul Tansey, that I do a feature on it.

Prudently, he replied: 'I'll bounce that off Douglas.'

It was Gageby himself who came to me. 'Do it,' he rumbled. 'But don't make it too pro-Brit.'

Mysteriously, neither the BBC, ITN, nor any British newspaper had identified the major threat to any British task force: Argentina's possession of the French-made Exocet missiles. Perhaps this was a case of patriotic reticence rather than ignorance. Feeling no such inhibitions, I opened my speculative assessment of the respective military strengths of the two sides (as I recall) with roughly these words: 'One name is about to enter the vocabulary of the Royal Navy for all time, and that is Exocet. This is the French-made anti-shipping missile that the Argentinians are likely to deploy against the British task force, and against which there is virtually no defence. This weapon could even bring about the destruction of the British aircraft carriers, and a historic British defeat.'

Gageby came out to me, copy in hand. 'This isn't bad, you know' – the second near-compliment I had received from him – 'however, our business isn't to predict the news, but to report it after it happens. I'm going to kill the opening par. Do a rewrite.'

Experiencing Gageby unsheathing his politeness sword was rather like being seduced by Stalin, so I compliantly downgraded the mortal threat posed by the Exocet to a possible hazard, not in the opening par, but deep into the copy. Furthermore, reluctant to appear too 'pro-Brit', I largely fudged my own opinion on the subject, which was that Ireland should join the European Community in unequivocally supporting the British demand for an Argentinian withdrawal.

The sinking of the Argentine warship *General Belgrano* turned the mood in Ireland from fake knowingness to authentic anger. Subtlety, nuance, balance were sacrificed as deeply anti-British feelings inevitably surfaced. My own opinions have not altered. I believe that the torpedoing of the cruiser in international waters without warning or a legal declaration of general hostilities, causing the deaths of hundreds of young conscripts, was a war crime. But this truth does not invalidate Britain's legal case against Argentina.

My colleague Olivia O'Leary, writing brilliant despatches from Buenos Aires, reported the pleasure that was evident in Argentina that Ireland had broken ranks with the European Community, thereby effectively siding with the junta. Then, one by one, British ships were sunk by the very weapon I had warned about, and, frankly, I didn't hear any exultation over that. No one – outside the ranks of the IRA, of course – relished the prospect of the British being defeated.

Gageby came up to me one day as the Falklands War was winding to its sorry and sordid conclusion, with, as we now know, a bayonet charge by the Scots Guards up Mount Tumbledown, a gratuitous barbarity that, like so much else about the war, defies all understanding.

'You were right about the Exocet,' he mumbled, a whispered 'Sorry ...' trailing faintly in his slipstream as he walked away. A near-apology from Douglas Gageby still ranks as one of the greatest achievements of my entire journalistic career. If I could have captured and framed it and hung it over the fireplace, I would have done. I just wish he had left it at that.

During that same week, the Israeli ambassador to Britain was shot by a Palestinian terrorist, thus triggering a long-prepared Israeli incursion into Lebanon. The usual candidate to cover that kind of stuff would have been Conor O'Clery, whose dauntless intrepidity had already taken him into Afghanistan with the *mujahidin*, but he was now the paper's news editor.

Conor came over to me. 'Douglas wants you to go to Israel and cover the war. I'd love to go, but I have to stay here.'

'What? When?'

'Now.'

'Now?'

'Immediately.'

'But why me?'

'He feels guilty for cutting your stuff about the Exocets. We've taken the liberty of booking you a flight to Israel.'

'You've done what?'

'We've booked you on a flight to Tel Aviv. God, I wish I was going.'

That made two of us.

'I know from experience,' he continued, 'that you're good at the war stuff.'

Good at the war stuff. He meant Belfast. Ha! That was *then*.

Six

THEN. I CAN SAY PRECISELY when *then* was. *Then* was at the high point of my infatuation with violence. *Then* occurred at the junction between the Springfield Road and the Whiterock Road. *Then* was a moment that was so insane that when I was writing my memoir about my time in Belfast, *Watching the Door*, I had buried it so deeply in my memory that I never mentioned it.

Here it is now. This – the early summer of 1972 – is *then*.

One Saturday lunchtime, a loyalist bomb had exploded outside the Catholic Kelly's Bar, at the junction of the Whiterock and Springfield roads. I was there within minutes, for war was my joy, my nightclub, my seat in adrenaline heaven. Kelly's was not merely in the IRA heartland of west Belfast; it was overlooked by the loyalist Springmartin estate, a handy 800-yard shot away. The bomb had injured sixty-three people, and during the clearing-up operation, loyalists had opened fire, killing a barman, Tommy McElroy.

His lolling body was being taken away as I arrived, a hand flopping from the stretcher. With the shooting apparently over, I went into the ruins of the pub. A barman showed me how Tommy McElroy had died. A bullet from Springmartin had come through a window, hit a wooden beam in the ceiling above his head, and flown down vertically into his brain.

'Not a lucky shot. A fucking unlucky one,' the barman said with the weary air of purest Ballymurphy.

The shooting erupted again. I ran out the back, towards the safety of the Turf Lodge estate, just as an Army Ferret armoured car entered it. A hideous burst of machine-gun fire engulfed the vehicle, and a soldier in the turret slumped sideways. More gunfire erupted from loyalists in Springmartin, as lines of IRA gunman approached from Turf Lodge, moving in groups like lawful infantry. They scattered and sought cover as more soldiers came on the scene, and a multilateral murderousness began.

Hours of shooting followed. At one stage, I saw a group of youngsters manoeuvring into position the Lewis machine gun that had been deployed with such deadly effect against the Ferret. It had a circular disk magazine sitting flat on its top, and since its cocking handle was broken, its operator was using a pair of kitchen scissors to draw the bolt back after each burst of fire. This done, he would empty a full thirty-round drum into the Protestant estate in one unbroken, deafening blast. He would remove the magazine with a tap from a hammer, and click in a replacement, while dutiful children hurriedly refilled the empty magazines, and then he would unleash another burst.

In all this insanity, no one was more insane than me. Deluded by the laws of ballistics that I had seen in Kelly's Bar and which I now assumed would prevail wherever fate took me, I rose from my place of cover and walked to where the Whiterock Road met the Springfield Road, and simply stood there amidst the hurricane of gunfire, bullets striking sparks from the ground and hitting walls beyond me. In my madness, and from the evidence of what had befallen poor Tommy McElroy, I had chosen to believe that the loyalists were firing high. Since I had no beam over my head, I was therefore safe, and with all the armed youngsters around me pausing between shooting to gaze at me in disbelief, I declared myself to be immortal. And for the course of that day, I was. Indeed, it stands out as a high point of my life: the moment when I felt I was in command of all nature, and even supersonic metal obeyed my silent commands. But in the coming months, these fantasies of youth were eroded by regular visitations of death beside me. I learnt that mortality was a matter of numbers, a lottery that I would sooner or later win. By the time I left Belfast, five years and fifty weeks later to the very day and hour of that insane séance, I was cured of all appetite for violence.

But now Gageby, and this bubbling, happy-go-lucky warrior O'Clery, wanted to send me back into the line of fire. It wasn't courage that caused me to say yes, but cowardice: I was afraid of being seen to be afraid. I privately swore that I would never enter Lebanon and would instead gallantly cover the war from a bar in Israel.

On the flight from London to Tel Aviv, I met David Blundy of *The Sunday Times*. A beguiling, hopelessly unreliable chap, he was very tall and routinely broke women's hearts with his charming attitude, his disarming altitude and his crooked smile – perhaps his raffishly scuffed leather jacket also helped. He was smoking his usual Gitane, as one could on planes in those days. We downed Bloody Marys like lemonades on a hot Sunday afternoon and agreed to mind one another in the coming war, of which he – being much more travelled than I – had more extensive, though perhaps not more personally intensive, experience. He had covered the 1978 invasion of southern Lebanon.

'Don't believe a fucking word anyone says to you here – the Israelis, the PLO, the Falange – lying cunts the lot of them.'

On the plane, there was a US network television reporter whom David knew from other assignments. He joined us, kneeling over the back of the seats in front of us, and ordered more Bloody Marys all round. He was loud and expansive and astoundingly obnoxious. The drinks arrived, and the stewardess began to walk away.

'Miss? Miss?' he called, clicking his fingers at her departing back. 'More drinks here, honey, like *now*, chop chop. Now let me tell you,' he said turning back to us, 'I got experience of war zones like this, and I'm telling you, you guys will need choppers to get around the place. Choppers – helicopters, you dig?'

'We dig,' said David equably.

'Do you? You can never tell with you Limeys. Well, I got choppers. I can hire all the fucking choppers I want. You guys need choppers, come to me. All I got to do is click my fingers,' and, rather obligingly, he again showed us how that complicated digital deed was done, 'and I got choppers. That's what my network thinks of me.'

'You know what I think of you?' said David charmingly.

'No. What?'

'You're a fucking asshole.'

With our fucking asshole having returned desolately to his seat, David talked about the worries of war.

'Getting shot is par for the course. Tall fucker like me can only expect it. The one thing I couldn't bear is one through the spine, then spending the rest of my life on a bag, knowing that I needed a shit only after I've fucking well smelt it. Heart or head, every time.'

We raised our glasses, and intoned together: 'Heart or head, every time.'

He then warned me not to get my passport stamped on arrival at Tel Aviv: if it had an Israeli stamp on it, I could never enter an Arab country.

'Even the Lebanon?'

'Even the Lebanon. But don't worry, they'll ask you if it's okay to stamp your passport, and you just have to say no.'

At Tel Aviv airport, I made sure to join a different arrivals' queue from David. The immigration official asked me if I wanted my passport stamped.

'Yes,' I whispered, my eyes scoping this way and that to ensure that David wasn't within earshot, 'on every page, if you please.'

And so, with a succession of inky blotches, he duly made my admission to Lebanon perfectly impossible. I then rejoined David in the airport concourse, loudly lamenting my violated passport, and we shared a taxi to the American Colony Hotel in Jerusalem. The next day, I hired a car and set out for Metula on the Israeli–Lebanon border. I was in for a very rude shock. I had supposed that the Israelis had actually launched a large-scale raid into southern Lebanon, an *in-biff!-out* commando assault, but it was now obvious that this was a full-scale invasion. There was enough room alongside the hundreds of static tanks and armoured personnel carriers for me to drive at reasonable speed towards the front. High on a hillside road, from where I could see much of the Bekaa Valley, I spotted a slight *poof* in the distance. I was still wondering what it could be when a shell exploded in the field right next to me. My car bucked upwards from the shock wave. The Syrians had had the entire fucking Israeli Army to shoot at – oh, many miles of it – but of course had chosen to fire at the only bit next to me. A moment later, the Syrian gun position was annihilated by Israeli counter-battery fire. So, clearly, I was not going to be as safe as I had intended.

Later, in a thrombotic traffic jam of APCs and tanks, I got out of the car. High overhead were a few vapour trails. An occasional ground-to-air missile snaked upwards from Syrian positions. There were various loud bangs and occasionally some burning things came spiralling slowly downwards.

'What's going on?' I asked a tank commander.

'Biggest goddamn fuckin' air battle since woild wahr tooo, you ask me,' he said respectfully in deepest Bronx. In silence, we watched and listened as the most one-sided jet-age air battle in history came to an end, with over eighty Syrian planes having been shot down and every one of their pilots killed. Even though it occurred miles above me, and all I witnessed were flashes, bangs and some spiralling debris, the harvest of so many young lives both sickened me and deepened my determination not to join them.

At Metula I did the most important thing that a journalist should do: I found a hotel. Next I discovered that a press convoy was about to enter Lebanon. Now I needed copy, though of course without putting myself in any danger, so I introduced myself to a most unsoldierly Israeli Army press officer. He nodded affably at me, even though tension between Ireland and Israel had been high since our Army had been deployed with the UN in southern Lebanon following the 1978 Israeli invasion.

'Irish? Excellent! We got a real treat in store for you.'

Soon a vast aerial armada was passing overhead, hundreds of helicopters, transport planes and fighter aircraft.

'What do you think, Mr Irish?'

'Ireland's population is the same size as Israel's, and you've got hundreds of troop-carrying helicopters. We've got just one – and it's borrowed.'

It wasn't funny, it wasn't meant to be funny, but he fell about laughing.

'I like you, Mr Irish. I like you very much.'

But now I had my colour story, all in the air, requiring no courage from or risk to me – war journalism at its most perfect!

The next day I visited a kibbutz, whose residents were sick and tired of incoming rockets from Palestinians, so they were happy about the invasion, though they had no answer to my query about what would happen once the invasion was over. That's a question that still hasn't been answered.

The next day, the press officer came up to me. 'Good news, Mr Irish! We go into Lebanon today!'

I said anxiously, but, believe me, not at all wistfully, 'There's no chance of any action, is there?'

Had he been a native English speaker, he would not have misunderstood my tone as he now so catastrophically did.

'You mad Irish. Always looking for danger! I like you. I come with you in your car. I show you things!'

Was he joking? It was hard to tell. A bus was waiting to ferry journalists across the border, but my press-officer friend insisted on accompanying me and, worse still, leading the bus. We set off, amid clouds of dust, past all the slowly moving tanks.

'Turn left here. We stay away from mad Army bastards. Cause trouble wherever they go.'

'Aren't you Army?'

'Fuck no. I mean, yes, like everyone else, but no, not like them. Nice here, no?'

On the horizon sat the vast Crusader fort of Beaufort Castle, which had just been taken by Israeli forces.

'Why are we in the front?' I asked. 'If the road is mined, we'll get it first.'

He roared with laughter. 'You funny, Mr Irish: you very funny.'

I shook my head. I had said nothing funny, though tears of joy were running in torrents down his cheeks.

'Maybe we deserve to be blown up,' he continued, in a philosophical vein. 'Who knows? Fuck, there goes the bus!'

The bus driver had decided that he didn't like the route we'd taken and had turned off our road.

'I'm going after him!' I said. I began to turn when I saw a mortar shell explode right in front of the bus.

'See?' roared the Israeli happily. 'Safer with me!'

We drove on for half an hour. There was a firefight going on north of Beaufort. We stopped, got out of the car, watched the shell fall and listened to the sound of calico tearing as machine guns unleashed streams of bullets where Crusaders had once wielded halberd and broadsword against Muslim scimitar.

'There now! I promised something special. Those yellow bastards there in that fucking bus, they think they got something, boom boom boom, but you got the siege of Beaufort! Exclusive! Scoop!'

Well, it was certainly a good colour story, and one gained with little danger – though it certainly wouldn't sound like that once I had dressed it all up with gallantly understated but nonetheless richly adjectival prose, which is the true art of war reporting.

Back at the hotel, reception told me to ring the news desk. I did so. Conor O'Clery said: 'You've got to go to Beirut immediately. The Israelis have started besieging the city.'

'What?'

'Beirut! You've got to go there immediately! We've booked you a flight to Cyprus! You make your own way from there! God, I envy you!'

Yes, he really did speak in exclamation marks, and yes, the lunatic genuinely did envy me.

Carefully, I drew my trump card from my hand and laid it on the table.

'Oh, Conor, I can't,' I murmured with atrocious insincerity. 'The stupid bastard at Tel Aviv ignored my *very* specific orders and stamped my passport. On every fucking page. Meaning of course I can't get into Lebanon.'

I smirked in invisible triumph in Lebanon, while a thousand miles away an O'Clery brain was whirring through options. Two point three seconds later, it had worked out a solution.

'You're an Irish citizen, aren't you?'

'Of course.'

'Good. So catch the first flight to Athens. We'll get Foreign Affairs to hurry through a passport for you at the embassy. But you must go now. There's not a moment to be lost.'

What? How? I unleashed a machine-gun belt of but-but-but-but-buts into the ether. I could actually sense Conor looking at his wristwatch impatiently. I finally managed to whimper: 'But what about my colour story ...'

'Fuck the colour story! Beirut calls! God! This is it! Action!'

Yes, the exclamation marks were back, and I was on my way to Beirut. As I rushed to my car, I met Blundy and told him my fate.

'Oh, well done, old fellow! What wizard luck! That really is excellent news. I just wish I was going with you. But look – don't forget to destroy anything that reveals that you've been in Israel. Otherwise ....'

And he colourfully drew an imitation knife across his throat.

Seven

IN BARELY MORE than a day, I was in and out of Athens and landing in Famagusta in Cyprus, accompanied by a new and tragically un-Zionised passport. A steamer that took deck passengers was leaving that evening for the Lebanese port of Jounieh. I shuffled aboard, paid my $20 and took my place at the taffrail.

'Excuse me, are you a journalist?' said a voice beside me.

Anne-Marie was from Brussels. She too was on her way to the Lebanese lunatic asylum.

'You know to destroy everything that shows you were in Israel?' she said.

'Yes.'

'Have you double-checked?'

Sure enough, in my shirt pocket I found a receipt for a coffee in Metulah. It was soon fluttering into the darkening Mediterranean as night fell – with it, a truly terrible cold descended. I had only a light jacket, so Anne-Marie and I chastely huddled and shuddered together as the steamer bounced in that nasty, short-waved middle-sea swell that had impartially brought ruin to Ulysses and to St Paul. The night lasted as long as December in Thule. At dawn – a filthy, bleak, exhausted dawn – an Israeli gunboat drew up alongside us and sent a robust burst of machine-gun fire across our bows. This, surely, was a clear hint to the skipper that he should put about and return post-haste to the safety of Cyprus! Instead, after Marines had boarded the vessel and searched individually us all, we were, quite appallingly, allowed to sail on for Lebanon.

From Jounieh, Anne-Marie and I shared a taxi to Beirut, passing through the militia roadblocks where no mercy could be expected for those of the wrong hue, but we were waved through, and went directly to the Commodore Hotel. It was, of course, full. We learnt of a small hotel off the main shopping street of Hamra, where we might find rooms. We were in luck. I hastily typed an account of the sea journey to Jounieh and the passage through the city of Beirut. As artillery shook the hotel windows, I went to reception to use the phone.

There was no phone.

No phone. Enter dreamland.

The female receptionist – who is also the manager, the chef and the porter – says that I must walk to the United Press International offices about four kilometres away. Night has fallen, and there are no streetlights or illumination of any kind. Gunfire is everywhere. I mean everywhere: loud, ear-hurting *BANG BANG BANG*.

'Who is doing all the shooting?' I ask plaintively.

She does a little Gallic shrug, suggesting that she is Christian. My first stab at tribal identification.

'Who knows? Welcome to Beirut.'

She draws a map and gives me directions.

'It has big columns on the front,' she says.

So I must look for offices I have never seen in a strange city full of shooting, with no streetlights, no torch and no knowledge of my destination.

'Be careful,' she cries as I stand on the steps of the hotel, summoning up the nerve to make the first step into the ink-black sea that awaits me. After a pause, she helpfully explains, 'It's very dangerous out there.'

Ahead of me there are gunfights, many gunfights.

I inch out into the dark night – rifle and machine-gun fire being exchanged with brainless ferocity all around – my copy glued to an already sweaty hand. I am walking in the dead of night along streets that I have never walked by day. I know I must turn right at the barely visible junction 20 metres away, but after that, the dark is almost total. Mentally, I am back on the Falls Road on a very, very bad night, but I knew the Falls Road, whereas I don't know Beirut. Besides, shooting at night in

Belfast is usually done with quiet, deadly purpose. Here, it is being done with wildly vocative glee, joyful howls accompanying the bullets. Also, in Belfast I know who is doing the shooting: IRA, loyalist or Army. Here, I haven't a clue. Are they Palestinian, Falange, Shia, Sunni, Druse, Lebanese Army, police, factions and/or combinations thereof? Not a clue. No Israelis yet, but maybe soon, and welcome to the party, lads!

In the starlight, I can see the edge of the pavement. I walk parallel to it, slowly. Just yards away, people are firing and shrieking. At what? I can't see. I just keep walking in this nightmare ocean, a dark seabed full of sound and fury, wrath and murder. I think about nothing except putting one foot in front of the other, ignoring the invisible cacophony that hurts my ears and echoes inside my cranium. I cannot hurry because I do not know where I am hurrying to, and I cannot, may not, must not fall, because then I would probably be doomed. And very quickly on a journey such as this, there is no going back, because filing copy is a non-negotiable and overriding obligation of any journalist on assignment. But, on the other hand, I do not know where I am going.

Then the shooting stops. Suddenly there is silence in the black.

One night in Belfast, rather like this one, I was parking my car off the Falls Road, the air like octopus ink. I could see nothing, but I could just about make out where I was going, by the outline of the buildings against the stars. Suddenly, as powerful and personal as an electric shock through the brain, there was a fusillade of Armalite fire. How? What was there to see in this blackness? What was the target? A street away, at that very moment, an entire British Army mobile patrol was being nearly wiped out by IRA men with new night-sights, which the Army didn't know their enemy had.

Now, the question for me is: do I want my gunmen here to have night-sights on their weapons? Will those night-sights enable them to see that I am innocent and unarmed, or will the night-sights enable them to shoot me more easily?

I am walking down Hamra to deliver a meaningless piece of copy for a newspaper that doesn't know where I am, for some subeditor just back from the pub to draw some squiggles on, for printers to interpret and then typeset for readers who will never know what I am going through in order to make this meaningless liturgy possible. No, no, do not ask why. There is no why; there just *is*.

The pavement comes to an end, and it is clear from the wide arc of starlight overhead that I am no longer surrounded by buildings. I am at a roundabout. But I cannot see the map in the dark, and I do not know which exit I should take. All I can do is follow the line of the kerb, just visible in the soft glow from the stones, as if light had been captured at noon, and was now guiding wayfarers here below. The final, pleading words of a hymn come back to me from Christ the King primary school, twenty-five years earlier: *Mother of Christ, Star of the sea, Pray for the wanderer, pray for me.*

No, I don't pray. Neither to God nor His Blessed Mother. But the words come back to me, and I intone them inwardly, like a drunk singing a half-remembered song as he meanders homeward. Home. What or where is home?

Roundabouts are not just circles that enable drivers to enter a series of instant contracts with other drivers, making complex decisions beyond the power of traffic lights. They are boundaries. They mark where some streets end and others begin. And humans, being primates, have a profound sense of territory. This roundabout is, I guess, a front line. There are men everywhere, watching the streets opposite. These men are not shooting. How do I know they are here? Because they are whispering. There is the clink of metal. A round being chambered. A rifle barrel touching a wall. A magazine onomatopoeically clicks into place.

The shooting resumes. I keep walking. Slowly. For an hour. Finally, I see the dark of massive monuments against the sky, and something of the receptionist's instructions comes back to me. Is it the third left? No, right. This is Lebanon: they drive on the right here, and roundabouts go in the same direction. I cross the road, leaving the sanctuary and safety of buildings and the reassuring glow of the kerb.

Thrown on life's surge, we claim thy care, Save us from peril and from woe.

Step by step I go, the perfect target for those who have not yet shot an Irish journalist and wish to carve that particular notch onto the butt of their Kalashnikov or M16. If there is shooting now, I don't hear it. My entire world is focused on getting across this road. I fully realise that if I am shot in certain ways, I will probably never know anything about it. A headshot.

One through the heart perhaps.

Not the spine, sweet Jesus, not the spine.

I have spoken to doctors in Belfast about this. A headshot should kill you immediately, in the sense that consciousness ceases the moment a bullet passes through the brain, sending supersonic shockwaves through the cerebral tissue. In a microsecond, the waves reach the skull, and are bounced back, with terminal effect. That would be okay, but not always. Belfast policeman Seán Hughes, a Catholic who always refused to wear a gun because he thought of himself as a community officer, was shot through the brain by an IRA gunman at point-blank range at his home in 1972, and was left a blind, incontinent, quadriplegic epileptic. For decades.

But he was shot with a handgun. Dear God, spare me the handgun.

No one dies from a bullet through the heart. You bleed out. Exsanguination it's called. But the shock caused by the kinetic energy transmitted by the modern round – the 5.56 M16 or the 7.62 Kalashnikov – is so great that you probably feel nothing until most of your blood is outside you, and your corpse begins to settle into the final composure that marks the dead from the living, and which I have seen too often.

But not the spine.

Mother of Christ, Star of the sea. Not the spine.

I've crossed one road, am back on the pavement again, and I follow the track of the kerb until it turns sharply right, and I must cross the road. Again. Fear has a unique intensity, almost limitless in its power and its scope, and the only thing that keeps me going is fear itself. I am terrified of the consequences of what I am doing, but am even more terrified of not doing it, not because of any duty to *The Irish Times* – that perished long ago – but my survival instincts, shaped and nourished and encoded on the long dark night of the Palaeolithic, tell me that the consequences of panic are far worse than the consequences of purpose. In adversity, these two Ps are always the fork in the road.

I come to another junction and gaze right: there on a wall is a sort of Tilley Lamp above a large door between some columns on a rather grand building. Columns! Just as she had promised! I head towards it, the seafarer bound for a haven, and I make it.

Do thou, bright queen, star of the sea
Pray for thy children, pray for me.

Inside, the lobby is full of refugees. I have no idea who they are. There is a burly security guard with a Kalashnikov, who looks at my press pass and waves me upstairs. I am immediately drawn into a set procedure. I pass my copy over to a clerk who does a word count and tells me how much it will cost to telex. I must pay before it is sent, but I may not leave until it is. These are the rules. No explaining. I hand over the $15 and sit down. There is a Coke machine nearby, but I do not have Lebanese coinage. Refugees – who they are, I never find out – are sprawled all round me. A full night passes, except it is actually only about an hour.

The clerk comes out, gives me a receipt for the money and my original copy. Is there a phone I can use?

Sure, but it's metered.

I ring the office and speak to someone on the foreign desk.

'Yes, the copy's through. But try to file a little earlier next time, would you? A bit inconvenient, this late.'

I pay for the phone, then go downstairs. I am exhausted beyond words. My aching feet are encrusted with ancient, desiccated sweat. I have not slept for three days and two nights. Clearly, I cannot possibly get any sleep here, so I must return to my hotel. Gunfights have resumed outside. I begin my journey back, through the violence and the boundless dark of the Lebanese night, and a repeat of the gun battles of my outward journey. Finally, at around two in the morning, I am back at the hotel. It is closed, dark and lifeless. I hammer on the door – in vain, for what is the sound that my fist can make compared to the brutal bark of rifle fire all around me?

I sit on the steps and spend the night shivering and dozing, shivering and dozing, in a hallucinogenic hell of gunshots and screaming, all the way through to dawn, when I am woken by the manager.

Eight

THAT AFTERNOON, the bombers came.

You get used to artillery fire. You get used to its sound; you know when it is shifting quarter. Israeli artillery had been firing from first light, just as the receptionist-manager-porter-cook was opening the door to let me in to crawl to my bed. The gunners kept firing through my sleep, from which my mind rose regularly, only to fall back again.

By eleven o'clock, further sleep was impossible. I rose, showered and went downstairs, where the receptionist-manager-porter-cook – a woman in her late forties, with comprehensively monochrome dyed hair – made me coffee and fed me pitta bread and humus, while the guns beyond the city continued to bombard faraway targets. But I didn't mind. I was safe.

Anne-Marie joined me. We each had the same assignment: to convey the feeling of a city under siege. The high politics was beyond us. We agreed to walk separately around the Hamra district, then to meet again and share our observations. I told her of the hell of filing copy. It would have to be done in daylight.

Around noon, and very abruptly, I discovered that the war was changing, with the clattering din of multi-barrelled anti-aircraft guns pointing vertically in the middle of a nearby roundabout. Moments later, bombs landed, not near me, but with shocking violence, the reverberations of which you feel through your feet and in the air, like windy caresses. Aircraft bombs are truly terrifying, because they have so much random energy, like an omnipotent Vulcan unleashing his wrath wherever he wants. Now I understood the rout of the British Expeditionary Force in 1940, pursued by mocking Stukas.

With the city shaking to the sound of the falling bombs, I hurried back to the hotel, and went up to the roof. There I sat watching as Israeli Phantoms and Kfirs circled overhead like silver fish glinting distantly in the sun. The anti-aircraft batteries were blattering away into the skies, but to no effect: the planes took turns to swoop down from beyond their range and drop their bombs on the waterfront about a mile away, and on the Palestinian refugee camps on the edge of the city. Safe and anonymous butchery, one of the twentieth-century's great military inventions.

I scribbled my thoughts on the rooftop until the manager came up to me: I would have to leave the rooftop. Her neighbours had seen me, and thought I was signalling to the Israelis.

'But ...'

'I know, I know, it is stupid, but please, for me.'

Of course, when I was gone, this Christian woman must answer to her Muslim neighbours. I obliged and went to my room. There I gazed onto a deserted street. I waited for Anne-Marie. And waited. No sign. I wrote my copy, finishing only as night fell, and the bombers departed, and the streets came alive again with the sound of rival militias disputing their patches in the only way they knew.

Once again, I walked through the Lebanese night to deliver my copy to the UPI offices. It was no easier the second time, for now I *knew*, and I was not sustained by the fatigue-reinforced ignorance of the previous night. The entire city was alert and deranged. Gun battles were being fought, the purpose of which was – and remains – beyond me. Suddenly would fall a silence, so sinister in the black, black night, because you can with eerie clarity hear the otherwise unhearable. A clink of metal on metal; the oiled steel sound of a gun being cocked. Who is the target? Me? Yes, maybe me. I continue walking, fear at its coldest and most purposeful filling every part of me, and the only way of defeating it is to reduce my world and my imagination to simply putting one foot in front of another, and continuing to do that until my night's duty is done. No kind words awaited me when I managed to ring Dublin, just a rebuke for not phoning earlier to tell them what I planned to write about, and a further complaint for filing late.

Why did I do it? Because I did. That is all.

Anne-Marie turned up at breakfast. She had met a Belgian camera crew in the street and had gone to the Commodore Hotel with them. When the bombing started, it was too dangerous for her to leave. She had slept on a colleague's bedroom floor. She was so sorry. No need to apologise. I would have done the same.

She told me she had put our names on a waiting list at the Commodore. We'd have to go there each morning to check if there were vacancies. We then went our separate ways, and I again wandered around Hamra. Street cafés were open, and I sat down and ordered a coffee. A lorryload of Palestinian fighters went past the café and then stopped fifty yards away. I watched them deploy, left and right, around the café. Ah, it looked as if I might have a story. An officer with a sidearm on his hip came up to me. He unholstered his pistol and pointed it at me.

Ah. *I* was the story.

I begin to explain. He cocks his pistol, the slide of the Makarov 9mm putting a round in the chamber, a deed that invariably commands instant obedience. I rise, and the officer leads me out. I am motioned onto the back of the lorry, and I get up. Beside me is a boy aged about fourteen. He has a tiny holster on his hip, containing an even tinier gun. He smiles at me in welcome. I sit down beside him. He smiles at me again, and then, with his hand, imitates drawing the gun from its holster, putting it to my head, and says '*Kaput*'.

The men around us laugh, and one of them speaks to the boy, who seems to obey by producing a real pistol from his holster. I am not an expert in these things, but it is, I think, a two-shot Derringer. It is not a battlefield weapon, and it has only one purpose.

We drive to a series of fine waterfront houses, and I am escorted up some steps into one, then downstairs to a basement, where groups of armed men are standing. They look at me coldly. I am ushered into another room, where I am made to sit at a table. The boy puts a chair next to mine. He places two fingers to his own temple, pulls an imaginary trigger, and says 'Poof'. Everyone laughs. I look him up and down. He clearly has an erection. For him, this is sex.

I am in deep, deep trouble.

They empty my pockets of everything. One of my captors speaks English.

'Why are you spying for Isra-el?'

Isra-el: not a diphthong, but two distinct vowel sounds, as in the Christmas carol of long, long ago, to rhyme with Emmanuel.

'I am not spying for Israel. I'm an Irish journalist. I'm here to report on what the wicked Israelis are doing to the people of Lebanon.'

'Of course. What else would you say?'

The boy beside me shifts keenly, his eyes wide and shining, the warm liquids of adolescent lust simmering: am I to be his murder-virginity? *Making his bones* is how the Sicilian mafia describe this dreadful rite of murderous passage. For the first time, I understand the full meaning of the phrase.

My interrogator stares at me coldly. His fellow judges do likewise: three sets of eyes, gazing implacably at me.

'Have you ever been to Israel?'

'Never! Never! The Irish people hate Israel. They hate colonialism!'

'Really? But your passport says you were born in England. You're English. And your name is Jewish. Myer,' his lips shaping the final sound with fastidious distaste.

'My family emigrated! Under penal laws,' I improvised, 'the Irish had to change their names from Irish names to English names. Our Irish name was Ó Midhir.'

All rubbish, of course.

'How interesting.'

He is holding my wallet, removing various receipts and pieces of paper and currencies. And suddenly, there in his hand, is the American Express counterfoil for my flight from Tel Aviv to Athens. He never takes his eyes off me as he fingers this potentially lethal piece of evidence, and neither do the two other judges. He puts the guilt-screaming receipt on the table, still without realising its significance. There, the folded piece of paper lazily uncoils to reveal the four cerulean letters, *El Al*, before rocking this way and that, silently urging my captors TO LOOK AT IT!

'You seem nervous.'

'I *am* nervous. I've been kidnapped. I'm being held by armed men and I've no idea who you are. I have this lunatic child beside me who clearly wants to kill me. Who wouldn't be nervous?'

The judge translates, and everyone laughs except the boy, who says something and glares at me.

The main interrogator speaks sharply to him, then turns to me.

'He is young and keen to kill the enemy, as is right.'

'Good. But I am not the enemy.'

'Maybe, maybe not.'

On the table, the El Al/Amex counterfoil still sways gently from the restless energy imparted into its molecules when I had folded it so carefully five days previously. Beside me is my teenage killer, apparently aroused by the prospect of an execution accompanied by ejaculation. I know these things can be related: William Manchester has described how he underwent the two experiences when he killed a Japanese soldier. But if the boy takes his eyes off me, he will surely see those four blue letters as the receipt slowly unfolds.

I am now as alert as a violin string, which is why I instantly know what is happening when the entire building and everything in it shifts minutely, *whoosh*, and I sense the downward arrival of a wall of compressed air. A bomb landing. A microsecond later …

BOOM!

A shattering roar sweeps through the basement, upsetting the table. A man comes rushing in from outside and bellows something to my interrogator. The familiar din of an anti-aircraft cannonade begins to bark deafeningly from the back.

CLATTER CLATTER CLATTER …

then …

… BOOM BOOM BOOM as a line of bombs falls along the street above.

The men around me rise hastily, reaching for weapons, then begin to rush outside.

'You can go,' barks my judge.

'May I take my papers?'

He waves a dismissive hand.

I scoop up everything, the El Al receipt especially. Everyone else hurries out into the rear, while I run back the way we had entered, up the stairs to the hall. The front door has been blown in, and there's rubble everywhere. Outside, a line of cars has been tossed upside down, and their scattered hulks are burning furiously. High overhead, the Israeli bombers are coming in for another pass. I screw up the El Al counter-foil and throw it into a burning car before sprinting away.

I have no idea how I found my way back to Hamra, but I managed to. It was a measure of the gallantry of the people of Beirut that some two miles away the cafés were still open, for it was clear to proprietors and customers that they weren't the target. I knew I had to return to the café and pay my bill and by my presence confirm that I was not an Israeli spy. This I did.

I have given long and hard consideration to that afternoon, which I have reported as factually as I can, exaggerating nothing. I don't know if anyone died in the raid. I think that it was the amateurishly conspicuous arrival of the truck on the waterfront that gave Israeli reconnaissance aircraft a clear target at which to direct their bombers. It was these bombers that saved from me the fate that had been inadvertently ordained for me by their aerial companions in El Al, though my own profound stupidity was the key contingency to the entire affair. It was not the last time that I would fatally lead the Israelis to their foes.

I returned to my hotel. Anne-Marie told me that the word at the Commodore was that Israelis were expected to stage an assault on Beirut over the coming hours, in which case the press would be taken as hostages or even killed. That night, I repeated the same journey to the UPI offices, with the same fear nearly overwhelming me. I knew I could not possibly do this again. I had reached breaking point. I got back to the hotel at midnight and surrendered to morbid fatalism. This being the night of my death, I opened the minibar in my room for the first time, and proceeded to drink every single little bottle within – Drambuie, Johnny Walker, Hennessy, Bacardi, Heineken, and why not a drop of this exquisite Gordon's gin to go with that delicious Jack Daniel's?

I collapsed on my bed, and sure enough, early that morning, the Israelis arrived, blasting their way up Hamra, firing their 125mm canon in flat trajectory into the buildings left and right, without discrimination. From my balcony, I saw the turret of a Merkava tank slowly swivel towards me and fire directly at me ...

BOOM!

The balcony roof fell on me ...

I woke. The tank was a dream. But the explosion was not. The hotel had been hit by a shell, and the entire ceiling was now on top of me, like a plaster sheet over a corpse. Lying beneath it, I had no idea whether I was dead or not. I heard Anne-Marie's frantic voice crying *Keveen Keveen* outside my door. I often wonder what might be the sweetest sound I've ever heard. It's probably *Keveen Keveen*, and not just because of that night.

Later that morning, Anne-Marie told me that she'd had enough and was leaving. She was going to the Commodore to say goodbye to her friends. I joined her. There was a large-scale departure that morning and I was able to get a room. I returned to the hotel on Hamra and said farewell to the manager-cook-receptionist-bottle washer, explaining that although I was very grateful for her kindnesses, the problems communicating with my office made it impossible to stay. She nodded in understanding, putting her hand on my arm. I kissed her cheek, then her lips. I briefly thought about it – maybe we both did – but instead I left.

Nine

IN THE COMMODORE, I ran into Robert Fisk, whom I knew from Belfast. He offered to buy me a drink in the bar, where he introduced me to a senior Lebanese police officer, presumably a Shia, whose name I don't remember. Bob isn't much of a drinker and he left the pair of us talking.

'I'm a policeman,' said the other. 'I know trouble when I see it. You're trouble. You get into trouble a lot?'

I told him about the abduction.

'See what I mean? Trouble. First, get rid of that beard. Makes you look like an Isra-eli.'

We got hammered together. Next morning, with no trace of a hangover, I went for a walk towards the university district. It was a Saturday, a day of rest for most journalists. Much of Beirut is lovely: palm trees abound, while jacaranda, oleander and bougainvillea create adjoining pools of fragrance. With a good night's drinking behind me, I felt refreshed and heartened.

I was rounding a corner when a young woman with a headscarf and Kalashnikov approached me. It wasn't hugely unusual to see women with guns, though I never really understood which faction they belonged to – and this one certainly wasn't telling. Instead, she started screeching at me, gesturing for me to put up my hands. Which I did. Two other young women swiftly appeared, similarly attired in Islamic headscarves, one carrying an AK, the other a handgun. All three of them began to scream at me, pointing me towards a house. They hustled me in and up some stairs into a room, where I was made to sit down, while they continued to shout hysterically and wave their guns at me. My captors were clearly determined that some harm should come to me, though they didn't seem particularly inclined to do it themselves.

A man arrived, listened to the women's bitter accusations against me, then went away. Several minutes passed, while the trio of Gorgons glared, unnervingly caressing the triggers of their weapons. I didn't think they would kill me, but I sensed a mounting determination that someone should.

Finally, a young man entered, obviously the leader. He was taller than me, dark, confident, handsome, a para-AK with a folding stock hanging from his shoulder by a canvas strap. He listened to the women shrieking their loathing of me, nodded and came over to me. He addressed me in Arabic, which was a compliment, I suppose. I shook my head. He then tried a hesitant French.

'Elles dites que vous êtes un espion Isra–élien.' ('*They say you're an Israeli spy.*')

I replied in improvised schoolboy French, saying absolutely not, that I was an Irish journalist, and that I had documentation to prove it. Here, I added, showing him my press card and my passport.

He smiled, and said in heavily accented French that an Israeli spy would hardly have a card marked Mossad, huh?

He had a point. An Israeli spy would probably have the same documentation that I had.

Then I chanced my arm.

'What's going on here? You're not Palestinians.'

This was taking quite an unnecessary risk. All right, so the Islamic scarves suggested that they were Lebanese, but since I knew nothing about the factions in the city, I could gain nothing by making such a dangerous observation. He looked at me steadily.

'Up,' he said in English.

I rose, and he pointed me towards some French doors that led to a balcony. I obeyed. Once we were in the open, he took my shoulder and turned me to face him. He gazed into my eyes from about a foot away, then stepped back, put the barrel of his AK against my lips, and jiggled it. The women were ululating their joyous approval. I shook my head. He smiled at me, raised an eyebrow, and turned the rifle around, with the iron butt end pointing at my face. He gestured with it, indicating that he would smash my teeth unless I complied. I opened my mouth and he put the barrel deep into it. The women were shrieking with the same libidinous appetite as the boy from the previous day. The last coherent question in my mind was: do women also reach orgasm when they kill?

No further thoughts rose in my brain: dullness filled it, while a secretary in my memory bank took notes. The women were howling. The gunman looked back over his shoulder at them and nodded. They cried with joy. Then he turned to look at me. He winked, whispered 'Bye' then paused for me to enjoy the moment, before he pressed the trigger.

Click.

There wasn't a bullet in the chamber.

He collapsed with laughter, his knees bent, his gun hanging loosely in his hand. But the women behind me were shrieking like brawling cats in their anger and thwarted lust.

'Très amusant, non?' – *Very funny, no?* – he chuckled, wiping away a tear.

The secretary in my memory, who had been coolly taking notes, spoke for me, in French, which in English roughly translated, 'For you, maybe, but not for me.'

'You're lucky,' he replied in French. 'I could have killed you.'

Yes, I was lucky; yes, he *could* have killed me. Like so many of these episodes, I have visited this one often, trying to examine what was going on in my mind, other than that dutiful secretary, memorising things and even speaking for me. I think the answer is that nothing was going on, and that in such circumstances a defensive mechanism causes the mind to simply shut down. I certainly didn't feel fear – and not out of bravery, but out of an utter lack of feeling. My mental receptor cells refused to receive and process the information they were being given, and self-induced anaesthesia reigned. When I hear of the killings of the unarmed and defenceless, once so rare in my life and now so commonplace, I pray that the stupefaction that colonised my mind on that balcony shares its merciful benedictions with those less fortunate souls.

I returned to the hotel, went to reception, borrowed a pair of scissors and went to my room to cut off the denser growth of beard before unleashing a razor on the stubble. The chambermaid had already put out the contents of my toilet bag. Beside the sink was the toothpaste that I had bought in Israel, its Hebrew writing loud and colourful. Clearly, a survival instinct was not written large in my genes.

'That is better,' my policeman friend said approvingly that evening. 'But you still spell danger.'

I was sitting in the lobby the next day when an American came over and sat beside me. He introduced himself, Paul, and asked if I would like a drink. No, thanks. He asked a waiter to bring him a bourbon.

'I been watching you,' he said. 'You don't seem to know the rules round here.'

'I do. I shaved off my beard.'

'The first time I saw you, I said, he's trouble. I wondered if you were a spook or a shill.'

'*Shill*? What's a shill?'

'Someone who isn't what he says he is. But Fisk says he knew you in Belfast. You don't sound all that Irish to me, but what do I know?'

A lot as it turned out. Paul was Jewish, and, unlike any Jew I've ever met, he drank morning, noon and night. He also smoked untipped Chesterfields, which he held halfway along their length, and so they invariably drooped in the middle. He'd won a Pulitzer Prize – or so it was said – though I've looked through the list of prize-winners for around that time and have been unable to find his full name. A pity, because he was a good friend and an invaluable companion with an uncanny nose for both danger and survival.

The war soon took a more serious turn as the Israelis embarked on a big push around the Palestinian refugee camps to the south of Beirut. It was everything: artillery, air strikes, infantry assaults. I bumped into Clark Todd, a genial, scholarly Canadian who had been an occasional colleague in Belfast when I was freelancing for Westinghouse Broadcasting. He always liked solid sources, and despised hacks' gossip. Clark told me that there were believable reports that a new weapon was being deployed: napalm B, globules of which would get lodged in the flesh and burst into flames hours later. Burn patients in their hospital beds, he said, were spontaneously catching fire.

'Can that really be true, Clark?'

'Not until you get it confirmed from someone who is *not* a journalist.'

Paul wanted to check out these reports. He took me to Sabra, where we were given a guided tour by the PLO spokesmen. Small silvery devices lay on the ground. Just as I bent down to pick one up, Paul violently pushed me sideways. 'Never touch anything here you personally didn't put down,' he barked.

It was a tiny anti-personnel device such as might be picked up by any child: it was too small to kill, but it was large enough to blow off a hand. We never got the napalm story confirmed, but it was nonetheless clear that Israel had lost all sight of reason and perspective and was deploying weaponry that must have been invented by the Israeli equivalents of my shrieking girlfriends and that charming lad with the Derringer.

Heavy fighting had taken place one Saturday night near the airport. The next morning, Paul and I shared a taxi to the nearby Bourj el-Barajneh refugee camp. We went to the PLO headquarters, where Paul was known; they were probably unaware that he was Jewish. A PLO officer offered to take us to a front-line position from where we could see the Israelis' overnight advances. The invaders had captured Katyusha rockets from the Palestinians, which they were now firing into the position held by the missiles' previous owners. Their howling din, like banshee dervishes, was almost as shocking as their kinetic effect when they landed.

So, while overhead the Katyushas wailed their demented chorus, *WHOO WHOO WHOO*, and the Israeli artillery fired their salvoes in solemn antiphon, Paul and I were taken to the most forward Palestinian post. It was heavily camouflaged and seemed undetectable. There were about a dozen young soldiers there, most of them teenagers, with a couple of grizzled veterans in their thirties. I furiously scribbled notes as they cheerily talked about the fighting they'd been through. There was one boy, who spoke a little English and who looked about twelve, for whom I felt a particular regard: his teeth were bared in a perpetual smile. We shook hands with them all, the boy laughing in excitement about meeting these apparently exotic, even important, strangers, and then we left.

We were barely a hundred yards away when the ground beneath our car rocked. As the driver struggled with the wheel, Paul and I both looked back. The post we had just left had been obliterated by a co-ordinated artillery strike. Our visit had apparently drawn the attention of Israeli forward artillery observers. Had we stayed another half-minute, we would have suffered the same fate as those young men and that laughing boy, whose hands we had solemnly shaken.

Later, at the HQ, Paul was spitting with rage, both at himself and the PLO. 'Why the fuck did you send us where we might be revealing where your goddamn forward positions are? Jesus, all those men are probably dead!'

'Inshallah,' said the PLO man, shrugging, loyal to the caricature.

'I don't know who the fuck I hate more in this goddamned place,' said Paul as we walked back to our taxi. 'The fucking Israelis or the fucking Palestinians.'

We returned to the hotel, both of us sickened by what had happened and our inadvertent role in helping to bring about the likely death of so many young men. Yes, trouble comes to me, but I also bring it to others.

And so, amid the dire midsummer Lebanese heat, I dreamed of Ireland, of going to horse shows, of the smell of dung and the scent of the rain falling on lush green grass. I was profoundly sick and tired of the war, for I was not like so many other correspondents who relished the hormone kick that fear and violence can give you. Some of these were demented war junkies, but Don McCullin, the legendary war photographer, was a deeply sensitive man. He and I spent an afternoon on the roof of the Commodore gazing at the artillery bombardments to the south, discussing his Irish origins, of which he was very proud. His name means 'holly', he told me, and his roots were in Armagh. He had seen many massacres, yet had remained intact. I knew I would not do so, mentally or physically, if I stayed there. Beirut Airport was closed by the fighting, so I joined an illegal convoy back into Israel through the Badlands of south Lebanon and ultimately arrived at Tel Aviv airport. I had done my bit, and I was going home, never – I swore – to return.

Ten

ONE OF THE GREAT COUPS for *The Irish Times* had been the appointment of Conor Cruise O'Brien as a columnist. Personally, I greatly disliked him: I found his manner odious and his speech contrived. At the very start of my journalistic career, I had gone to watch an Apprentice Boys' rally outside Derry. I spotted O'Brien amongst the spectators and heard some loyalists declaring that he was an IRA man who needed seeing to. So, I went over to him and warned him that he could be in trouble. He disdainfully pooh-poohed me, and, believe me, an O'Brien dismissal has never endeared him to the dismissed. I walked away, but nonetheless kept a distant eye on him. Soon, half-a-dozen men went charging towards him. He tried to flee, but he was soon caught and knocked to the ground. Several men began to punch and kick him, at which point – I was young, remember – I allowed a suicide gene to intervene. I raced over, and began to haul the assailants off their target, crying with what now seems like astonishing naivety that I was an Apprentice Boys Grand Marshal from Leicester, and that this Conor Cruise O'Brien was actually an enemy of the IRA.

'If you're an Apprentice Boy, where's your fucking sash?' hollered a burly rustic.

'It's against the law in Leicester,' I improvised with preposterous optimism. I lifted the injured O'Brien to his feet, escorted him away, and once he was safe, I returned to the rally. I later went to the City Hotel, the main meeting place for journalists, and told them what had happened. The next day, several newspapers quoted me as an eyewitness, saying that I had seen O'Brien running from the mob.

A week later in Dublin, I happened to see O'Brien walking along Merrion Square. I went over to him and introduced myself, expecting him to favour me with a few words of thanks. I had, after all, taken some risks on his behalf.

'Are you the fellow who said I was running away?' he lisped.

'Yes, I am.'

'I've never run away from anything or anyone in my life! How dare you, sir, how dare you!'

'Of course you were running. Anyone with any sense runs from a mob.'

He raised his umbrella above his head, waving it as if it was a scimitar.

'You lie, you lie! Now stand back, sir, stand back, before I smite you as a liar and a cad!'

He wide-eyed me like an angry frog, his equally indignant brolly quivering with its own designs on my cranium, whereupon I concluded the meeting, and we never spoke again. Nonetheless, although I found O'Brien to be personally loathsome, I admired him politically, both for his unwavering hostility to the IRA and his penetrating critique of the nationalist mythology that underpinned republican terrorism. It was then the fundamental position of Fianna Fáil that the state of Northern Ireland was purely the creation of the British, and all that was required for a united Ireland was a British statement of intent to withdraw, whereupon all the pieces of Irish unity would fall neatly into place. From my years in the North, I knew of the power of unionist aversion to a united Ireland.

It's an odd feeling, simultaneously respecting a man for his opinions, while thoroughly disliking him as a poltroon. Journalistically, O'Brien was the right man in the right place that summer, when the murderer Malcolm MacArthur was found in the flat of the government attorney general, Patrick Connolly. We might reasonably ask what sort of officer of the court would ally himself to such an enemy of the rule of law as Haughey? The latter had called the MacArthur affair 'grotesque, unbelievable, bizarre, unprecedented'. Any of us could have redeployed those words to our advantage, but it was Conor Cruise O'Brien who saw the acronymic gold glinting amid the tawdry gravel of Haughey's excuses, and coined the term 'GUBU' to describe Haughey and his sordid government. GUBU was to haunt Haughey for ever.

Meanwhile my columns on that far more distant war in Picardy and Ypres had aroused different responses amongst *Irish Times* readers: frank ridicule and disbelief, outright hostility, relieved welcome. Jim Milton, one of the foremost PR consultants in Ireland, asked me to escort a group of his friends to the Western Front. I am far too chaotic a person to be able to assemble a group of Eskimo even for a snowball fight: Jim was the direct opposite. All I had to do was draw a campaign plan for a group of men whom I came to call The Chaps over my years of battlefield tours – Jim, Mick McBennett, Mark Wilkinson, Eddie Shiel and Tony Moore. Fine men all, loyal friends and future stalwarts in both my campaign and many future travails.

Where to begin? The first British shots in the Great War in Europe were not fired on land, but at sea, two days after war had been declared, when HMS *Amphion* sank the German minelayer SMS *Königin Luise*. Having rescued some German sailors, the *Amphion* sailed into a mine that its quarry had just sown, blowing off her bows. Sinking yet still circling, with her engines still working, the surviving crew and captives were taken off by another RN vessel. And just as the *Königin Luise* had a sting in her tail, so too did *Amphion*: a fire spreading through her hull reached a gun which still housed an unfired shell. The blaze detonated the gun, and its shell hit the deck of the neighbouring ship, crowded with survivors of the two vessels, impartially slaying both the British and their German captives. If ever there was a metaphor for the entire war, this episode – part squalid, part heroic, part farcical and wholly tragic – provided it. One of the twenty Irish dead was Pierce Murphy, from a tiny row of tenements called Thorncastle Place in Ringsend, Dublin.

The land war for the British began a fortnight later, as the British Expeditionary Force (BEF) made its tortuous way north from the Channel ports of Calais and Dunkirk to head off von Kluck's vast right hook heading towards Paris. The German barracuda ran into the BEF minnow south of Mons, where the first British Army's shots of the European war were fired by a patrol of the Royal Irish Dragoon Guards.

Shortly afterwards, 19-year-old Second Lieutenant John Denys Shine of Dungarvan, County Waterford, led a platoon of the Royal Irish Regiment in the British Army's first bayonet charge of the war, with an entirely predictable outcome as eighteenth-century ironware met twentieth-century munitions. Most of his men were casualties, and young John Denys – the youngest of three soldier-brothers – was mortally wounded. Within two years, the other two boys had been killed, followed by their mother, Kathleen, who presumably died of whatever it is that mothers die of when all their sons are dead. The boys' uncle, a Catholic chaplain, also died in the war, leaving their father wifeless, sonless and brotherless.

One of the men young Shine had led to a common doom just south of Mons was Stephen Corri, the grandson of an Italian choirmaster who had been brought to Dublin from Italy to teach the boys of the Pro-Cathedral to sing. The Corris had fallen on hard times, ending up in a tenement in a tiny dead-end street called Thorncastle Place. Yes, he had been a neighbour of Pierce Murphy, killed in the first naval engagement of the war. Of the million or so British and empire dead of the Great War, that almost the first two killed in that vast harvest – one a sailor, the other a soldier – should come from the same tiny street in Dublin not only defies arithmetic and belief but should have merited a special place in the mythology of the war.

Instead, silence. No plaque has ever been erected to commemorate these boys, not even for the centenary of their deaths in 2014. However, the Mons-Bergen cemetery, wherein Corri's officer, young John Shine, lies, is a good place to start a battlefield tour. Four years after his death, they were still burying bodies here – now of Russian POWs who were retained as battlefield slaves even after the Treaty of Brest-Litovsk of March 1918 should have resulted in their freedom. And, mysteriously, Romanians and Italians also. In its own way, this single graveyard tells a larger story of German intentions. Once Belgium declined to allow German troops to pass through its territory, it was doomed as a state, for it soon became the conquerors' intention to colonise Flanders east to west, with Ostend ultimately to become the westernmost base for the *Kaiserliche Marine*. This would have effectively made the Kaiser the Admiral of the English Channel and the harbour-master of the Port of London.

I am not saying that the prevention of this justifies the Great War, with all its monstrous horrors, but am merely observing that this was Berlin's intention. However, a declaration that each side was equally guilty for starting the war is satisfying, for such a stance acquits one of hubristic war-mongering while aligning one with the Hibernian angels of neutralism. This invocation of a plague on both your houses was certainly the formal view of Official Ireland, despite the Easter Proclamation's idiotic identification of Germany as 'gallant allies'. But this is no more absurd than the British claim that the war was about 'freedom', when its actual outcome was the enlargement of the British Empire, with the further creation of a string of subservient satellite states across the Middle East. However, the larger truths of these times are far too complex to be conveyed in a few declamatory paragraphs, any more than the circuitry of a radio can be. Yet myth attempts to do just that.

So much to see from a cemetery called Mons (Bergen). Bergen is not a suburb of Mons, but the same place: Bergen is Mons' Flemish name. Two names, one place, just as rival histories compete around the same events, but viewed through different lenses. Another citizen of this cemetery is Robert McIlvenny, of the Connaught Rangers, who died four years after young Shine. He was a Catholic from Primrose Street, Belfast, and presumably a National Volunteer, who joined the British war effort in the belief that Home Rule for all Ireland would be the result. So much for that. In his choice of regiment, we can see the hand of cultural partitionism. Instead of joining the locally recruited Royal Irish Rifles, thereby becoming a regimental colleague of his Protestant neighbours, he opted for the Rangers, drawn from the very heartland of Celtic pre-modernist mythology.

In 1926, Robert's brother named a son after poor dead Bobby, and the boy went on to become a professional footballer in England. Thomas McIlvenny, a stonecutter and a Catholic who appears to have been a cousin of Robert's, was killed on the first day of the Somme with the 9th Royal Irish Rifles, which was based on the west Belfast UVF – clearly, only in part. Once again, there are no clear truths here, only shards, like tiny crystals from which to assemble a home-made radio that might possibly enable one to hear the remote crackles of some distant truth.

European civilisation shattered when it hit the iceberg of the Great War, and here in Mons (Bergen) we can see some of the results: all these dead Russians, Romanians and Italians, plus of course the first Shine, killed at the war's beginning, the down payment on an entire family, and next young McIlvenny, who died a month before war's end. It takes no particular wisdom or sensibility to understand that the gravestones of Mons (Bergen) provide a lapidary lens on both world and Irish history, not least when you consider that amongst its citizenry is Pilot Officer Anthony Michael Dillon, aged eighteen, a Hurricane pilot clearly of Irish origin, shot down and killed in May 1940 when the Germans returned yet again, but this time staying for four and half years.

The St Symphorien Military Cemetery nearby is an altogether more beautiful place, where Irish, English, Germans, Scots and Canadians mingle companionably in the loam. Here lie James Brennan MM of Ballyaise, Kilkenny, a railway worker's son, and William Welby, of Dublin, a belt maker's son, both killed at war's end. Here rests Edward Ellison of the 4th Irish Dragoon Guards, killed shortly before 11 a.m. on 11 November 1918, in the last cavalry charge on the Western Front. That fatal burst of gunfire also injured Thomas Farrell, of the 5th Royal (Irish) Lancers, from near Navan. He died the next day, the last Irishman to be fatally injured in the war, though by no means the last to die from its effects. He is buried in the nearby military cemetery at Valenciennes. And here again the hand of history moves on. In the 1930s, Robert Armstrong, a Church of Ireland ex-Irish Guardsman from County Roscommon, became a gardener in the cemetery, perhaps preferring to spend his life with dead soldiers rather than living humans. Despite being of presumably unionist sympathies, he had acquired an Irish passport, and so was not interned when the Germans returned in 1940. Nonetheless, he joined the French Resistance, and his network was betrayed. His fellow resisters were all shot, but he was not because he was Irish and so suffered a far worse death in Waldheim concentration camp in Saxony in 1944.

History is not set in stone. It is not a series of facts, but a series of tales, which is how we relate facts, in narrative form. And since the Irish are such extraordinary storytellers, it makes the successful abolition of all public memory of Ireland's involvement in the Great War even more astounding.

Ypres is the epicentre of the British narrative of the Great War. Each evening in the town, buglers of the Fire Brigade play the last post at the Menin Gate through which so many men passed for the last time and now pilgrims nightly stand, amid the granite cliffs that commemorate the tens of thousands of graveless dead. When we toured these cemeteries, ours were the only Irish names in the registers. Two generations before, widows and mourning mothers in their weeds of grief might have slowly paced through the lines of stones in the cemeteries that dot the landscape like unharvestable crops alongside the potatoes, barley and beet, looking for their man, their boy, but no longer, just memories in their minds and molecules in the entire food chain.

Poelkapelle Cemetery is the home of the grave of Private John Condon, once wrongly believed to have been fourteen at the time of his death, and therefore the youngest British soldier to die in the war (he was in fact eighteen). Beside him is the grave of Thomas Carthy, aged forty-seven, of 34 River Street, Clonmel, County Tipperary, also of the Royal Irish Regiment. Both died in the great gas attacks of April–May 1915, which inaugurated another phase in the development of human civilisation. A thousand Dublin Fusiliers fell in these attacks, slain, butchered, maimed and gassed by the empire the insurgents of 1916 would hail as 'our gallant allies'.

Later, back at home, I wrote to 34 River Street, asking the occupant if they knew what had happened to the Carthy family. It says something about that great organic miracle, the Irish social memory, that the postmistress – it is almost always the postmistress – in Clonmel clearly knew what to do with the letter, for I got a reply a month later from a woman in Nenagh who was Carthy's great-grandniece. Her great-grandmother had been Carthy's young sister, who, when she married, changed her religion (from Church of Ireland to Roman Catholic), her name and her town. When her daughter married, she too changed her name, and it was the daughter of this second lady who had been tracked down by the gallant postmistresses of County Tipperary and who contacted me.

Thomas Carthy belonged to a caste which a ferocious state-backed Catholic religiosity and the barbarous *Ne Temere* rule have since almost eliminated from Irish life: the small-town Protestant poor. He was the oldest of eleven children, but he and his wife had no offspring. In one sense their line ends in Poelkapelle, but in another a certain immortality is now his lot: Condon's grave is the most visited on the Western Front. Some of those who visit must surely pause and wonder about the 47-year-old Irishman lying alongside the teenager.

Some months after the Nenagh reply, I received a letter from Texas that was an essay in the art of mythologising. The letter writer, named McCarthy, said that he was a member of Carthy's family. He said that, under the penal laws, the British made it illegal for anyone to retain 'Mac' in their name. The family had pretended to be Protestant under comparable proscriptions, while remaining covert Catholics. Thomas (Mc)Carthy had enlisted in the Army in 1914 simply to get weapons training in time for the 1916 Rising, of which he clearly had a mysterious foreknowledge.

It would be too easy to mock such confabulations: was the Irish state not guilty of confecting comparable falsifications from the 1930s on? Within a generation, there was no awareness whatsoever of the Irish losses in a war in which Ireland was a lawful combatant. Not merely had Ireland withdrawn from the world in a catastrophic experiment in cultural and economic isolationism, it had created its own autonomous history: discrete, austere and profoundly authoritarian.

The 40,000 forgotten Irish dead were only part of the price that Ireland paid for its insane journey into an invented yesterday; for in the midst of an economic and cultural collapse, cronyism and philistinism became driving forces in the post-independence society. Sitting at the top of the table was the new elite: the political and professional classes, whose status was assured by restricted access to the new state's markets, universities and the law. They had no interest in art or music, but they did have an interest in banning things. Free Ireland created the most unfree society that any democracy has ever known, and when Fianna Fáil lost power, Fine Gael and lesser parties in the Dáil could be relied upon to maintain the same tragic political culture. The placemen would be different: but they still rode the broken old jades of failure, strutting as if they were astride thoroughbreds, bringing ruin to the land they had fought to rule.

In essence, the state had been captured by adherents of a pre-Christian cult of Fenianism which had been fused with an armed version of Irish Catholicism. This had begun during the Easter Rising, as insurgents recited the decade of the rosary when not shooting people, and rapidly mutated into a full-scale alliance. Of the thirty-five Catholic bishops – a well-stocked hierarchy indeed; the same number of Bavarian Catholics had to make do with just five episcopal hats – only four unequivocally condemned the Rising, and these soon became mute as gravestones as events overtook everything, including commonsense and reason.

Thomas Ashe, who had been responsible for the ambush and massacre of an RIC column in Meath in 1916, but had nonetheless been released, was later charged with making a seditious speech. No, I can't explain why sedition merits prison and mass murder doesn't. Claiming prisoner-of-war status, he embarked on a hunger strike and died after being force-fed, a brutal and stupid process, though precisely what reaction to a hunger strike combines wisdom with humanity? Ashe's self-inflicted death sealed the pact between Fenianism and Irish Catholicism: *130 priests concelebrated his requiem mass.*

So the basis for a Haitian accommodation between Fenian voodoo and Rome was laid, as the deities of each came to be revered by the other. Catholic priests would annually gather to recite the rosary over the bones of Wolfe Tone, who must have been shrieking in horror in his secular hereafter, for in life he detested Rome, and in death no doubt detested it even more, as Romanised Fenians enforced Catholic laws in his name. These twin forces would become so fused that it was unclear where the myths of Cuchulainn ended and those of Calvary began. And what better place to contemplate this moral and cultural absurdity than the grave of John Denys Shine in the cemetery at Mons (Bergen)?

Eleven

ONE OF THE MOST ATTRACTIVE features of writing 'An Irishman's Diary' were the freebies. This system of bribery – open and accepted within the trade – could not be reconciled with honest journalism, and I did not try to do so. I simply availed of whatever came my way. I flew on an executive plane hired by Quinnsworth supermarkets in that appalling gimmick, the Beaujolais race, and squared this with that great organ of humbug, my socialist conscience, by not mentioning the name of my capitalist host in my report. Hypocrisy is unedifying enough at the best of times: infused with self-righteousness, it is capable of almost any infamy.

Over the years, I was given free trips to Thailand, Malaysia and Barbados. I went skiing in the Alps, visited Stockholm in mid-winter and Paris in autumn. In a trade that can be deeply dishonourable, I learnt that the bottom of the moral barrel is most often scraped by two species – wine writers and travel journalists. I don't say that from any lofty perspective, but from deep within the barrel itself.

It was on one such free trip that I found myself in a car with a Norwegian journalist outside our hotel around midnight. She didn't want to be seen entering the hotel with me, so we embarked on the usual capers in the front seat of her little Fiat.

On this particular occasion, my head ended up on the floor after I had fallen off my seat attempting some intimate gallantry, while a carburettor was kebabbing a kidney and my feet were touching the roof.

I was trying to work out where the little Norwegian's mouth was when, out of the corner of my eye, I spotted an empty bus silently cruising by. I was just about to yodel my congratulations that our four-limbed entanglement had not been witnessed by any passengers when I noticed a lamp standard sailing past us.

Lamp standards do not move. Indeed, they are paid not to.

This meant one thing. It was *we* who were moving. I wrenched my neck upwards. Yes, we were silently proceeding past a line of parked cars down a steep incline towards the glass doors of the hotel. The handbrake had been freed by our exertions and was trapped beneath our bodies, which were inseparably spliced together in the kind of complex knot with which sailors would once bind captured octopuses to the mast. We were gathering speed at such a rate that we would not merely hit the hotel's glass doors, but would probably explode into reception, where we would be greeted by our press party shedding tears of gratitude for giving them such a world-beating story. Only by some miracle (which I am not so blasphemous as to call divine, but by heavens it is tempting) was I able to free a hand, and, with the tip of an extended thumb, reach the footbrake. The Fiat halted just an inch from the glass doors, but that was the only good news. Firstly, we were mostly naked, though I noted with some pride that I was still wearing socks: it's rather reassuring to see how the last vestiges of Catholic decency never quite leave one. Secondly, we had to extricate ourselves swiftly from our complex knot – an octoshank? – before anyone tried to exit the hotel, thirdly clothe ourselves, fourthly start the car, fifthly reverse it, sixthly park it and seventhly (and finally) enter the hotel separately and as piously as a brace of winged seraphim visiting the baby Jesus in his crib. And, by gum, we did it, going to our separate, celibate beds in a condition of far greater ecstasy than we could possibly have enjoyed had the car remained stationary.

It was on a freebie to Brussels, sponsored by the EU to mark the foundation of Euro-Toques, the association of European chefs, that I first met the wonderful Myrtle Allen. The food revolution which she had helped begin was finally gaining ground, in Cork especially, where the great (and now, alas, late) Veronica Steele had already devised the pioneer Milleens cheese. Along the coast, Kinsale was setting dramatically high standards for restaurants, with Brian and Anne Cronin and Gerry and Marie Galvin at the fore. In Tipperary, the Grubb family were taking the first steps towards making the extraordinary Cashel Blue cheese. In Dublin, the redoubtable and fearless Patrick Guilbaud (supported by his splendid wife Sally and his chef Guillaume Lebrun) had opened his restaurant serving classic French cuisine, the only concession to Irish tastes being butter on every table. It was impossible then to foresee that these revolutionary forces would one day triumph, making Ireland a home of fine restaurants and wonderful raw products.

Myrtle was leading the Irish Euro-Toques delegation. She was charming but exacting, a shrewd, keen-eyed Miss Marple of the kitchen. In the first Euro-Toques session, the conference received opening lectures in gastronomic sanctimony from a pair of bureaucrats of the kind that grows in Brussels like conkers on horse chestnuts. Their subject: protecting basic products. Then we broke for coffee, which was accompanied by capsules containing something that resembled the effluent from the rotting toes of an old man dying from gas gangrene, namely UPC milk.

After we resumed, Myrtle rose, her face cold and austere, as if she was about to point an accusatory Marple-like finger at the murderer. She began to address the assembly, and when she wanted to be particularly contemptuous, she audibly and disdainfully italicised.

'Mr Chairman, we have just had the rare pleasure of being lectured by two of your *functionaries* about the virtues of Europe's raw products, and then we retired to coffee, accompanied by these strange *capsule-devices*' – she held up an example rather like a Mother Superior exhibiting the used condom she had found under a bed in the postulates' dormitory – 'apparently masquerading as *milk* or perhaps *cream*. Mr Chairman, it is neither, nor is it any substance known to a civilisation worthy of its name. What is it doing here, pray, in the company of some of the finest chefs in Europe? Why was there not a violent uprising at this *impertinence*? Why were the *perpetrators* not beaten to death with these loathsome objects in concrete form?'

I paraphrase, of course, Myrtle being a Quaker; nonetheless, the massed assembly shied with terror. Myrtle was one of the greatest people I have ever met, and as time has shown, she and the pioneer chefs of

Ireland were triumphantly the future, in an extraordinary victory of excellence over mediocrity. But that was not so clear then, for the past is always a mystery, even to those who have lived through it.

Throughout this period, the great scandal of the Birmingham Six and the Guildford Four – ten innocent people jailed in Britain for their involvement in IRA atrocities – dominated the public consciousness in Ireland. The Irish anger was both thoroughly justified and hypocritical, for the terrorists responsible for the Birmingham massacre were living in their Dublin homes, untroubled by the government or gardaí. To have acted in both directions, to vigorously seek the release of the innocent and with equal vigour pursue the guilty, would have required too much courage. Instead, a campaign of one-sided advocacy was followed. A petition was actually passed through the *Irish Times* newsroom demanding the release of the Birmingham Six, which I agreed to sign if its organisers added a demand for the arrest and extradition of the terrorists responsible. With a huff and a puff, the petitioner withdrew his scrap of paper.

To be sure, a comparable tribal fealty was being exhibited by the British, who refused to accept that they had imprisoned innocent people, primarily in order to protect their police, their judiciary and, most important of all, their institutional self-esteem. However, that this scandal finally ended was due only to investigative efforts by British journalists, not Irish ones.

The thornily incomprehensible relationship between the islands was evident in the strange agreements between the two government-owned airlines, Aer Lingus and British Airways, which had a state-protected duopoly over the flights between the capitals. Flight prices were governed by something called 'APEX', for which the passengers were expected to be grateful, rather as the canary in the mine should sing with joy at being spared the horrors of sunburn. APEX flights had to be return, booked a fortnight in advance, had to include a Saturday night away, could not be cancelled and would cost 244 times the price of *The Irish Times*. Without the exonerative Saturday night away, a 'budget' fare would cost 411 times the price of *The Irish Times*. When I protested in my column about a new airfare with free drinks and a free newspaper that had been launched with much fanfare by both airlines, but now at a newspaper multiple of 444, the Aer Lingus press officer was incredulous: how could I? The airline had a very simple relationship with journalists: it gave them free flights and they, in return, said how wonderful it was. And so it remained a national doctrine that governments and trade unions were best suited to run airlines. (At the time of writing, thanks to the great Michael O'Leary, Ryanair's standard fare to London was ten times the price of the newspaper.)

Other insights into that strange yesterday were provided when the English writer Anthony Burgess wrote a saucy libretto to celebrate the life and works of James Joyce. Some members of the RTÉ Chorus refused to sing the word 'masturbation', and were given personal exemptions from uttering the dread noun in public, rather as Catholics in Protestant churches might fall silent as the hitherto ecumenical 'Our Father' departs into the heretical 'For thine is the glory ...'

I wrote a column about visiting a nudist beach in France, an admission which caused a minor sensation. Some Irish naturists contacted me and said how *daring* it was of me. Could we meet? We did so in one of their homes. They all used pseudonyms or first names only, as if this was a pioneer meeting of Chainsaw Killers Anonymous. It rapidly became clear that they were all Protestants; they had had a few Catholic male applicants, said a Douglas or a Myrtle wistfully, but had been unable to attract a single Catholic woman. Nor was such general prudery a question of full nudity: the annual ladies' underwear fair at the Gresham Hotel had to import models from England, for Ireland's plucky mannequins refused to appear in public wearing just knickers and bras.

With Pope John Paul II having breathed fresh life into Monsignor Horan's Basilica at Knock, a serious campaign to build an airport began. Absurdities conjoined and competed here, for the airport's proposed runway was long enough to permit a fully laden B52 to take off. As Fine Gael and Fianna Fáil went in and out of government like American football squads swapping places on the bench, Horan shrewdly played the two leaders off against each other. Haughey promised boundless bounty to honour the Virgin Mary, and he would certainly have put her on the state payroll, with a generous pension, if he could have. FitzGerald, a barely less ambitious individual than Haughey, was nonetheless curtailed in his munificence towards Knock by a residual – if flickering – devotion to the principles of fiscal prudence. Either way, Horan got his runway, yet even this was then turned into further proof of the world's conspiracy against Ireland: according to that Official Balladeer of Irish Victimhood & Perpetual Sorrow, Christy Moore, NATO was the secret and profoundly *sinister* funder of the airport, which would presumably be used as a base from which to napalm orphans in South-East Asia. It is no coincidence that the acronym NATO in Ireland usually meant National Association of Tenants' Organisations, thereby invoking a winsome combination of the Land League and the Famine, fortified by a fastidiously unarmed (and therefore defenceless) neutrality.

In this endless festival of sanctimonious self-regard and populist piety, the moving statue of the Virgin Mary at Ballinspittle, County Cork, not far from Kinsale, proved to be the most excruciating element of all. For here we had yestermorrow in all its glories – the forward-looking present and, tugging at its coat tails, this reactionary, hysteria-driven optical illusion. To add to our common mortification (and the delight of the scores of outside reporters whose presence made this a global story rich in embarrassing Paddy caricatures), the Department of Posts and Telegraphs supplied a bank of phone boxes to enable the pilgrims to bawl the news that they had actually seen the Blessed Virgin move! Meanwhile, people wanting a phone at home would have to join a two-year queue.

However, I was the inadvertent trigger for the most bitter clashes between the past and the present. I had met President Hillery at the Wexford Opera Festival, where he told me that he had read my columns on the Great War. He had no idea of the huge scale of Irish involvement: was I writing a book? My ability to organise or keep track of accumulated documentary material rivals the ice-sculpting skills of the Bedouins, and I admitted as much, but I said I would continue to write newspaper articles on the subject.

'Most fascinating – a worthy venture, and I wish you much success with it.'

I had already befriended the head of the British Legion in Ireland, Lieutenant Colonel Brian Clark. A generation older than me, he had won a Military Cross with the Royal Irish Fusiliers in Italy in 1944, but, most importantly of all, he shared with me an almost preternatural deficiency of diplomatic skills. I told him that it would be an excellent idea to invite President Hillery to the Remembrance Sunday service. We two idiots took neither procedural realities nor existing, strongly held feelings into account. The president, as was the convention, forwarded the British Legion's invitation to the government, whereupon Haughey blew gaskets in all four green fields.

There followed an eruption of disbelief and anger, most classically represented by great soldiers such as General Mickey Joe Costello and General Seán MacEoin. These men had been raised, schooled and indoctrinated in the old traditions of the Christian Brothers. As one letter to *The Irish Times* declared, 'I believe in the values of the Republic, as expressed by the men of 1916 and the sacrifices of Tomás Mac Curtain and Kevin Barry. What business has the head of state of this Republic attending a service to remember men who died serving a foreign king, and head of the empire that oppressed us for 800 years?'

No matter how factually absurd some of those assertions might be (800 years?), this letter reflected the deep beliefs of genuine patriots who had served their country during the war years of 1939–45, and who had been prepared to die for it. Worse was yet to come. Haughey had hitherto been unaware that the Army, as a military courtesy, had traditionally sent a couple of middle-ranking officers to the Remembrance Sunday service. In addition to vetoing the president's attendance, he ordered the Army to cease that practice, and instead send a full colour party to attend a memorial service for Germany's war dead at Glencree, County Wicklow.

We had reached a moral nadir: the government of this Republic, through its armed forces, was honouring the dead of the Third Reich and ignoring the tens of thousands of Irish dead of the two world wars. My attempt to advance the cause of remembrance had, catastrophically, set it back. I wrote the following:

There it sits, right in the heart of the national psyche: implacable, unregenerate, unforgiving, forgetting no past injustice; ever-sensitive of betrayal, it suspects treachery in every attempt to modify the received canon of nationalism and perceives only vile heresy in every attempt to embrace broader notions of Irishness than those exemplified by the men in 1916. One flag, one people, one form of nationalism, one single, unwavering loyalty, one noble band of heroes, and, in effect, one permissible religion. The Truth. It is one seamless garment, admitting no adulteration by other cloths. And those born on the same island who do not choose that particular weave automatically become part of some alien fabric, forever isolated. There can be no accommodation with those who belong to that alien fabric, no reconciliation, nor even peace. For they do not acknowledge The Single Truth.

World wars come and go. Entire populations are herded to camps set in distant forests, where they are vaporized into the skies over central Europe; cities are levelled and their populations burnt alive; armies in strange uniforms strut in other people's capitals, and country after country is enslaved, their treasures looted, their peoples subjugated, their patriots murdered.

But in Ireland there remains One Truth, unique and inviolable, one band of heroes, solely one cause to serve: and those who wear any uniform not associated with that Truth cease somehow to be Irish; their valour neglected; their deaths ignored. For such matters are unrelated to The Truth; and memorials to such men are a violation of The Truth, which allows of service to solely one flag, one loyalty, one form of nationalism – one tribe. And the very essence of this Truth is hatred – hatred for England, to be sure, and Englishness, but more than that: the real hatred is for those who do not share that hatred. Traitors. Lackeys. Worse than the Brits.

We have been seeing a great deal of The Truth of late, all to do with the Army's participation in last year's Remembrance Service in St Patrick's Cathedral. That event has been the subject of such misunderstanding, and, much worse, such deliberate misrepresentation, that I despair. For the whole business arose out of a desire for reconciliation, no more; and in how many countries in the world would a desire for reconciliation lead to so much acrimony?

And the acrimony is there because The Truth is at work. Though by no means are all those opposed to Army involvement in Remembrance Sunday motivated by hatred. They are disturbed at what they feel is a submission of national honour to a foreign flag and a foreign organisation.

If that were true in spirit or deed, I would agree with their objections; but it is not true. There was only one national flag in evidence in the St Patrick's service, last year, and that is our own; and it was not, as one writer recently suggested, in an obscure part of the cathedral. It was next to the pulpit.

But I recognise an honest doubt is at work for many people on this matter, and uneasiness that the Army and the flag are not being put to proper purpose. I assure them; if they were present at St Patrick's they would almost certainly recognise there was no ground for such qualms.

But for the adherents of The Truth, there can be no such reassurance. Their hatred burns unquenchably. No quarter to be given, no ground yielded. Simple desires for reconciliation are incomprehensible to the devotee of The Truth. For them, there is the grim litany of history, their Nicene Creed – the Penal Laws, the Fencibles and their pitch-caps of 1798, the evictions and the Famine. Coercion, the Curragh Mutiny, the 1916 executions, the Black and Tans, Partition, and the North; all unfinished business on the agenda, and business which can never be finished while the Truth holds the memory fast.

That column is still relevant today. I am proud of it still, not least because the mood at the time was remarkably ugly, and I was subject to much personal obloquy, both from a few colleagues and many readers, not least on the grounds of my 'non-Irishness'. Gageby came up to me with the copy in his hand. 'This is good: very good. I don't agree with it, mind, but it's written with great power and passion, and no editor has to agree with everything in his newspaper.'

This was the only time that Gageby ever paid me an uncompromising compliment.

But it was a later war that had temporarily put me in the public eye, as I was to discover when the figure of Gageby came sidling up to me.

'Have you heard from the Benson and Hedges people?'

'Benson and Hedges? No.'

'Ah.'

He paused, grief clearly etched on his face. He cleared his throat of some solid lump of unhappiness.

'You've been made journalist of the year for your stuff from Beirut.'

I think these were the most grievous tidings he had ever had to communicate in his entire life. However, the old soldier bore himself well, for he added with rare generosity: 'I thought O'Leary's stuff better. Much.'

He turned, and with shoulders gallantly back, took his broken heart away with him. He was probably right: Olivia's reports from Buenos Aires had been outstanding, but I suspect that she had not submitted them for assessment. That was the degrading way the system operated: journalists who wanted to win an award had to enter their articles like homework for a teacher. And though I detested this system, I was desperate for money. All attempts to get my stockbroker friend to explain what had happened to my investments had come to nothing. A financial raid on the Gallaher tobacco company, to whose financial welfare I had over the years made substantial contributions, seemed morally appropriate.

However, my writings about the Irish involvement in the two world wars led to my being asked to do a series of articles for the fortieth anniversary of the D-Day landings. I interviewed various Irish veterans; this was the first time this had ever been done by the newspaper. They were touchingly delighted that someone was *finally* interested in their stories, which they had long since folded and put away in the airing cupboard. Most of those I met were soldiers or seamen of principle, like the Parachute Regiment's Paddy Devlin of Moycullen and the naval officer Michael D'Arcy of Dún Laoghaire, who were prepared to fight and die in defence of European freedom.

That June I went to Normandy. The French tourist board had placed me in a delightful château, some 60 kilometres from Caen. The proprietor was – like most French people, in my experience – extremely friendly, and very curious about my presence.

'Was not Ireland neutral?'

'Yes, but many Irish volunteers served in the British Army, and died in the liberation of France.'

'But I thought the Irish hated the British.'

'It's more complicated than that. I'm named after my uncle, who died on active service with the Royal Army Medical Corps, and my cousin was with the Irish Guards in Holland and Germany.'

'Your *cousin?*'

'But old enough to be my father.'

During this trip, I learnt the still undiscussed secret of Normandy: the many thousands of French civilians who were killed by Allied bombing. The entirely justifiable anger at this colossal loss of life was still largely taboo, and only with great difficulty could I prise an admission of such feelings from locals. Occupation, arduous though it was for the people of Normandy, was never so onerous as to justify the appalling loss of life so that it might be ended. In my despatches, I reported on these tragic and hitherto neglected aspects of the Liberation.

My most emotional experience was meeting veterans of all nationalities in the cemeteries, often weeping at the graves of their fallen comrades. The day these men landed in Normandy, totalitarianism governed the Eurasian landmass, from Narvik to Vladivostok and the South China Seas, a rule of secret police, torture chambers and death camps. Aside from some footholds in Italy and the Alpine ambiguities of Switzerland, these were the opening acres of freedom, carved by living human flesh and bones – and one of the very first Allied soldiers to render his body into the soil and soul of Normandy was Irish. Private Edward Delaney O'Sullivan, of the 22nd Independent (Pathfinder) Company of the British Parachute Regiment, had been tasked with marking the most distant drop zone for the landings. Separated from his comrades, he fell amongst German troops at Touffréville at around 3 a.m., was caught in a brief fire fight, shot dead, and was then forgotten.

Similarly, one of the first ashore was Redmond Cunningham from Waterford, a Royal Engineer tank commander whose job was to destroy beach defences. Alone of his troop of four, his tank survived the day, and he was awarded a Military Cross, the only Irishman so decorated during the landings. He was to add a bar, plus a Croix de Guerre, to his campaign medals, and he survived into the 1990s. The greatly respected writer Peter Cunningham, Redmond's son, and his wife Carol thereafter became friends of mine, and remained loyal supporters through the many personal trials that lay ahead.

In June 1944, at least 301 Irishmen were killed in action with British and Canadian armies in Europe – ten per day. Sixty-eight of them were killed with the Royal Ulster Rifles, the only regiment in the British Army to supply two battalions on D-Day. The other 230 or so Irish dead were killed in many regiments. Private Michael O'Connor was with the Somerset Light Infantry, Private Bill Liston with the South Lancashires, and Trooper Thomas McClelland with the London Yeomanry (Sharpshooters). Patrick Toolan was a young working-class Catholic from north Belfast who had won a Military Medal with the Gordon Highlanders before being commissioned into the Queen's West Surrey Regiment. So, there he was, Lieutenant Patrick Toolan from Ardoyne, holding the King's Commission, commanding soldiers from the Home Counties, aided by his warrant officer, Company Sergeant Major Daniel O'Connell, from Ballineen, Cork. Both would fall within twenty-four hours of one another in mid-June 1944.

Presidents Mitterrand and Reagan, and Prime Minister Thatcher, attended the huge and deeply moving commemorative ceremony on 6 June. Security requirements meant that I could not leave until late, and I arrived at my château at 11 p.m. The restaurant was closed, so the proprietor made me a sandwich, and then put a bottle on the table. He had watched the ceremonies on television, and, like me, was in a highly emotional state.

I told him of the sacrifice of so many Irish servicemen on the shores of France, in the bitter cold of the Atlantic and in the fire-filled skies of Germany.

'All those Irish boys, who died to make us free. It is terrible but wonderful. Are they remembered and honoured in Ireland?'

'Maybe they will be one day.'

'Do you like Calvados?'

'I've never had any.'

'You shall have some now.'

He poured two glasses.

'Calva, the drink of freedom,' he said, and we toasted those forgotten Irish who had fallen in the liberation of France four decades earlier.

'And to your uncle and cousin: heroes of France.'

We raised our glasses to them too, and then we fell silent, not a little tearful, as old ghosts gathered to remind us of the unbearable price these men had paid to enable us to be toasting them as free men.

There was a payback for all this one June weekend a few years later, when the RTÉ radio producer Caroline Murphy invited me to assist presenter Donncha Ó Dúlaing on a tour of the beaches and cemeteries. Donncha's usual form was to be as politically and sentimentally green on air as the Broadcasting Act allowed. Yet even he was reduced to tears beside the graves of the dead Irish of the Crown. With little time to spare, Caroline edited the hours of tape through the night, right up to the moment of broadcast. The result was a wonderful programme which, going out on the sizzling morning of 6 June, a Bank Holiday when the potential audience was fleeing to sun-kissed beaches, was heard by about 112 people, my dog Diesel, my cat Tensing and the slice of apple pie I was eating at the time. But I'm still proud of it: I hope she is too.

Twelve

MY DRINK PROBLEM had not gone away. There was a strange rhythm to these valueless, brooding lucubrations, normally finishing at 3.45 in the morning, which meant I seldom surfaced before midday. I can't maintain that I was consciously trying to repress all memory of the things I had experienced in Belfast and Beirut, but this must have been part of it.

Grania and I were invited to the Westmeath Hunt Ball in Mullingar, and later we left for a house-party. We were welcomed by a tall handsome man in a dress suit, whose lordly hospitality was tinged with a patrician charm. His very attractive wife served the drinks. I retired to bed around four. Grania got up at seven, along with most of the household, for the hunting field. I lay unconscious until midday, then rose. There was just one person remaining when I trickled downstairs.

'Hello. I'm Richard Flynn,' the man said affably.

'Forgive me, there were so many people last night – you are …?'

'I'm your host. I own the place.'

'Sorry – I'm a little confused. Who was the fellow serving the drinks?'

'That was Father Molloy.'

'*Father?* You mean he's a priest?'

'And a family friend.'

Richard cooked me brunch and chatted about his life. He had been a farmer, but had contracted brucellosis, and so, unable to be near cattle, had gone into business, at which he had been remarkably successful. I asked him how the illness had affected him.

'Aches all over, a terrible lassitude, which I have to fight every single day.'

I did not ask about the third symptom, impotence, and our conversation then affably toured the world until the hunting party returned, yodelling greedily for beakers of gin. I liked Richard enormously, so much so that we stayed in touch, and I visited him a couple of times at his auto-spares shop in Blackrock, County Dublin.

A few months later, after the wedding party for one of the Flynn daughters, Father Niall Molloy was found beaten to death in the Flynns' bedroom. Richard was charged with assault and manslaughter. The case went before Judge Frank Roe, who ordered the jury to acquit, and Richard walked free. Personally, I felt happy for him, though justice clearly had not been done. It was later alleged that Roe had been a friend of the Flynns, but I doubt whether any Irish judge would have accepted a case that could have so fatally compromised him. However, Roe was an ardent Catholic who would probably have done his utmost to protect the 'good name' of the Catholic Church, a term which had not yet become risible. The clearly sexual relationship between Niall Molloy and Teresa Flynn might have been fully exposed in any trial, which Roe was apparently determined to forestall. It was, in Charles Haughey's imperishably worthless aphorism, an Irish solution to an Irish problem. Or, if you like, GUBU.

Haughey – hypocrite, crook, tribal bigot and one of the founding financiers of the IRA – had forged a strategic alliance with the Catholic Church. The two referendums created by this alliance – one installing a ban on abortion in the Constitution, the other reaffirming the existing constitutional ban on divorce – seemed to copper-fasten the apparently unassailable, crozier-wielding power of the Catholic Church. During the perfectly loathsome debate on divorce, children were coming home from school in tears, having been assured that if divorce were allowed, their daddies would leave them. A young, small-town solicitor I knew who had campaigned against a ban on abortion being inserted into the Constitution became the victim of a pulpit-backed boycott and her practice was destroyed.

Inevitably, I would encounter Haughey's mistress, Terry Keane, around Dublin. She embodied all the hypocrisy and deceit of this foul era. Born in England to an Irish family, she had briefly studied medicine at Trinity College, Dublin, before abandoning that for an early marriage to a rising young barrister, Ronan Keane, a wise man in all matters save connubial selection. As he rose through the ranks of the bar, she sank into the bed of Charles Haughey. The two men could not have been further apart: Haughey I have already described, whereas Keane was a gentleman of honour, not an accolade I would crop-dust upon the bar. I suppose Terry Keane sensed Satan's tang in Haughey's company: that illicit combination of cordite, criminality and cash. Though, by then, this no longer included sex.

'He can't get it up any more, darling,' this model of personal loyalty once lamented to me. 'Such a baw.'

A self-proclaimed paragon of republicanism, she had been trying to get her son Tim into the British Army, specifically, the Irish Guards, but the other Irish Guards – An Garda Síochána – told her that they simply did not have the manpower to protect him while he was home on leave.

'It's so unfair,' she complained. 'We pay our taxes. We deserve the full pwotection of the state. The guards are being simply wotten about it all.'

She finally got a divorce in London, which did not, however, prevent her from campaigning to keep the constitutional ban on divorce in Ireland. She even appeared on RTÉ radio, lispingly complaining: 'Ahland is a Chwistian countwy, and the family is the woot of Ahwish life. If we allow divaws in Ahland, we are attacking our caw Chwistian values.'

'But some maintain that in a republic one shouldn't have rule by the Catholic Church,' said the interviewer, who must have known – as almost all of Dublin did – that she had just got a divorce in perfidious Albion.

'I'm a wepublican, to the caw of my being! I believe in the Ahwish Wepublic, for which good men pewished,' proclaimed this wepublican pawagon. 'Why should we abandon the Chwistian values which have made this countwy gweat, and slavishly copy wotten ones from acwoss the water?'

94

The constitutional bans on divorce and abortion thus became jewels within the crown of Irish jurisprudence, to add to the sceptre that was the existing ban on contraceptives. Moreover, an attempt to end this latter provision, just as the AIDS virus was landing in Ireland, was defeated in the Dáil. It seemed as if we were irretrievably sunk in falsehood, deceit, cowardice and lies – and this was also true at a more modest level. When my phone calls to my stockbroker were never returned, and my letters went similarly unanswered, I sought the advice of an accountant. He listened to how I had been persuaded to hand over my savings.

'I'm giving the same advice as I just gave a client who lost over two hundred thousand pounds to the same fellow. Forget it. It's lost. You'll spend the same amount of money chasing it, and that's just throwing good money after bad. You've been very foolish. Now put it behind you.'

So, I was doomed to remain in my freezing flat above the family planning clinic – my condominium, as I so wittily called it – saving anew to buy a house. Meanwhile, my stockbroker-thief went on to earn millions and much esteem.

Thirteen

WHAT I DREADED came to pass: a return to Beirut. Suicide bombers had levelled the US embassy, killing sixty-three people, and later attacks killed over 250 US Marines and seventy-eight French soldiers. No one even suspected at the time that two entirely different value systems were beginning their great continental collision. I certainly thought of events there simply as an extension of the Lebanese Civil War. I could have said no to Conor O'Clery's request to return, but a blue funk prevented me. Behind so many acts of apparent bravery festers a deep cowardice that dare not speak its name. I felt reasonably certain that this time I would finally be killed, which sounds silly and melodramatic, but it is the truth. You can't keep taunting death without it getting irritable in the only way it knows how.

I was to stay overnight in London and catch the dawn flight to Beirut. I put in an alarm call at my hotel for 5 a.m., but then drank far too much wine. I woke at 8 a.m., my plane long gone. I had received no alarm call. Half-delighted, I rang reception, faking anger, and the response was simply appalling. Management accepted full responsibility for the failure to wake me. Since the next London–Beirut flight wasn't for three days, they offered to fly me to Paris that day, give me a suite in their sister hotel in the Trust House Forte chain, La Plaza Athénée, thus enabling me to fly to Beirut at dawn the next day.

Good God, what is a poor fellow to do when he encounters such probity? Did every employee have to emulate Charles Forte's legendary honesty? And was the entire world determined to kill me?

That night, I dined dolefully in the Michelin-starred restaurant of La Plaza Athénée: for all the pleasure I derived from it, I might have been eating *fricassee de sheepshit* in a *jus de shoe polish*. After a couple of hours of astonishingly horrible sleep, at dawn I took a taxi to Charles de Gaulle, whence I flew to Lebanon.

Beirut airport had become a major battleground. US Marines of the 22nd Marine Amphibious Unit were living beneath tarpaulins stretched over water-filled trenches, just as they might have done at Khe Sanh or St Mihiel in earlier wars. Firing into the airport compound was constant as armed immigration officials hustled the few passengers through a disturbingly unbulletproof Nissen hut, the main arrivals buildings having been reduced to rubble. The taxi drive to the Commodore was truly shocking, close-range gunfire every second of the way. My driver told me that he was only working because his wife was desperately ill and they were penniless. He was weeping when he dropped me off – not with relief, but because he would now have to return to the airport along the via dolorosa on which we had just travelled.

True to form, as I arrived at the Marine headquarters the next day, the sentry post overhead came under sniper fire, and I entered the building at speed and on my hands and knees. The Marines' press officer, Major Denis Brooks, was extremely formal. In my time in Belfast, I had met very senior officers, such as General Ford, the idiot who was essentially responsible for Bloody Sunday, and General Frank King, a hero, a veteran of Arnhem and a charming gentleman, and they both called me by my first name. Now, it was strictly Mr Myers and Major Brooks. A few minutes into the conversation, he took a phone call. When he finished, he said: 'That shooting when you arrived? Killed a Marine. Strange. Cos it's been kinda quiet recently.'

He told me he was Irish, a Notre Dame boy, and asked what part of Ireland did the name Brooks come from. Wexford, I improvised, the sunny south-east. That pleased him. He outlined the main dangers in Beirut; first, the terrorists, and not far behind them, the police. The latter had just been equipped with American tracked armoured personnel carriers, and their drivers had taken to roaring around the city streets like Indianapolis 500 wannabes.

One of Brooks' observations dealt a death blow to my clichéd view of the Marine Corps. Jane Fonda had been in the news again. Of course, she was detested by the US military for having posed over a decade previously in the firing position of a north Vietnamese anti-aircraft gun that would be used against American pilots. Did she not enrage him?

'Course she does. But I joined the Corps to protect American freedom, and that includes the freedom to oppose US policy abroad.'

No answer to that.

The next day, I had an appointment at a hospital near the Chatila refugee camp. My taxi was sitting in the usual Beirut traffic jam when I caught the eye of a teenage girl in a long purple dress. She was pretty, and, as our eyes met, we exchanged innocent smiles. Suddenly gunfire erupted. She promptly collapsed onto the red Lebanese clay, in that familiar, terrible way, her legs simply folding like bed linen. In that same evil second, my driver started cursing, head-swivelling, horn-hitting, reversing. Around us, others were doing likewise: chaos, gunfire, car horns, tiny collisions, swift exits, no looking back, as we sped towards my rendezvous.

There I met Dr Hawami Amir, an imposing yet kindly, pro-Palestinian Lebanese man. He asked for my impressions of Beirut. I told him of the shooting at Chatila.

'Shootings every day there, and they never get reported. The world has done nothing for these people,' he told me bitterly. 'And the Arab world *in particular* has done nothing for them.'

At that point, a nurse came to the door. They spoke urgently, before he turned and said: 'Come with me.'

I followed him into casualty. Victims were being brought in. One of them was a teenage girl in a purple dress, her arms lolling from the stretcher. She had a hole in her neck. Yes, her. Even though she was clearly dead, blood was still pouring from the wound. Her family was wailing, transfixed with shock and grief, and yet the blood flow seemed to have given them a deranged and baseless hope, their eyes flickering beseechingly.

'Is this ...?' Dr Amir asked.

I nodded. I had seen her briefly in life, and now I saw her in death. Could my taxi have taken her to hospital? Was this the difference between what might have been and what actually was? Admittedly, I had had no control over the taxi driver, nor had I known *for sure* that the girl had been hit, even though I had seen her go down. Hadn't others in that very same second? But still …

I later mentioned this to Dr Amir.

'She would never have survived that wound. You could not have saved her.'

Maybe not, but did that half-second during which she paused to smile at me put her in the line of fire? All those contingencies in our respective lives, every one of them vital to that final fleeting encounter. I see that smile now, registering the briefest of unions before our respective journeys diverged for ever. I described this shooting in my report to *The Irish Times*, but I did not tell how the girl in the purple dress and I had briefly exchanged looks in the very last moments of her life.

Some people never leave you. She is one of those people.

Later that same terrible day, I visited a Palestinian graveyard for 'martyrs'. On each headstone was a slightly larger-than-life-size photograph of the dead, all young, mostly male. Was this where my girl in purple would soon reside, her unflinching picture gazing at future visitors like me, who might well wonder how it was that her martyrdom came about? And was I perhaps the only person in the world who could testify to its utter randomness? I was possibly the sole custodian of the final truth of this girl's life.

The graveyard was on a slight slope, and gazing upwards from the lower end, I could see all these unchanging faces gazing stoically at me. I did not know, could not know, that death was to be the growth industry of the region, and that these graves were just seed plants for a far vaster harvest yet to come.

My general assignment was to give readers a sense of Lebanese life and history, not a detailed day-by-day political assessment, which was beyond my powers. A CBS man suggested I contact Malcolm Kerr, the heroic president of the American University of Beirut. I phoned Kerr's office a few times and left messages, but to no avail. He was a much acclaimed and very busy man, with no Irish connections – why would he return my calls?

Some journalists in Beirut were virtually indistinguishable from soldiers, but having been mistaken for a combatant twice previously, I wanted to be as unmistakably a civilian as a wimpled baby nun in her cot. Each morning I would put on a clean shirt and tie with pressed trousers. My attire soon won the undisguised disdain of John Hoagland, a photojournalist who affected the full regalia of combat-fatigues. Perhaps because of my decisively non-military appearance, Denis Brooks had taken a shine to me, even asking me privately if I would like to join a flight of Marines to the USS *New Jersey* battleship.

'Marine Corps rules,' he stipulated. 'We say, you obey.'

I reported to the USMC base at dawn. It had been mortared overnight and the sentries were keenly alert. While I was being processed at reception, there were more incoming rounds. Next, I was in a USMC helmet and heavy body armour, sitting in a hangar while the helicopter was readied, and then I was patted on the shoulder. Like an ungainly turtle crossing a beach to lay its eggs, I waddled over to the back door of the Sikorsky ch-53 Sea Stallion, where a huge black air-gunner hauled me aboard, as other Marines hurried past my bucket seat. The gunner gravely signalled for me to belt myself in, which I did, and the Sea Stallion rose amid a plume of ochre dust, then banked almost at right angles. Even as we turned sharply over Bourj el-Barajneh, we got incoming fire, and the gunner unloosed half a belt into something down below. I knew enough about angles of attack and deflection-shooting to be aware that firing at anything from a helicopter rear door while moving rapidly in a rising vortex through three different axes serves no military purpose, other than to make everyone aboard feel a little happier. In my case, it succeeded hugely.

I spent the day as a journo-tourist talking to the all-male naval crew. They were precisely the kind of Americans I had met when hitchhiking through the States as a student: immensely likeable and polite, if a little baffled at the murderous ways of foreigners – and excuse me, sir, might I help you to some more coffee? What became obvious to me was that this vast, ponderous battleship had no useful function in Beirut. All she was good for was firing car-sized shells into the civilian-packed villages in the Chouf – which is what she occasionally did. But liking these Americans so much, I did not – as I really should have done – dwell upon that. What would later be termed 'embeddedness' is usually the enemy of truth, as being in bed with anyone so often is.

The bugbear of the Irish Army contingent of the United Nations Forces in the Lebanon, Major Saad Haddad, head of the South Lebanon Army, had the bad grace to die during my stay, obliging me at least to *try* and visit his home village of Marjayoun, near the Israeli border. However, to my unspeakable joy, the taxi drivers outside the Commodore refused to take me, protesting that Marjayoun was too far and the road too dangerous. I was just turning back into the hotel when a driver volunteered to drive me.

He spoke strangely, so I asked: 'Where are you from?'

'Sydney, mate. And I need all the money I can get.'

Grimly, I went back inside the hotel and rang the news desk, telling them that I would be heading south, and might be some time. I returned to my chipper little Lebanese-Australian, frantically nurturing hopes that the Israeli Army would prevent my journey. Joy of joys, my taxi was stopped at an Israeli roadblock outside east Beirut, where a middle-aged Army reservist, whose demeanour cried out *teacher teacher teacher*, told me that no journalists were being allowed any further. I wanted to kiss his lovely pedagogic face in gratitude: now I could write about the cruelty of the Israeli invaders preventing me from doing my duty! I began to protest, solely to create – if only in my own mind – the verisimilitude of righteous indignation.

'You don't want to be here, I guess,' said the Israeli. 'Neither do I. You got a job to do, so have I. But you didn't go through here, okay?' And with appalling generosity, he stood back and waved us on.

What? How is this remotely possible? I was silently shrieking to myself, though my driver felt differently: 'Fantastic, mate. Well done! Looking forward to this. Never been to south Lebanon before.'

'You don't know how to get to Marjayoun?' I whispered in horror.

'Haven't a clue, mate,' he said cheerfully. 'My cousin, he came down here last year, or so I'm told, and was never seen again. Funny old place, south Lebanon.'

We took more wrong turns that morning than even my mother and I – two spectacularly bad map readers – combined would normally take in a year, endlessly reversing back up the wadi-lined tracks we'd just come down. Throughout, the solemn thwack of artillery shells on distant hillsides reminded us of the high price of being in the wrong place at the wrong time. Finally, we found our way to the Major's village, where clusters of women were shrieking in discordant unison and militia men were unleashing mournful volleys of automatic gunfire into the air. All the local communities with whom he had warred – Druse, Greek Orthodox, Maronite, and others – were represented. Accordingly, by the same Levantine alchemy, I was now an unofficial ambassador of the people of Ireland. So, with a facial mien that – I trusted – was fusing gravitas with grief and mourning with majesty, I met Haddad's senior warriors, who escorted me to his wife and daughters. There, I conveyed Ireland's unspeakable sorrow at their great loss, before joining them in their ululations, even waving my hands in the air. I felt rather like a turf-cutter, loy in hand, sharing the stage with Yehudi Menuhin.

I went over to the man himself, his face like wood ash, his lips sewn shut. Under his command, perhaps half a dozen of our lads on UN duty had been killed, and I wordlessly cursed his departed ghost.

On the road back to Beirut, we were flagged down by a UN patrol. There was fighting up the road. It was too dangerous to proceed. I got out of the car to discuss our options with the UN officer, and a burst of fire nearby drove us to take cover in a wadi while my driver set a world record for the 100-metre reverse from a standing start.

'Where you from?' I asked the officer, as we crouched low, him peering keenly over the edge, me skulking beneath it.

'Denmark. You?'

'Ireland.'

'Ireland. Always blahdy Ireland. Denmark's population is the same size as blahdy Ireland's. I go round the fahking world, but I never meet a fahking Dane. But I'm always meeting the blahdy Irish, smiling and laughing and knowing every fahking body. How the hell is this blahdy possible?'

I don't know. But it's true. As the firing abated, my Ozzie-Leb came back like a bad penny, looking a little sheepish about his earlier exit, and we returned to Beirut.

One afternoon in the Commodore, I saw an Irish Army officer talking to a French officer, and I went over and introduced myself. The Frenchman, very courteously, invited me to join him for dinner at his barracks the following evening. I was delighted for many reasons, all of them obvious.

Late the next afternoon, I got a taxi outside the Commodore. The driver and I exchanged names.

'Keveen!' he said delightedly. 'Keveen Keegan.'

The Beirut night fell as swiftly as the blackout curtains of the London Blitz. At the French headquarters, against the starlight, a block of flats 400 metres away was just about visible. As I alighted, a shot was fired at the sentry post directly above the main gate.

Here we go again.

'See you at ten,' I said to the driver, then crouch-scuttled over to the main gate, hastily pressing its bizarrely suburban bell push. Moments later, a sentry opened a small shutter within the gate.

'Bon soir. Je m'appele Kevin Myers.' *Good evening. My name is Kevin Myers.*

'Documentation, s'il vous plaît.'

I gave him my passport, and then asked for the officer by name. 'Il m'a invité,' I finished lamely: *He invited me.*

'Dommage. Il a été abattu cet après-midi.' *Too bad. He was shot this afternoon.*

'Abattu? Est-il mort?' *Shot? Is he dead?*

'Peut-être; sais pas.' *Maybe; I don't know.*

Of course, I felt sorry for him, but not nearly as fucking sorry as I felt for myself. I gabbled my explanations, seeking admission until my taxi returned.

'Désolé, monsieur.' *Sorry, sir,* said the sentry, closing the shutter on me.

Christ alive. I was on the outskirts of Beirut, location unknown, night had fallen, I had no idea how to get to my hotel, and the taxi was not due back for *four hours*. Using my feet as a blind man would his stick, I tap-tap-tapped away from the gate, where I might yet be assessed as a threat, and lay down in a shallow ditch. What was I to do? Night had camouflaged everything in deepest black, apart from the flats, and, above me, the sentry post. I lay deep in the cold clay and watched, incredulous, as an extraordinary exchange occurred. A sniper firing a round from the flats would be spotted by a very upright sentry with binoculars motionlessly standing on the parapet, for my night eyes could now detect his silhouette against the stars. He would intone co-ordinates and a colleague elsewhere would return fire. Then another enemy sniper would open up from elsewhere in the flats, and his position too would be calmly identified, and so on. Sometimes a bullet would hit the gate that I had just left, and I would burrow even deeper into the cold Lebanese soil, knowing that no taxi driver would ever come and rescue me here. Only dawn could bring respite – if I survived that long.

Winter nights in Lebanon can be bitter, and I was wearing no overcoat, just my studiously civilian sports jacket. Soon cold gnawed at my bones and ate into the marrow of my shins. What would happen when sentries changed and a new man spotted what might appear to be an intruder just yards from the front gate? The French had lost many men to suicide bombers. Would I not appear to be one?

My wristwatch was invisible in the dark, and I felt my liver starting to freeze. I needed to move to stay warm, but any movement might be lethal. A Lebanese night in January lasts about thirteen hours. How long could I stick this? My hair was frosting over, and I could feel the digital tendons in my hands shortening in the cold, irresistibly curling my fingers. I doubted I could survive the night but if I tried to return to the French gate, might not a sniper of either side claim me?

Hours passed as slowly as glaciers ascending. Cold does in time bring its own consolations, because as your brain cools, it no longer registers the scalding ice forming on your shinbones, or the Stalingrad-clench of your hands. As the intermediary between the equally frozen loam and air, I found that if I kept my eyes shut, the dark even became soothing. The seductiveness of slumber: an end to cold and fear. As I slipped downwards to that delightful place of ease, I became aware of a bright light rudely forcing its way through my eyelids. I started awake and raised my head an inch or two. Headlights were approaching. Was it a French mobile patrol returning to base? Unlikely. That would consist of no less than four jeeps, and this was a single vehicle.

As the sniper fire crackled overhead, the car drew up at a safe distance from the front gate, sounding its horn.

'*Keveen! Keveen!*'

I tried to rise, frozen, stiff-limbed, my legs collapsing beneath me. I uttered a pathetic cry. With his headlights still on, my driver drove slowly towards me, sounding his horn to let the French sentries know that nothing sinister was afoot. He drew alongside, got out of the car and helped me to my feet, while I, with mind-numbing fatuity, cried out in mangled franglais to the sentries: 'Ne tire pas! C'est moi, la journaliste Irlandaise!' *Don't shoot! It's me, the Irish journalist!*

My driver bundled my collection of uncoordinated limbs into his blissfully warm car and drove hurriedly away, to parting salutations from the rival snipers. As my hands warmed, I wrote my driver's name in my notepad, determined never to forget the former or lose the latter; and, naturally, I did both.

Next morning, as the Marine briefing was about to get underway, John Hoagland asked loudly: 'What the fuck is this Irish guy up to? Why does he always look like a fucking clerk?'

'That's Mr Kevin Myers you're speaking of, and he's no "fucking clerk",' said Denis. This was the only time I had heard him use a swear word, even in quotations. 'Our French colleagues report that he lay out for four hours under fire last night. Had he been wearing military attire, he probably would have been killed. Gentlemen, please remember, this is a Marine Corps briefing, and the press will observe Marine Corps etiquette. Thank you.'

Thank *you*, Denis.

Walking down Hamra later that morning, I came across a limbless boy, a torso, his arms and his legs gone, propped on the pavement. Carefully drawn on the pavement in front of him – by whom? – was a begging chalk circle. A great colour story? No. Anything I wrote about this unspeakable tragedy would merely be a voyeur's charter, a licence to feel empty, egregious sympathy for a few meaningless minutes over the morning coffee in Dublin.

I went back to the Commodore, deliberately faxed the office rather than phoning, thereby courting a possible negative, and irreversibly announced that I was coming home. There were no taxis outside the hotel, so I began to walk down to the British Airways office, near the American University. My heart was singing: I was going home! A CBS camera crew stopped beside me. They were hurrying *away* from the university.

'Hey, Kevin, get the fuck out of here. They've just assassinated the university president. Anyone who looks like an American could be a target.'

'What? Malcolm Kerr?'

'The very same.'

That such an admirable man, a true hero, could be murdered merely confirmed my decision to leave. But if I turned back as advised, I might not get a flight booking that day. So I hastened onwards, and soon heard the whirring din of heavy-duty diesel engines. I turned. Some Lebanese police APCs came racing around a corner on the slight hill above me, their metal tracks skidding on the tarmac – yes, the terrifying drivers that Denis Brooks had warned me about. I began to run to the British Airways office, now one hundred metres away, as the APCs raced towards me, at right angles to my intended path.

Too fast, too fast, I knew they were too fast.

I stopped and turned, with my back against a wall for safety, just as the lead APC started to brake. But instead of stopping, the vehicle went into a long downhill skid, sparks flying like bow waves from its metal tracks as it came hurtling towards me. I was trapped. I could see the appalled face of the driver above the sloping armoured plate of his vehicle as it fishtailed in my direction.

I instinctively stepped backwards towards the solid brick wall, only to find that a miraculously Kevin-shaped alcove had been waiting there – apparently purposelessly all these years – for this very contingency. In that same microsecond, the APC slammed into the wall to my left and right, but instead of cutting me in two, it left me unharmed in my little brick enclosure – though thoroughly shit-shaken. The driver, his head still out of the front of the APC, invisibly wrestled with the differential gears down below, left right, left right, and sheepishly reversed, engine howling.

My destiny thus decided by a variety of historical accidents that remain beyond any explanation, I looked over at the British Airways office, where a woman was just locking up.

'Excuse me,' I cried, as she turned to leave. 'Don't go! I want to book a flight to London.'

She paused a half-beat.

'You're in luck. Twice over. There's just one seat left. Quickly now, before the whole fucking place goes mad,' she called in a Home Counties accent, hurriedly reopening the office door. 'God clearly wants you to live. I just hope he wants the same for me.'

She handwrote – as you could in those days – or rather scribbled in a frenzy of biro hieroglyphs – the last BA ticket out of Beirut for a week. I kissed her briefly at her office door, and she kissed me too, an odd spasm of requited passion, before our two young lives went in their different directions.

Fourteen

SHORTLY AFTER MY RETURN from Beirut, Val Lamb took me to the bloodstock sales in Goffs. This provided a rare insight into a secret aspect of Irish life, for it seemed that every single racing stable in Ireland bought a Haughey yearling, though none of them bought two. Michael Osborne – a fine man and a true patriot, who had abandoned a lucrative career in Kentucky to become the modestly paid manager of the Irish National Stud in Kildare – later explained the auction to me. As Minister for Finance, Haughey had made the industry wholly tax-free. Every racing stable would duly thank him by buying one of his yearlings.

'But one only. They're all useless. They'll all be fed to hounds by the summer. He doesn't have an eye for bloodstock, though he thinks he does. Even the inflated prices he's getting will never repay his idiotic outlay on mares and getting them covered. And, believe me, no one is ever going to buy a second yearling from him. Once is enough.'

Haughey understood the underside of Irish life perfectly. Contrary to the foreign perception of Ireland, it is not always a *nice* country. For all its outward charm and voluble gregariousness, there is too often a steady drip of poison in daily discourse, especially in relation to those who step out of line. This is a miniature expression of a larger condition in Irish life: the lack of organised, statutory solicitude for others. It is classically an example of the *Gemeinschaft/Gesellschaft* dichotomy that Ferdinand Tönnies proposed. Kinship, as expressed by the term *Gemeinschaft*, comes before all else, first most visibly and toxically expressed in clientelist constituency politics at home, but also Tammany corruption in the US. The notion of *Gesellschaft*, quotidian duty towards the unknown, helpless and nameless, within broader Irish society is either sporadic, spasmodic or electorally driven. The Irish are spectacularly generous in time of famine, but there is more to charity than coping with emergencies. The Jesuit Lambert McKenna said in 1913 that 'nowhere in Europe is social charity as distinguished from alms-giving charity less known or practised than in Ireland'.

That 'social charity' is a reflection of a structured moral ethos, which Ireland has largely lacked. The informed debates that led to the formation of welfare states across Europe are almost inconceivable in Ireland. The emulation of those welfare states in Ireland had no philosophical or philanthropic blueprint, but largely consisted of vote-buying gimmicks that were gradually encrusted one upon another. The resulting coral reef of state-run, union-protected welfare and medical institutions, both by definition and intent, lacked any intellectual coherence or central moral imperative. Irish Catholicism had been predicated on ethical authoritarianism, institutional power and wealth, and it no doubt developed that way within the gross societal distortions caused by violent conquest, exclusion and the penal laws that essentially prohibited Catholics from participating in public life or owning substantial properties. Following emancipation, Catholicism expressed itself in two main forms: physically, in the creation of buildings that conferred and enforced ecclesiastical power – churches, schools and hospitals – and through the hierarchical and confessional control over the tiniest details of people's lives. Almost completely absent were abstract thought and moral theology. This has been true both at home and in the diaspora: a basic Google search reveals that of the 200 foremost moral US theologians, fewer than ten are of Irish origin.

If you had political power in Ireland, you were allocated resources and a recognised place in the pecking order; if not, not. For example, in 1973 there were 7,000 blind people in Ireland, only twenty of them with guide dogs, all supplied through Britain. For most of the twentieth century, deaf girls and deaf boys were taught two different sign languages in their separate homes, which were organised around the needs of their administrators, religious orders, which were segregated, of course: the original apartheid.

From the outset, Ireland's 'health service' attended to the interests of its employees as much as to those of its patients. Dysfunctionality was inbuilt, for the pioneering template – combining outwardly pious purpose with inwardly fraudulent intent – was the Irish Hospitals' Sweepstake. This vastly complex scam was founded in 1930 by the former gunman Joe McGrath, and supervised by another former gunman, Charlie Dalton. Both had killed people during the viciously vacuous campaign of murder that led to 'independence' – in reality, a change of empires, from London to Rome. But one triple murder by Dalton is really worth recalling. As a young officer in the new Free State Army in the autumn of 1922, he caught three teenage boys pasting anti-government posters in Dublin's northside. He took them to the Red Cow crossroads west of the city and shot them dead with his service revolver. The ideal fellow to put in charge of a health service.

A decade later, the Sweeps began its fund-raising across the English-speaking world, with at least 10 per cent of the proceeds going directly into the pockets of the bosses. McGrath ruthlessly used the laws of libel and contract to protect his operation. This was possible only with the complicity of the Irish political classes. Naturally, almost the last people to benefit from the Hospitals' Sweeps were hospital patients, and any journalist who tried to expose the scandal would face ruin in the courts. This was yet another scandal that *The Irish Times* never ever touched – not an elephant in the room, but an entire herd.

So, the Sweeps scandal was not some departure from a basic Irish decency, but a norm, and the corruption was usually concealed behind a mask of conversational affability and good cheer. Donagh O'Malley became a national hero in the 1960s for introducing free secondary education, some twenty years after it had been granted to students in Northern Ireland. That such a modest step is still hailed as a historic breakthrough says a great deal about the melancholy expectations the public have of their politicians. But that public respected power. O'Malley, a notorious drunk, was stopped by a garda driving the wrong way down a one-way street after leaving a late boozing session in a Dublin hotel.

'Did you not see the arrows?' asked the garda.

'Arrows? I didn't even see the fucking Indians.'

The garda insisted on prosecuting the minister and was duly sacked by the commissioner. It is often said that O'Malley was contrite about this, but not enough to stop him from repeating the arrows and Indians story, amid much hilarity, and down the years the story was repeated approvingly by party apparatchiks. Its purpose was condign: *this is who we are.*

Even during the Tiger years to come, the underclasses in their sink estates were never given the higher teacher–pupil ratio that might help lift their communities out of the degrading isosceles triangle of low expectations and low achievement on an unshakable base of state dependency. It remained easier to settle with the powerful unions that represented the government workforce than to direct resources to the genuinely poor. The Labour Party had become little more than an advocacy group for upper-middle-class liberals whose preoccupations were dominated by their grisly debates over whether the local primary school in their leafy Victorian *arrondissements* should be interfaith or non-denominational. Naturally, it was a Labour Minister for Education who gave Ireland's middle classes free university education for their children, while schools in poorer areas still had leaking roofs, outside toilets and forty pupils per teacher.

Ireland's semi-state companies – in fact, they were wholly state-owned and for generations board memberships were paid sinecures for party placemen – almost revelled in such dysfunctionality. In the 1980s, the Electricity Supply Board had around twenty-five unions: RTÉ had some twenty, with two employees belonging to the Irish Seamen and Port Workers' Union, so entitling them to climb the mast. Such state institutions would function rather like self-licking lollipops. As I pointed out in one column, the Dublin train pulled in at Galway at 16.50, just five minutes after the last bus for Clifden had left. Similarly, the morning bus from Clifden arrived at Galway at 11.35, in time to see the back of the train leaving for Dublin. Passengers on the Dublin to Wexford train arriving at 15.50 had a similarly melancholy view of the bus for New Ross. Visitors from Fishguard on an afternoon sailing could revel in the beguiling vista of the last train to Dublin that day departing just as their ferry was docking. However, it was not all bad news: the Dublin train arrived at Cork at 18.05, five minutes *before* the bus for west Cork departed – alas, not from the railway station but from the bus terminus a mile away. And Irish people privately grumbled about such bizarre practices, but nonetheless complied rather than complained.

This was the society that Charles Haughey understood thoroughly. He knew that the best results within such a disordered society were often achieved directly, through bullying and coercion: after all, had he not got the Revenue Commissioners to help form the Provisional IRA? As Taoiseach, he effectively controlled most of the main departments of state through glove-puppet ministers. Yet, appalling though he seemed at the time, what we actually know now about Haughey's financial shenanigans vastly exceeds any contemporary rumours. However, the real scandal was not Haughey's antics, but the almost complete silence of the press. What the press did cover were the repeated attempts by a handful of plucky individuals within Fianna Fáil, usually led by the Limerick grandee, Dessie O'Malley, to overthrow Haughey. The latter's response was to use the gardaí to tap the phones of those political correspondents writing the stories.

Like most journalists, I was aware that Haughey was a bigoted crook, a flashy spiv who lived on a politician's income in a beautiful Georgian house, above a cellar of allegedly astounding quality, with, of course, bloodstock stables and parkland. But it was Michael Osborne's revelations that prompted me to write a column, wryly wondering about the source of Haughey's spectacular wealth, and asking how he managed to cope with such vast and endless outgoings when his known income was so modest. Did the Revenue Commissioners never inspect his books? Gageby soon erupted out of his office, almost like projectile vomit, my copy trembling in his hand.

'Who the fuck do you think you are? You're *not* one of our political staff. You don't belong to the financial pages. You have no business intruding on their territories. I pay you to write light chatty pieces on the lines that "An Irishman's Diary" has been written for about a hundred fucking years. Never ever stray in that territory again, do you hear?'

'I can see you're very angry.'

'Not as fucking angry as I'll be if you try this on again. Leave politics alone and leave Haughey's money alone. Have you got that?'

'Yes,' I whispered abjectly.

It certainly wasn't bravery that caused me to return to the subject some months later, but a slightly hungover belief that Gageby was away. This time, I asked wryly whimsical questions about the source of the Haughey wealth. I assumed that Gageby – since he despised me – would never bother to read any of my back columns when he returned.

The problem was that he wasn't away. Minutes after I had submitted my column, he emerged from his office.

'Are you fucking deaf or fucking stupid?' he barked, his eyes probing into mine like lasers. 'What did I tell you about Haughey? What did I fucking tell you?'

'Not to write about him,'

'*What the fuck is this?*'

'Questions,' I whimpered, in a little voice.

'*What?*'

'Questions,' I repeated in an even tinier one.

'Short of sacking you from the newspaper's staff, I can do almost whatever I like with you – is that clear? Now, never ever attempt to pull a stroke on me like that again. You're lucky I was here. If I had found that this column had gone into print, you'd be emptying bins here and sweeping the fucking floor.'

Thereafter, I left Haughey's money off my personal radar; however, Gageby was not done in his protection of Haughey. Soon afterwards, Conor Cruise O'Brien told his page editor, Paul Tansey, that the *Irish Independent* was offering him more money. He really didn't want to go, so a small increase in pay might indicate that he was at least being respected. Paul sought the extra money from Gageby, who instantly saw his chance. He told Paul that there would be no money, and merely by entering into talks with the *Independent*, O'Brien had revealed a fundamental disloyalty. He had to go.

O'Brien had been foolish: he needed the money less than he needed the *Irish Times* readership, which needed him just as much. Thereafter, throughout the most depraved regime independent Ireland has ever known, *The Irish Times* said almost nothing about Haughey's finances or his apparent immunity from investigation by the Revenue Commissioners. I discovered why only after leaving *The Irish Times*.

In 1974, the Irish Times Trust was formed. At its heart were two major shareholders, Douglas Gageby and Major Tom McDowell. The trust certainly had some benevolent intentions – namely, the protection of the newspaper from a hostile or predatory takeover. But unlike *The Guardian*, which had been put into the protection of a trust without a financial transaction, the creation of the Irish Times Trust involved the purchase of the equity of the three main shareholders. To buy these shares, the Trust borrowed the requisite money from the Bank of Ireland, with the newspaper itself undertaking to repay the loan over the coming years. The need to generate profits to cover these payments proved to be a major driver of the newspaper's property pages, which thereafter unquestioningly endorsed the puffery of the country's estate agents, who then supplied the paper with vats of advertising revenue.

The beauty of this scheme was manifest and manifold. The men who ran the Trust were also the men who were selling the shares to it – primarily Gageby and McDowell. The Trust was a charity, and therefore would not have to publish accounts, meaning that the cost of repaying the loan would remain secret. Perhaps most beautifully of all, the Trust's founders had insider information about the start date for the introduction of capital gains tax, and the deal was signed and sealed just minutes before the new tax regime began.

Gageby's share of the deal was worth around £350,000, tax-free; a fine Georgian villa in Dublin was sold at the same time for under £15,000. Thirty years later, it would sell at £900,000, namely a multiplier of sixtyfold. In other words, at 2004 property prices, Gageby had netted himself £24 million, or €30 million, tax-free. Yet he retained control of the finances of the newspaper both through the Trust and as editor, for which of course he earned a generous salary. McDowell's take was around 50 per cent larger, even while he continued to take staggering amounts of money out of the newspaper, with most of his household costs, his laundry and dry-cleaning bills, and his wine cellar, being paid for directly as untaxed expenses by *The Irish Times*.

Why did the other newspapers not leap on this? Well, firstly, the three Dublin daily newspapers worked a protective cartel, one of whose provisions was that if one of them had a strike, the others would close for its duration. Secondly, why poke one hornets' nest when all three titles had comparable infestations in their attics? The *Irish Independent* had always been a prime supporter of the criminal conspiracy through which Joe McGrath had founded the Irish Hospitals' Sweepstake, the proceeds of which had enabled McGrath to found Waterford Crystal, which had long been a jewel in the crown of Irish commerce. For *The Irish Press*, it was the theft of hundreds of thousands of dollars collected in the 1920s in the US by Eamon de Valera, through the issuing of two kinds of shares to the donors in exchange for their money: the worthless 60,000 A stock went to the mugs, while the 200 B stock, though notionally worth only $1,000, nonetheless gave de Valera complete control over the monies raised. An emergency slush fund was even established to buy off any investors savvy enough to complain. De Valera's vision of a rustic Ireland composed of sturdy smallholders with modest financial expectations clearly did not extend to his clan. Thus were the fortunes of the de Valera family transformed for ever.

Why didn't the Revenue Commissioners investigate Haughey? Colm Condon, the Fianna Fáil attorney general who had prosecuted him in the Arms Trial, later became a good friend of mine. He told me that he had uncovered irrefutable evidence that the Revenue Commissioners had assisted in the transfer of money from the Department of Finance to the new Provisional IRA. However, this information was irrelevant to the prosecution of Haughey and might have irredeemably damaged Ireland's international reputation, so it was kept from the court. To the end of his days, Colm regretted that omission, for, as he said, the unplugged iron doesn't get hot a second time.

So there it was: Protestant Ireland, Fine Gael Ireland, Fianna Fáil Ireland, all helping themselves at the trough, and saying nothing about one another's little capers. Tammany Hall didn't lick its corrupt ways off the streets of New York. And, of course, most Irish people knew of the intrinsic corruption within Irish culture at some level.

Faith is the enabler that turns fiction into fact in all societies. A violent Blessed Trinity dominated countless rural Irish households until recently: one was a picture of the thorn-bound and bleeding sacred heart of Jesus; another was a picture of Patrick Pearse, who had been shot by a firing squad; and the third picture was of JFK, who had been assassinated by a sniper. This was pure Fenianism in triptych to match the other Trinity. The Irish have basically been polytheists down the millennia. The real historical significance of the shamrock is probably its attempt to incorporate existing Celtic deities into the new religion, rather than its use as an explanation of the Blessed Trinity. Hence the continuing religious and cultural reverence shown towards the Virgin Mary, St Patrick and St Brigid, or *Bríd*. St Brigid was so revered that Irish monks proselytising in the ruins of Rome's Londinium even dedicated a spring to her, which gave its name to the church alongside it. With the dissolution of the monasteries, the church became a prison, from which the term 'Bridewell' derives. There is something enchantingly contingent about a saint giving her name to a prison. It serves as a useful reminder of how evolution can mutate all things, turning them around 180 degrees, as legged mammals returned to the sea, and Irish newspapers conspired to hide the truth.

That said, the *Irish Times* duo were not mono-dimensional crooks. Thomas McDowell was, on one level, a posturing poltroon, all ironed tweed, fob watch, waxed moustaches and winged tufts of hair over the ears, like an Eastbourne con man about to relieve a brace of elderly dears of their life savings. (His sartorial role model could almost have been his fellow Ulsterman, John Bodkin Adams, though *he* went a little far in bumping off his victims.) Yet McDowell also had his good points: when poor Harry Saunders, the portly, whey-faced security man who feasted on life-prolonging onions, was diagnosed with inoperable stomach cancer, McDowell sent him on an all-expenses-paid holiday to the West Indies. While Harry was sunning his pallid, greying skin beside the pool, a man came up to him.

'Stomach cancer?'

'Yes. How could you tell?'

'Because I've got it too. Three months, at best.'

'Same here.'

Poor Harry lasted two.

As for Bruce Williamson's thoughts about the McDowell–Gageby depredations, he took those to the grave, along with his intact sense of honour. The last serious conversation we had was about an interview I had done with Group Captain Leonard Cheshire VC, the undiluted enthusiasm of which had earned me a few epistolary sneers from the newsroom and a beetle-browed glower from Gageby. I mention Cheshire because he remains the most mesmerising, purposeful, valiant man I have ever met, an extraordinary synthesis of mental intent and neat, anatomical purpose. As an RAF master bomber leading a raid on Munich, in order to minimise German civilian casualties he flew directly beneath the bombers as they passed over their aiming-point, calling on them to release their loads directly on him, so that they would hit their target.

During our talks, his pupils vanished in his unwavering brown eyes. His very presence radiated authority as uranium emits gamma rays, and he was possessed of an almost perfect unity; a small smile played on full, sensuous, almost womanly lips, and his delicate, long-fingered hands were folded neatly before him, like those of a pianist laid out in an undertaker's.

As a teenager, I had worked in a Cheshire Home, and had witnessed the horrors of progressive illness, the gibbering patients marooned in their beds, their facial muscles turning to mush, their jaws hanging open as they dribbled pendulums of saliva. Coping with these terrible illnesses must test the most demanding of faiths, yet Cheshire had become an utterly dedicated Catholic, a conversion which his biographer Andrew Boyle attributed to the deep faith of the Irish aircrew he had flown with. I once met Nelson Mandela, if only briefly – indeed, I even held a chair out for him – and he possessed a comparable charisma, but Cheshire nonetheless outshone him. Incredibly, Cheshire, who had minded so many with progressive illnesses, not long afterwards succumbed to perhaps the most evil of them all – motor neurone disease.

'A fine job my boy, a fine job,' said Bruce of my piece. 'I've read many profiles of Cheshire; yours was up there with the best. Well done indeed.'

Those were amongst the last words he spoke to me before he retired, though he still wrote short, diamantine film previews from home. His first stint in *The Irish Times* had been in the 1950s. Opposite the editorial offices stood the large windows of the Munster & Leinster Bank. One night the editor had sex with his secretary on his desk, with the lights on. On the floor below, the men of the case room silently watched the lovers' reflections on the darkened windows of the building opposite. Word soon got out, and the secretary was sacked, but not the editor. Bruce resigned in protest. That was the terrible world of yesterday – and not just in Ireland, but almost everywhere – and no matter when and where such injustices occur, there were and are far too few men who make a stand, as Bruce did. The only unimpeachably honourable journalist I have ever known, he made it to sixty-nine before his heart succumbed to the insuperable challenge of keeping such a vast body alive. But that he lived so long was largely due to the intervention of that most perplexing man, Douglas Gageby.

Fifteen

THE FOLLOWING CHAPTER might seem rather puzzling in a personal memoir, but I include it to give a modern reader a historic sense of the forces that had been working on Ireland. One might say that the failure of *The Irish Times* to exploit its position on the sill of the national house – of, but not in it – was one of the great tragedies of independence. Would such a deed have been possible? Even though four of the five Nobel prizes won by men from southern Ireland went to Protestants – Beckett, Shaw, Walton and Yeats – independent Ireland was no place for artists or dissenters, and from the outset it was clear that Protestants (and therefore *The Irish Times*) really should know their place. Perhaps the clearest statement of national intent was made in 1928, when de Valera, the father of so many institutions of the Irish state, lamented: 'We will, unfortunately, not be able to cut off ourselves completely from the world economy.'

This strange desire for isolation surely bespeaks great trauma, like a wounded animal seeking sanctuary in a cave; in other words, the voice of the Famine. In this post-cataclysmic epoch, most forms of 'republicanism' were in fact subspecies of Irish Catholicism, and the mix was usually imbued with a perplexing moral superiority. Ireland was seen as God's great Catholic experiment in insular salvation, and for decades this was almost the defining dogma of Irish identity.

Astonishing acts of vandalism could be overlooked or forgotten in the new Ireland. One atrocity towers above all else, serving as a template for so much that followed: the destruction of the Four Courts and Ireland's national records in 1922. The common ignorance of and silence about this monstrosity suggests that it remains too terrible to understand. Rather like the Emperor Chin's destruction of Chinese writings, it is absolute and irreversible. Not merely were the archives lost; so too were their catalogues, and with them went all knowledge of what had been burnt. We cannot ever know what it is that we do not know. True nihilism results when the flame of passionate ignorance devours the Platonic gnosis of parchment.

This appalling act of cultural sacrilege was also the foundational deed of Ireland's largest political party, Fianna Fáil, which, within rather more than a decade, would become the natural party of government of a state that it had originally set out to overthrow. Little wonder that dysfunctionality became almost an expression of governmental aspiration in Ireland, and that Fianna Fáil administrations, time after time, have driven the state onto the rocks. Deep in either its DNA or its subconscious, or perhaps in both, there seems to be a desire for auto-destruction. De Valera's achievements were magnificent: thrice over he wrought ruin on the people of Ireland. Haughey, twice over, once as co-founder of the IRA, another as Taoiseach. Lynch managed it a modest once. Ahern/ Cowan together, likewise.

With so many Irish historians grinding axes in defence of the 1916 Rising, various other vital truths were lost amid those ferrous sparks. One such truth so profoundly rebuts the validity of almost all historical narratives that to this day it is not spoken of. That Easter, the authorities had just learnt that a rising was imminent, but the only man empowered to deploy the Army to forestall it, Major General Friend, had gone to England to celebrate his fiftieth birthday on Easter Monday. Thus a sexual act in a house in Halfway Street, in Sidcup, Kent, in late August 1865 was a vital ingredient of the Rising and all the myths that followed. This reminds us that history is as much about contingency as it is about intent, while the myths that result from collisions between the two are not about any underlying truths, but about our need for legends that justify both past deeds and present opinions. Elisions are needed to sustain those myths: who in the years after his execution would learn Pearse's poem?

I forgive, you child
Of the soft red mouth:
I will not condemn anyone
For a sin not understood.

Raise your comely head
Till I kiss your mouth:
If either of us is the better of that
I am the better of it.

There is a fragrance in your kiss
That I have not found yet
In the kisses of women
Or the honey of their bodies.

Lad of the grey eyes,
That flush in thy cheek
Would be white with dread of me
Could you read my secrets.

He who has my secrets
Is not fit to touch you:
Is not that a pitiful thing,
Little lad of the tricks?

Just who in their right mind would entrust their son to such a man? Was James Connolly any less mad? He greeted the prospect of an even larger world war than the one they already had with unrestrained glee: '... Ireland may yet set the torch to a European conflagration that will not burn out until the last throne and the last capitalist bond and debenture will be shrivelled on the funeral pyre of the last war lord.'

He infused his Marxism with Golgotha: '...in all due humility and awe, we recognise ... as of mankind before Calvary, it may truly be said "without the shedding of blood, there is no redemption".'

Was there a single unionist, sane or otherwise, who could identify with such bloodthirsty gibberish? So perhaps the most important element within the myths that emerged after 1916 was the respect accorded to violence, on many levels, for the custodians of 1916 mythology would, once in power, resort to sub-homicidal forms of violent coercion. Almost the defining act of Irish independence was the project to make people speak Irish, whether they wanted to or not. A ferocious regime of corporal punishment drove this project, and economic ruination was to be visited on the non-compliant: if you failed your Irish at Leaving Certificate, you failed *all* your subjects. It is so hard to disentangle the Irish revival movement from its conjoined twin of *means* that I am tempted to believe that the relationship is not just metaphorical. Fenianism was essentially violent; therefore, re-establishing the language of the Fenians could be authentic only if it was violent too.

Moreover, the Romanised neo-paganism that seized control over Irish nationalism after 1916 further muddied the lexical waters by adopting much of the political vocabulary of the French Revolution, though remaining quite ignorant of its meanings. The resulting mental confusion was exemplified on St Patrick's Day 1923, the first to be celebrated by an independent Ireland. Across Britain – from Aberdeen to Bournemouth – local, pre-BBC radio stations dedicated their entire evening's broadcasts to a celebration of Irish poetry and traditional music. In Ireland, however, the commemorations took on a rather different tone. At noon that day, on a radio command from Dublin by the Chief of Staff of the Free State Army, General Richard Mulcahy – who had helped conduct the massacre of a squad of mostly Catholic RIC men at Ashbourne, County Meath, in 1916 – Major General David Reynolds hoisted a tricolour over Cork barracks. Emblazoned in its centre was a huge bleeding Sacred Heart, pierced with thorns, that had been especially woven by Les Soeurs de la Société des Oeuvres du Sacré Cœur de Lyon.

From 1870 onwards, the long-standing devotion to the Sacred Heart in France had mutated into a specifically anti-republican cult. Its author, Bishop Fourier, had proclaimed that his country's defeat by the Prussian armies was a divine judgement on the century of moral decline caused by the Revolution. That the republican Irish tricolour could in 1923 be adorned with such a specifically anti-republican symbol as the Sacred Heart can mean only that profound intellectual contradictions animated the new state's leaders. We do not need to leave that barracks to see what these contradictions could lead to. For just the day before, across the country, another six 'republican' captives had been executed by government firing squads. One of them, a teenager named William Healy, was actually shot in Cork barracks, where the republicanism of the tricolour was to be so implicitly rejected the next day. The previous week poor Healy had been caught scattering petrol around the Blarney Street home of a 'Mrs Powell'. Executing this pathetic would-be arsonist was perhaps made a little easier by the fact that Mrs Powell was the sister of Michael Collins, who had been ambushed and killed the previous August.

Healy's execution brought to sixty-three the number of men shot by Free State firing squads in under nine months – nearly three times as many as the British had executed over *five years* of insurgency. That night, in apparent if somewhat incoherent revenge, a 16-year-old boy named Ben McCarthy was taken from his Bantry home and shot dead by some 'republicans' – though that term is clearly meaningless – with the usual admonition being placed on his dead body: 'Spies beware.'

A couple of weeks earlier, the first customs posts had been erected along the Border – not by the Northern Ireland government, as is generally believed today, but by the Free State, a keen co-author of partition. Tariffs soon followed, the first on margarine and rosary beads – the former to protect Irish farmers, margarine being the cheapest fat available for the poor of the teeming tenements, and the latter to shelter the hapless Irish rosary industry from beads made in Buddhist Japan and Hussite Czechoslovakia. Tariffs duly followed on almost everything, though surely the most delightful, a duty on second-hand shoes, was introduced by Fianna Fáil in 1934. A universal tariff on all imported glass jars, even ones containing preserves, created a minor currency for the very poor: into the 1950s, children could get into Saturday cinema matinees by handing over two jam jars.

This Ireland managed to be both isolationist and intrusive. One of its first deeds was the creation in 1926 of the Committee on Evil Literature, which proposed: 'The sale and circulation … of books, magazines and pamphlets that advocate the unnatural prevention of conception should be made illegal, and be PUNISHABLE by adequate penalties.' So too should be 'any description or picture that relates or refers to the generative organs of either sex or to any complaint or infirmity arising from or relating to sexual intercourse or the prevention or removal of irregularities in menstruation, or to drugs, medicines, treatments or methods for procuring abortion, miscarriage or preventing conception'.

The law that resulted went even further, forbidding any public mention of the words 'menstruation', 'contraception', 'divorce' and 'abortion'. Tragically, menstruation itself proved a little harder to ban. *The Irish Times* mentioned the word during its account of the report of the Committee on Evil Literature, but not again until 1946, when it appeared in an agency report on the after-effects of the atom bombs on Japan. Presumably either a subeditor on the foreign desk had nodded off after one pint too many across the road or the contextual incineration of 150,000 people was considered proof against any possible aphrodisiac effects the word might have on the young and impressionable. The word 'menstruation' did not appear again in *The Irish Times* until the 1970s.

Intrusiveness in independent Ireland rapidly became a governmental norm. All incoming parcels were opened by Customs, and their contents scrutinised. Thus, as *The Irish Times* reported, a Christmas package containing a pennyworth of sweets, a rosary, a candle, a handkerchief and a necktie, total value 5 shillings (€12.50 in today's money) would not merely cost 15 shillings (€37.50) in duty, but a further one shilling and threepence (€3.10) in additional postal costs. Even the bereaved were to be punished: duty on coffin mountings amounted to 66 per cent, though a widow might console herself with the knowledge that her undergarments had attracted a mere 60 per cent duty.

In part, these new tariffs were designed to raise revenue for a government that was starved of funds. In 1923, pay cuts of 10 per cent had been imposed on public servants in the Free State because British subventions were gone and the Irish people were forced to pay for much of the cost of years of war, including compensating homeowners whose houses had been burnt by the IRA. For example, the ratepayers of Meath had to pay Colonel Rowley £76,000 – €10 million in present-day money – in compensation for the IRA's destruction of Summerhill, perhaps the greatest house in Ireland. Happily, however, the ratepayers of County Galway didn't have to compensate the ninety homeless Protestant orphans after the IRA burnt down the boys' orphanage in Clifden. They simply left Ireland, as thousands of other Protestants would: 17 per cent of the population of Dublin in 1911 were Protestant. Within a generation, the figure had dropped to around 5 per cent.

De Valera acceded to power shortly after Seán T. O'Kelly had successfully – and futilely, as it turned out – negotiated, in Ottawa in 1932, a protection for Irish exports across the Empire. The economic war that de Valera soon afterwards began with the United Kingdom and the British Empire was hardly noticed by its intended 'victims' – not least because the Roca–Runciman Treaty with Argentina of 1933 supplied all the beef that Britain needed. Indeed, Britain gained from the conflict: Guinness built the world's largest brewery in London simply because its Irish base was now politically too unstable.

Unsurprisingly, between 1926 and 1936, 166,000 people – the equivalent of the then population of Donegal – fled the new state, and the number of children in it fell by 6.8 per cent. A food-growing nation could no longer afford to eat. Between 1931 and 1938 bacon consumption fell by 31 per cent and flour consumption by 40 per cent. With impoverishment came undercapitalisation and underdevelopment. Live cattle were still being exported for English factories to get the value-added benefits of butchery, bone exploitation and leather manufacture. By 1949, after twenty-seven years of self-government, in which the state had done almost nothing to develop food-processing, adults in the west on average drank seven litres of milk a week but ate only a gram of cheese.

Contrast this with Denmark. In 1946, the German occupation over, it resumed exporting to the rest of the world, selling 67,000 tons of butter, seven million tons of cheese and nearly 100,000 tons of meat, while Ireland simply had no food to sell. Between 1941 and 1948, Ireland exported no butter whatsoever: this contrasts with 42,000 metric tons annually before the Great War, and, yet more unbelievably, 22,600 metric tons before the Famine.

So if we were not exporting our butter, surely we must have been eating it? No. In spring 1952, the government had to import 1,500 tons of

New Zealand butter to meet domestic demands. Ireland, a grass factory, was importing butter almost from the Antarctic. Not to be outdone by its polar rival, the near-Arctic circle then spoke up: in 1957, both Sweden and Finland sold more butter to Britain than Ireland did. By 1956, there were 3.5 million fewer head of poultry and 1 million less of cattle, horses and sheep than in 1939, and Dublin regularly ran out of eggs. When agricultural exports did finally resume, they had to be subsidised. The wretched Irish taxpayer was effectively bribing the British consumer to eat Irish butter. Between 1956 and 1957, the impoverished Irish state spent £355,016 underwriting the sale of 22,000 tons of butter to one of the wealthiest countries in the world.

The Irish Times witnessed these calamities, and duly reported them, but, in its meek, laodicean way, failed to challenge the underlying reason for them. Maybe this was prudent, and not just because of the paper's Protestantism: the political culture of independent Ireland was still dominated by the agricultural lobby, and this in turn was bewitched by the power of herd-ownership. Possessing cattle was almost more important than their economic value, and this culture probably had its roots deep in the quasi-Minoan culture of the first settlers to Ireland, as suggested by the primacy in Irish folklore of the Cattle Raid of Cooley.

Conspicuous neglect of the sea was the concomitant of herd-worship. At the Treaty talks in 1921, maritime matters were swiftly despatched to an unimportant sub-committee. Some fifty years later, we further bartered away our fishing rights to the EEC to protect our dairy and beef interests. Indeed, Ireland is the only Atlantic country – from the North Cape of Norway to the Straits of Gibraltar – that has no ocean-going, deep-sea fishing tradition. Even now, the population of our west coast per head eats less than one-tenth the amount of fish of the average citizen of Madrid, 200 miles from the nearest sea and 2,000 feet above its tallest waves, just as in times of hunger, the Irish seas washed unfished on the shores of a famine isle.

In 1924, an appalled Minister for Fisheries, Fionán Lynch, told the Dáil that there was not one single commercial buyer of fish in the whole west of Ireland, and no retail market for fish existed at all in the inland counties. A Norwegian company was offering nine shillings a hundredweight for cured mackerel – in today's prices, a ludicrous €45 for 50 kilos, *but no one in the west even knew how to cure fish.* A generation later, in 1950, the annual consumption of fish in Ireland was 4.5lbs; in Britain, it was 32lbs. The Republic's 3,200 kilometres of coastline had only 1,600 fishermen, or one for every 2 kilometres of shoreline. The English fishing port of Grimsby alone had 3,500 fishermen.

In 1950, *The Irish Times* published the observations of a Russian visitor. The Army – he noted – had nearly 1,500 officers and 2,500 NCOs to supervise just 4,500 private soldiers: effectively, one officer per soldier. Or, to put it another way, there were as many state-dependent commissioned officers (with government-funded pensions to follow) as there were wealth-creating fishermen, and the commissions were largely reserved for the sons of independent Ireland's middle class, the state's *nomenclatura*, within what was clearly a collapsing economy.

Between 1926 and 1961, the population of Northern Ireland rose by over 168,000, the population of Spain rose by nine million, through wracked by civil war, and the population of France rose by seven million, though that country had lost two million men in the Great War. The population of independent Ireland fell by 154,000. Even more dramatically, over the same period the Catholic population of Northern Ireland increased as a proportion of the state from 33.5 per cent to 34.9 per cent, while the Catholic population of the three westernmost counties of Northern Ireland rose minutely, going from 146,128 to 146,437. The Catholic population of the neighbouring counties of Monaghan, Cavan and Donegal meanwhile fell by 61,000, from over 250,000 to nearly 189,000. In the 1950s, three out of five young people in the Republic emigrated. As Archbishop Lucey of Cork observed: 'Rural Ireland is stricken and dying.'

Almost the defining moral deed of the new Ireland had been the wretchedly cynical use by de Valera of the Emergency Powers Act to allow his son Rúaidhrí to relinquish his commission in the Army in 1943 so that he could succeed his brother-in-law Brian Ó Cuív, husband of de Valera's daughter, as permanently tenured lecturer in Celtic languages in Maynooth College, which was the primary educator of Ireland's priests. In this new Ireland, Army and Church marched together. In 1958, for example, the Officer Commanding Western Command, Colonel Fox, dropped dead during an Army pilgrimage to Lourdes – an interesting insight into military priorities. That year, a group of Catholic zealots attacked and beat up three absurdly optimistic Protestant missionaries in Killaloe, County Clare, knocking one of them unconscious and kicking out several of his teeth. At the assailants' trial, District Justice Gordon Hurley observed that Roman Catholicism was *above* the law and that Protestant 'street-preaching' was an abuse of religious freedom. He allowed the assailants to walk free. A handful of Protestant clerics complained, but since they did so in the dulcet tones of evensong in a cathedral close, they were unheard amid all the papist braying filling the air. One public dissenter throughout this time was Senator Owen Sheehy-Skeffington, the son of the martyr of 1916, whom the Dublin Vocational Education had already banned from all their premises, even forbidding staff and students from having any communication with him. The speaker of the Senate rejected Sheehy-Skeffington's request for a debate on the Killaloe scandal. Meanwhile, the few southern Catholics who did comment critically on this affair added the irrelevant caveats that things were much worse for Catholics in Northern Ireland.

Such an observation might have had some merit had the Irish government formally complained to the British government about the position of that minority. From 1922 to 1969, no such representations were ever made. Instead, youngsters were taught deluding fictions about the violent 'successes' from 1916 to 1921, which many of them took as gospel, aided by a lack of any reference to the Civil War that had followed these martial triumphs. The isolationist Catholic nationalism that resulted found its apotheosis in Seán South, a personal fusion of all the malignant forces that independent Ireland had been cultivating. A leading light in the Limerick Sodality, an association of zealous Catholic laymen, South would regularly lead a bunch of vigilantes armed with blackthorn sticks around the city's cinemas, beating up courting couples. He was a member of various right-wing Catholic groups, such as the anti-Semitic Maria Duce and the Knights of Columbanus. He was both a lieutenant in the FCA, the Army reserve defending the Republic, and a foremost figure in the IRA which opposed that Republic for its territorial and spiritual imperfections. On 1 January 1957, he was killed in an IRA attack on Brookeborough RIC station.

South's funeral procession through the Republic occasioned a vast outpouring of Catholic–Republican hysteria of the hybrid Cork barracks variety. Dublin County Council passed a vote of sympathy for him and stood for a minute's silence. One Protestant councillor, Lionel Booth, dissociated himself from the vote of sympathy, but the chairman, Senator James Tunney of Labour, ruled him out of order. Tunney may have better understood the mood of the country, for hysterical, rosary-chanting crowds were acclaiming South's hearse as it passed from Dundalk to Limerick.

In South's home place, fresh variants of the flag of 1923 were on display. The city was festooned with hundreds of tricolours emblazoned with black crosses, as tens of thousands of mourners lined the streets. Six priests officiated at the funeral, which was attended by most members of Limerick City and County Councils, including the chairman of the Limerick Mental Hospital Board, of which institution South might properly have been a guest. In all the hysteria sweeping Ireland, there was no mention of the Catholic RUC man John Scally, killed in the near-simultaneous IRA attack at Derrylin, County Fermanagh.

Other, more worldly priorities in the meantime required attention. That Thursday, as South's funeral cortège moved to Limerick, the government granted special licences to fish traders to import 500 stone (3,200 kilos) of plaice and 100 stone (640 kilos) of black sole to supply the elites with their Friday fish. In 2018 prices, the plaice cost €100/kilo, and the sole fillets nearly €200/kilo, as Dublin's tenement urchins were still going shoeless.

Meanwhile, Seán MacBride's Clann na Poblachta explored fresh depths of irrationality, observing meticulously that 200,394 people had emigrated from the state in the previous four years, and, furthermore, Britain's 'intolerable' claim to govern the North should now – and possibly even 'therefore' – be ended. In 1948, MacBride, as leader of Clann na Poblachta and Minister for External Affairs (and only twelve years after being chief of staff of the IRA), had penned the letter to Pope Pius XII on behalf of the new Taoiseach, John A. Costello: 'On the occasion of our assumption of office and our first cabinet meeting, my colleagues and myself desire to repose at the feet of Your Holiness the assurance of our filial loyalty and devotion as well as firm resolve to be guided by the teaching of Christ and to strive for the attainment of social order in Ireland based on Christian principles.' Now, in 1957, this bizarre little creature withdrew his support for the government, not over the atrocious conditions in the tenements, but in protest at its few tentative moves against his former colleagues in the IRA, and the government soon fell.

Not coincidentally, four months after South's death, gardaí raided a theatre mounting a production of Tennessee Williams' *The Rose Tattoo* and arrested and imprisoned the director, Alan Simpson. The charge? That he had mounted a 'lewd' production, in which an actor pretended to throw an imaginary condom onto the stage floor. Simpson was ruined by the ensuing court action, and his marriage foundered. Meanwhile, the Catholic hierarchy's ruthless auxiliaries in the Knights of Columbanus had captured the Censorship Board and had raised the number of books banned to nearly 6,000 titles.

This was a society that flourished on lies and censorship. There are many days one could select to commemorate the triumph of bad ideas, but I choose 20 February 1951, when the Censorship Board announced that it had just banned another seventy publications. An inquest heard that Patrick Flanagan (aged 14) had been killed at Artane Industrial School 'while sliding down bannisters'. After hearing almost no evidence, the coroner delivered his verdict: accidental death. Next, he heard how Nellie Lee of Dublin, who was 'prone to fainting fits', had been found gassed to death beside a gas oven that had been turned on without being lit. Verdict: accidental death. So here we have the Censorship Board doing the usual, while – at a guess – and who can be sure at this remove? – the Coroner's court was hushing up a homicide and a suicide.

These were amongst the forces that had shaped the public memory of the Ireland that I was later to live in, and, though with the great Whitaker–Lemass reforms of the 1960s, Ireland had opened up hugely, many of the attitudes forged in the long bleak winter of isolation remained powerful. It was going to take a far greater stimulus than a few articles by an English-born journalist to rock the intellectual status quo, and that stimulus, in all its moral majesty, came from the spiritual and cultural successors of Seán South himself – the Provisional IRA.

Sixteen

THE FIRST REPORTS were so unbelievable that decent brains rejected them as some lurid fantasy concocted by deranged anti-republican propagandists. In truth, the IRA's attack on a Remembrance Sunday service at Enniskillen in 1987, in which eleven people were killed almost immediately, and another sixty-three were injured, one of whom, Ronnie Hill, spent thirteen years in a coma before succumbing, was a thoroughly intentional barbarity. A second bomb at nearby Tullyhommon failed to explode just as the Boys' and Girls' Brigades were gathering alongside it. But for the grace of an imperfect detonator, a dozen children would have been slaughtered.

Enniskillen and Tullyhommon were a deliberate and murderous assault on the entire process of commemorating the Irish dead of the two world wars. I have thought very carefully about this. I believe that these outrages were a culmination of all the forces and attitudes outlined earlier in these pages and intensified by the Haughey government's overt and outspoken hostility to the Remembrance Sunday commemorations. For, within the deviant and psychotic Sinn Féin–IRA mindset, Haughey's loud denunciations of my cause had provided a subconscious authorisation for the Enniskillen barbarity. Such attacks on commemoration were deep in the IRA's gene pool. In the 1920s, heroes would snatch poppies from the lapels of grieving mothers and widows, and one of the first targets in the 1950s' campaign was a Remembrance Day service on 11 November thwarted by the bombers blowing themselves up at Edentubber, County

Louth, which, cleansed of all murderous intent, thereafter became a place of republican martyrdom and pilgrimage.

The wave of revulsion, incredulity and anger that swept across Ireland after Enniskillen proved to be culturally transformative. This was the watershed moment. The core of moral decency that guides the average Irish person like a lodestone seeks the Arctic pole was irrevocably violated by this IRA atrocity. Every set attitude now came under critical review. It also gave the Haughey government both the opportunity and the moral obligation to close down the IRA, root, bark, bough and branch, with the support of most of the Irish people. Instead, once again, Anglophobic equivocation was preferred, and the IRA remained in existence for another two decades. The conjoined power of Romanism and Fenianism was gruesomely evident at the funeral of that devious little goblin Seán MacBride some months later. As *The Irish Times* was to report: 'Gerry Adams and Seán Mac Stíofáin received communion from the Bishop of Galway Eamonn Casey.'

Adams is Adams. Mac Stíofáin was the deracinated English Protestant psychopath who became an Irish Catholic chief of staff of the IRA. Casey had secretly fathered a child with his troubled second cousin Annie Murphy, who had been put in his care after she had suffered a miscarriage and divorce. He later cassocked £150,000 from the Third World Charity Trócaire to pay her hush money. When this theft was made public, he was not charged. Another of the funeral guests (it would be wrong to call them mourners) was the cackling assassin Vinny Byrne, who used to joyously tell interviewers of the final moments of the pyjamaed man he had murdered in 1920. 'I says to him, "Put up your hands, Mr Ames, your time is up", and then I plugged him, ha ha ha!'

Was there ever a funeral graced with such murderousness, corruption, depravity, sexual exploitation and grand larceny which nonetheless spoke a quite spectacular, if unintended, truth?

By this time, Conor Brady had been made the first Catholic editor of *The Irish Times*. This was initially very much to my advantage. Brady actively encouraged me to steer my column towards serious issues and to challenge conventional thinking. He also brought in fresh blood and waved farewell to old blood, such as our Washington correspondent, Seán Cronin, a manifold traitor. He had been in the Irish Army during the war and had taken an oath to serve the state. He later dishonoured this oath by joining the IRA and was the architect of the 1950s' Border campaign. He was therefore directly responsible for the murder of Constable John Scally, mentioned earlier. After his release from internment in the Curragh in 1962, Cronin moved to the United States, and became the *Irish Times'* Washington correspondent, regularly promoting the general cause of the Provisional IRA and its foul auxiliary NORAID. Of all Gageby's editorial delinquencies, Cronin's appointment remains the most incomprehensible.

Sadly, with the arrival of Brady, the columnist Sam McAughtry also got the chop. I liked Sam. The sane voice of Protestant Ulster, he was a witty, kindly man whose columns and company I enjoyed greatly. I believe that he reciprocated my affection. Brady introduced new columnists, such as Nuala O'Faolain and Fintan O'Toole, and increased the profile of Mary Holland. I knew O'Faolain from UCD, where she was a very youthful and overtly sensualist, miniskirted assistant lecturer. She had been flagrantly promiscuous at a time when Irish agony aunts were proclaiming that any female interest in lustful sex was perverted, deviant and un-Irish. So, clearly, in liberational matters, I admired her, not least because she was now involved in an open lesbian relationship with the feminist Nell McCafferty.

However, it soon became evident that O'Faolain was both a fraud and deeply neurotic. Her very first column was about the amazement of a French couple she had driven around Ireland at the number of building societies they saw. She explained to them that this was how Irish society worked: boys went to a couple of well-established schools, such as Clongowes and Blackrock, and eventually took over control of building societies, with huge salaries for very little work.

I never really challenged other journalists on their opinions, but this was too much. I went over to O'Faolain and said: 'You can't have driven them because you can't drive. And building societies are not run by Clongowes boys. You've created a fiction about a public-school nexus that might apply in England, but it certainly doesn't here. If anything, building societies are run by Christian Brothers boys.'

'Possibly, but I wasn't speaking a literal truth. I was dealing in metaphors.'

Well, those metaphors went down a treat with a great many readers. O'Faolain unfailingly found a tone of bewildered poor-me innocence: why are those beastly men getting ahead while we oppressed women are being held back? Of course, women had experienced much deplorable injustice in Irish society; however, she eschewed factual assessments in favour of a wheedling and imaginatively self-pitying note that struck a resonating chord with many. In time, with perfectly predictable perfidy, she publicly betrayed and disavowed her former lover, Nell McCafferty.

O'Toole was a laureate of left-liberal sanctimony. Unlike O'Faolain, who, underneath all her flim and her flam, was full of self-doubt, he had a reserved space in the car park for *The Morally Superior Monthly*, while his sermonising prose style similarly had one in the bike rack of *Turgidity Weekly*. John Waters was another addition. No friend of the IRA, he was nonetheless an uncompromising nationalist and – long before I was – a critic of the political feminism that was gaining so much power. There were issues on which he and I were allies, and others in which we would disagree, but without doubting one another's integrity. To my mind, he was the most important journalist to emerge in Ireland at that time, and the fate that awaited him was emblematic of the terrible era that we were now entering.

Holland had a background rather like mine: born in England to Irish parents, she very much espoused the notion (as I once had) that it was the physical conditions of Northern nationalists which explained the IRA. I now felt that it was a cyclical process: the very fact of the IRA, and the nationalist mythology that it was able to deploy, explained the IRA. Any state reaction to its excesses caused that mythology to be intensified. In other words, it was armed victimhood, whose circular arguments justified its existence. Holland had been a closet supporter of the IRA: early in the Troubles, she told me that she approved of the murder of British soldiers as a strategic necessity, though later her position on this softened.

Another change followed: the introduction of new technology. I had never learnt to type properly, and still hunted and pecked inaccurately, :ing two or even three adjoining letters, then having to disentangle the mesh of keys trapped in the single typing space. New technology brought my digital incompetence to a new and exhilarating level. I would often inadvertently but unknowingly hit Alt A, highlighting the entire text without knowing what I had done because my eyes were still on the keyboard. To hit any key would delete everything, and suddenly I would have a blank screen, with no knowledge of how to retrieve what I had lost. As then, so now; I still hammer the keyboard inaccurately, thereby regularly achieving the annihilation of my work.

At a national level, the Progressive Democrats – largely a breakaway from Haughey's Fianna Fáil, but with a few recruits from elsewhere – had become a new force in Irish life, determined to tackle the absurdly high levels of tax in Irish life. The government was deducting well over 60 per cent of my modest income at source. Quite iniquitously, civil servants and politicians were paying half the level of social insurance that employees in the private sector were, on the disingenuous grounds that they couldn't get sacked, so they didn't need the 'protection'. Those were reasons for paying more tax, not less. Senior civil servants had simply devised a scheme whereby both they and their political masters retained more of their incomes than the hopelessly quiescent taxpayers who were making those incomes possible.

When I wrote a column criticising the tax system, both O'Faolain and Holland told me how proud they were to be paying higher taxes to aid the destitute. Such pious nonsense was everywhere: the state was there to help the poor, went the theory – yet amazingly, the more money the state handed out, the number of poor people increased. The equation was simple: dole wasn't taxed, income was – and in a depressed economy, anyone who took a modest job would find themselves earning less money than the feckless layabeds.

It was around this time that a new American creed, 'political correctness', arrived on our shores. This fad seemed to be so vapid and counter-intellectual that I assumed it would soon find a place in the Museum of Ephemera, along with the hula hoop, the Davy Crockett hat and hot pants. I certainly had no sense that it would soon pose the most coherent threat to western values since the defeat of the Third Reich. Instead, almost overnight, so many of the apparent gains of the 1960s

– tolerance, personal liberation, the abolition of doctrinaire thought – were being confronted by the opposite forces: cherished victimhood, a new puritan priggishness and growing intolerance. Moreover, egalitarian feminism had begotten a new and delightfully self-refuting oxymoron. This was the term 'offensive to women', though, naturally, in this new world of asymmetric equality, nothing could be 'offensive to men'. Whenever a woman journalist wanted to make a man she was writing about sound ridiculous, she would say he had 'harrumphed' something; another killer verb was 'guffaw'. You will rarely find either word applied to women, who meanwhile had monopolies on approving terms like 'feisty', 'gutsy', 'sassy' and 'fiercely intelligent'.

My first experience of the new PC dogmas arose from a description I gave of a cow being examined internally, in which the vet (a friend of mine, Caroline Berry) had inserted her arm up the cow's rectum to check on an embryo transplant. A page editor came to me with the copy in her hand. 'I've been discussing this with women colleagues. This line will have to go,' she said sternly. 'Any intimate description of the female anatomy is highly offensive to women.'

'Cow-readers, maybe, but surely not women-women readers.'

'Don't be frivolous. I'm not here to discuss this with you, just to tell you it's going. If you want to write about the female anatomy in future, a safe rule is: don't.'

Another sign of the future was the boastful opposition to free speech at Trinity College Dublin, academic home of Edmund Burke, Swift and Wilde. An alliance of the left, Sinn Féin, pacifists and various lunatics with wet rot in the roof space managed to prevent the English historian David Irving from addressing the college's Historical Society, because he was allegedly a 'Holocaust denier'. Unlike this sundry shower, I had read most of Irving's works and spoken to him. I pointed out that he himself had used words such as 'holocaust', 'extermination', 'devil's work' and 'extirpation' to describe what the Nazis did to the Jews, of whom, he said, the Nazis had murdered three million. However, I refused an invitation to appear on a platform with him because I profoundly disliked many of his opinions about the Third Reich, which were either very bad or very mad, and I didn't trust my ability to rebut them in public.

One of the people who justified the silencing of Irving was the president of TCD's Students' Union, Mark Little, who later became RTÉ's Washington correspondent. Clearly, censoriousness was the future, and in more ways than one, for he later became MD of Twitter Ireland. But perhaps the most ignoble contribution to this affair came from six members of Trinity's Modern History Department, who justified silencing Irving by declaring that it was the duty of historians to 'help support democratic society'. No, it is not: it is the duty of historians to support historical enquiry, and to let democratic society look after itself.

Yet the words of the Trinity Six were mere straws in the wind. Airborne haystacks would follow in due course. The most recent victim of what is now called 'no-platforming' at Trinity was my friend the Israeli ambassador, Ze'ev Boker, who is of German–Jewish ancestry. Deny free speech to Irvine for his 'Holocaust denial' and sooner or later you are denying free speech to the survivors of the Holocaust.

Yet even as both PCs – political correctness and prudent cowardice – were knocking at the door, economically and politically Ireland had been achieving Paraguayan levels of ineptitude, as governance had passed back and forth between FitzGerald and Haughey. In the twelve months up to 1988, over 100,000 young people emigrated, mostly to Britain, while the Irish government benefited from their departure twice over – by not having to pay their dole, and by extracting the absurd 'travel tax' on their departure. What was and remains most striking about the Irish people was their docility in the face of such widespread ineptitude – yet the young were nonetheless willing to travel vast distances to find jobs and better themselves. Such resilience – requiring stoicism, enterprise and courage – would in time save the Irish nation.

Seventeen

CURIOUSLY, THE WELFARE of what was then called the Third World remained paramount in Ireland throughout this period of domestic economic failure. I certainly approved of all aid for Africa, never wondering why this continent should still uniquely expect to be the constant beneficiary of western moneys. It just seemed to be part of a natural and mutually solipsistic contract: we gave, they took, and each felt morally enriched by the deal.

No doubt this was why Gorta, which specialised in long-term development rather than famine relief, asked me to report on their projects amongst the Pokot people in the village of Kositei in northern Kenya. The Pokot turned out to be perhaps the most beguiling, enchanting people I have ever met. Yet for all the regard I still feel for them, the irrefutable truth, which rapidly became evident to me during my brief stay there, was that the land around Kositei was as uninhabitable as the Great Blasket Island, which was why the latter was abandoned. But the Pokot insisted on remaining on their ancestral lands, and the only reason they could do so was because of Irish money. This was a dependency as absurd and demeaning as it was addictive. It might still be, for all I know.

As with most African societies, Pokot women appeared to do all the work, while the men, ornamental studs in their chins, sat in companionable circles all day and talked. I don't know what they talked about, or indeed what there was to talk about, because nothing seemed to happen there, apart from regular visitations of drought, the death of the latest Gorta-planted trees, and occasional skirmishes with the Turkana. The men's cattle were looked after by boy-herds, as were a species of strangely sybaritic donkeys whose function was to flaunt their owner's wealth. These beasts were not even used to carry the skin bags of water from the distant wells. No, these were borne by the women in a slow, and often luscious way – for young Pokot women, even when burdened, sauntered like panthers down a Paris catwalk.

When I asked the men (through a translator) why the donkeys were not carrying the water, they laughed: 'Why? Carrying is women's work: donkeys are valuable.' All said very pleasantly, for the Pokot people laugh a lot – even the able-bodied warriors were able to see the bright side of things while a most unfeline and arthritic old woman tottered by beneath her wobbling freight of H_2O. However, we might take some minor comfort from the Pokot women's secrets, about which I can write because Seán McGovern, the very fine priest Gorta was maintaining there, showed me a thesis written by an American female anthropologist. Apparently, the men think that 'their' women – having been circumcised – are sexually inert: however, the cuts are in fact symbolic, and though obviously painful and bloody, the important bits remain. Aunts teach teenage girls how to please themselves sexually, which, along with lesbianism, is the primary source of erotic pleasure for Pokot women. Their menfolk remain gloriously unaware of the parallel universe 'their' women inhabit. The idea of a female getting pleasure from sex would be as culturally ludicrous to the Pokot male as making a donkey do women's work.

Some characteristics of the Pokot were striking: the fear of night and of snakes, and their habit of not making habitual pathways, which is what V.S. Naipaul observed of Africans in Tanzania. But these phenomena are easy to explain. The animals of Africa co-evolved with Man. They developed defences against Man as Man grew hungrier and wilier. Africa, with its homicidal carnivores – lions, leopards, hunting dogs, hyaenas, crocodiles – also has the only professionally homicidal herbivores on the planet: elephants, buffalo, rhinoceros and hippopotamuses. They will naturally devour any agricultural produce, and with equal enthusiasm kill farmers that get in their way, and the farmers who survive their killing rampages will soon be finished off by one or more of the many carnivores. So why would night not be terrifying? Why create paths that advertise where you or your child might be safely taken? And who would not fear snakes where lethal reptiles abound, when the only cure is juju? It is absurd to expect Africans to start behaving like Europeans simply because European schooling has arrived. After all, for how long did Iron Age Fenianism remain a powerful cultural force in Ireland?

Nonetheless, despite all I learned about the downsides of the Pokot project, I wrote with warm approval about every aspect of Gorta's operations in Kenya; this was effectively both justifying and subsidising the moral ethos that esteems the value of asses above the toil of women. So instead of being sceptical, as I should have been, for the acquirement of wisdom is impossible without organised doubt, I simply sought to remain within the consensus that embraces the dogmatic pieties of Irish life. These socially coercive norms protected so many national projects by making any examination of them taboo. Beneficiaries of these universal dogmatic pieties have, at different times, included the Irish language, Catholicism, censorship, the Shannon stopover, the rejection of contraception, the sanctity of marriage and the reintegration of the national territory. All these have since perished, only to be replaced by other equally adamantine values usually, of course, with 'equal' in their name. But the one value that has survived has been the virtue of aid to Africa, the very pinnacle within the hierarchy of universal dogmatic pieties. At the time of writing, famine has again struck Kositei, as it was bound to, with several women (of course) dying of hunger, while some Pokot youths murdered a British–South African businessman named Tristan Voorspuy, who was trying to encourage tourism in the area. So much for that.

I regret one more thing about that trip. Outside the Masai Mara game reserve, I met a naked Masai boy, aged about eleven. In almost perfect English, he asked me where I was from. I told him, and then began to describe this 'Ireland'.

'Thank you,' he interrupted. 'I know what Ireland is. Dublin, Belfast, killings. You don't seem to get on very well, do you?'

'We have our problems.'

'Like the Pokot and the Turkana, I suppose.'

'I dare say. Your English is very good. How many languages do you speak?'

'Thank you. It is passable. I speak Masai, of course, plus Swahili, Luo and Kikuyu. As for my English, it's not so good. I'm only third or fourth in my class, maybe.'

'What are you going to do when you grow up?'

'That's a long time away. I've got to be circumcised before that happens. And I like this' – he pointed down at himself – 'the way it is.'

'Have you any choice in the matter?'

He laughed. 'Don't be absurd.'

Confident that I was talking to a future head of the entire world, or at least the world's pioneering brain-transplant surgeon, I asked for his address, which he wrote down in elegant copperplate.

'I'll write to you,' I said.

'Do. I'd like an Irish pen pal.'

Pen pal: what an extinct world that term conjures up.

I folded the piece of paper and put it in my shirt pocket, from which it duly vanished in the laundry in Nairobi. What is that lad up to now? Making human cell tissue out of seaweed to help those with severed spinal cords? Or, more probably, minding cattle?

My abject capitulation to unprincipled Third-Worldery in due course led to my being sent to Ethiopia in 1988, where again the goodness of the people there, and the obvious 'virtue' of all charity to Africa, further seduced me. Naturally, I set about writing really juicy famine porn. I think the money shot in these matters is seeing a wizened baby die, preferably with a fly supping at the corner of her eye – little dead girls being slightly bigger box-office than boys. Tragically, from my point of view, no African child was considerate enough to expire in front of me, so, in the absence of such mortal munificence, I resorted to stereotype – I used the lazy, almost contemptible, metaphor of the Irish Famine. Even then, I knew that there were no points of contact, for both causes and consequences were different. Over a million people died in the Irish Famine, a catastrophe without comparison in Europe as almost an entire society collapsed. There can be no understanding of Irish history or psyche without the Famine as the centrepiece. My own feeling has moved towards a harsher view of British policies: that, as the Famine endured, the Westminster government tacitly accepted that nature should be allowed to dispose of millions of Irish people, through death or emigration. It was not the Holocaust, but, on the other hand, in a strictly metaphorical sense, it was not *not* a holocaust. The furies of twentieth-century Ireland were born amid the Golgotha of the 1840s.

In comparison, relatively few died in the Ethiopian famine: indeed, the population actually doubled over the next twenty years. Nonetheless, my weepy, intellectually barren *Irish Times* essay on Ethiopia was years later republished in a selection of the 'best' Irish journalism of recent decades – presumably because it was a restatement of the single surviving item from the original set of Universal Dogmatic Pieties, even though I had long since disavowed that one as well.

Nonetheless, I retain a huge admiration for the Irish people I met in Ethiopia, while despising the vast aid industry that had been established in Addis Ababa, with its career structures, its offices, its hierarchy, and its fleets of four-by-fours, even for local administrative work, when bicycles would have sufficed. Anyway, when does any multinational organisation, with vast numbers of careers and pensions to protect, ever say, *Our job is done – it's time to fold our tents and leave?*

The Finucane brothers, Jack and Aengus – the backbone of Concern's operations in Ethiopia and amongst the most selfless, splendid people I have ever met – wanted me and a Concern nurse named Kay Walsh to visit one of their remoter operations, a two-hour flight away, beyond that huge geological cleft, the Great Rift Valley. The pilot of our small single-engine Pilatus Porter aircraft was an elderly American in mandatory Ray-Bans. Previously with the USAF and American Airlines, on retiring he had decided to See The World & Do Good.

After the usual checks, he took off and was soon wrestling with charts on his lap while peering this way and that below. An hour out, his voice came through the earphones of his two passengers.

'Any of you folks flown this route before? My maps don't correlate with the terrain below, and I can't seem to pick up any navigation beacons.'

'There are no navigation beacons here,' said Kay. 'You have to read the land.'

Audible cogitation filled our earphones, followed by a slightly thin voice: 'No beacons, eh? No one told me that.'

'You have to read the land,' Kay repeated.

'Read the land? How can I do that? I only arrived here yesterday. Also, someone gave me the wrong maps. Plus, I keep calling Addis Ababa, but I get no reply.'

'That's what happens in the Great Rift Valley,' intoned Kay. 'Its magnetic field prevents communication. You surely know that.'

The pilot was silent for a few moments.

'There's another small problem.'

'What?' said Kay, lowly.

'The fuel gauge is faulty. It said full at Addis. It's nearly empty now.'

'Anything else?'

'That's it. I think we need to find an airfield real soon. Otherwise, I might just have to land her in a field.'

A *field*? Beneath us lay the vast broken landscape of the Great Rift Valley, which appeared to have been created by an axe-wielding Miocene madman, bringing his blade down every 50 metres. The Pilatus can land in 120 metres. It would plummet down a Pilatus-wide crevasse in under half that distance.

Kay cleared her throat.

'How "soon" is "soon"?'

'Max, ten minutes. Maybe eleven. We're running on smell.'

Even amid the roar of the Pratt and Whitney turboprop, an odd silence inserted itself. Ten minutes went by. Then eleven. Below us stretched a nightmare mountainscape, as if the Himalayas and the Andes had hurtled into one another, before being blindsided by the Pyrenees.

The pilot whispered. 'I'm sorry, guys, real real sorry. Looks like I fucked up big time. I'm jet-lagged, and this is first time I've ever been out of the States. No navigation beacons. Wow.'

Kay and I sat wordlessly, gazing at our knees, digesting the amazing news that, even though he had never been out of the States before, our pilot nonetheless thought he could get into a plane in Africa, with no real planning or maps, and head off over one of the most formidable landscapes on Earth. I was also wondering if one could beat a pilot to death mid-flight without condemning oneself to a comparable end.

'I got a wife,' he said conversationally, 'Molly, and a grandchild I've never seen.'

He suppressed a choke.

Fuck me: he was feeling sorry for himself.

The plane flew on. Fourteen minutes. Twenty. One thing I knew was that if we ran out of fuel, and the thrumming Pratt and Whitney ceased to thrum, there was little prospect of us 'gliding' anywhere. Without power, the Pilatus flies like a crocodile. I waited for the cough as a spark futilely flew into the fuel-less void of an empty combustion chamber. Would we spiral or would we plummet? What questions.

'Airfields everywhere back home, in Tacoma, Washington,' our pilot reminisced fondly over the intercom. 'Seems like every second field is an airfield in Tacoma, Washington. Not here though. We're on empty. Empty. Sorry. I am truly, truly sorry. Anyone care to join me in a prayer?'

That was probably the closest he ever came to death – from behind, sixteen fingers on the throat, four thumbs into his spine, Kay and I gallantly doing our final duty. Nonetheless, the Pilatus flew on, until we were clear of the Great Rift Valley, and he was able to make radio contact. We were one hundred miles off course, and were believed missing, possibly down. He was given directions to an airfield. As we neared it, we saw smoke rising; the people there were burning oil to guide us safely in. We landed and taxied to a bowser, and the pilot got out to buy some fuel. Presently he returned.

'Problem solved,' he said brightly. 'Apparently, the Ethiopians use metric. I did not know that.'

As an explanation, this fails the first test, for all useful metric units are smaller than their imperial equivalents, so he couldn't have under-filled at Addis. No matter. With such deranged and untried characters coming to the country's help, it's no wonder the Irish were needed. Of course, there are no simple solutions to Africa's many dilemmas, because aid endlessly defers the creation of sustainable long-term solutions, until, inevitably, a continental famine leads to a global catastrophe, as it will. But for the moment, the most pressing problem of all is politico-cultural: what may one say about or propose for Africa before all discussion is effectively halted by the accusation of 'racism'? That is the ultimate veto, to which there seems little answer.

Eighteen

AFRICA WAS NOT ALONE IN welcoming my uncritical presence. Panama was similarly blessed. Not merely does it have a certain canal and is a convenient place to buy a folding straw hat or register a dodgy vessel, it is also the home of both an almost impenetrable rainforest, and of Darien, from whose peak stout Cortes (we are oft told, though inaccurately) silently first beheld the Pacific.

I wasn't entirely happy about receiving the hospitality of a charity yet again, but I did fancy a free trip to Central America, my job being amanuensis for the visit of the chief executive of Gorta, Ronnie Smiley. We were accompanied by the photographer Aidan Meade. Once there, we were met by the bearded septuagenarian Desmond Goode – who, I soon discovered, was when sober a delightful and scholarly agronomist of gentry stock, but once drunk became a braying socialist pest. On our first night there, Goode invited Aidan and me to join him for a drink – the teetotal Smiley having retired to bed. Within an hour, Goode was on a table, singing the Internationale, toasting Daniel Ortega of Nicaragua, plus Castro, Mao and Lenin. Our attempts to subdue him led to threats with bottles, and various communist anthems from the Spanish Civil War, bawled from the hotel bar, on which he had managed to haul his withered old frame. I then abandoned my efforts to keep the old fool out of jail and went to bed.

Next morning, instead of deservedly hanging by his thumbs from some dripping dungeon wall, Goode was sitting at the breakfast table as primly as a ten-year-old convent schoolgirl attending a tea party to celebrate the Virgin Mary's birthday.

'What happened when we left you?' I asked.

He looked puzzled.

'Left me? Dear boy, I left you, if you remember. You wanted a drink, but an old chap my age can't manage that anymore, so I toddled off to bed. Have a nice night, did you?'

Soon we were joined by Ronnie Smiley, wearing tiny, tiny skin-tight shorts that approximately stopped where his legs began. In a gay bar in San Francisco, they would have been a little ripe, and in Ireland they would have been a violation of our entire criminal code, including torts, malfeasance and delicts. But in Panama, which is steeped in the Hispanic traditions of sartorial appearance and respect, they were as shocking as a Papal striptease.

Goode suggested to Smiley that he might perhaps wear more restrained apparel.

'I'm wearing tropical gear for the tropics,' Smiley simpered. 'I got them specially made.'

Four of us – myself, Aidan, Desmond and David Tolliday, an English aid worker, and like so many people engaged in such work, a thoroughly delightful person – set out for the airport, where we met Pedro, a local Gorta employee. We all shook hands and began a cordial, getting-to-know-you conversation. Pedro was a stalwart: decent, respectable and friendly, the kind of fellow you instantly like. Then Smiley arrived, as, most of all, did his shorts.

'Who is this man?' whispered Pedro into my ear.

'He's your boss.'

'No, no, he cannot be. That is not possible. Is he here to say goodbye to you?'

'No, he's coming too.'

The poor fellow went all silent and lip-trembly.

'On the plane – *with us?*'

I nodded, adding: 'And remember, he is your boss, and he controls all the money.'

Outside, the rain was now like a dam burst.

'I would do anything to get away from him,' Pedro whispered.

'It's all right. We can't fly in this,' I replied, just as our pilot appeared, and departure announcements in Spanish and English followed. Though flight was clearly impossible, like zombies we walked outside, and were instantly soaked: the raindrops hit my skull like gravel, while the underside of my chin was being showered from *below* by rain bouncing upwards from the tarmac.

The Trislander is a twelve-seater commuter aircraft with no aisle and with doors along its length to allow access to each row of seats. I was seated at the back alongside a head-high heap of dead chickens. In front of me was Pedro, next to a young but unusually fat woman. Aidan, David and Smiley were further up front, and sitting right alongside the pilot was Desmond.

Pedro turned around to speak to me. 'Ees very dangerous, this plane?'

'Not remotely dangerous. There's absolutely no chance of the pilot taking off in this storm. Never you fear!'

Whereupon the Trislander's engines clattered into life, and the plane began to trundle towards the runway. The wings directly in front of me were invisible, but I *could* see the wipers on the pilot's windscreen forlornly sweeping back and forth, like bamboo canes trying to dispel Pacific breakers.

We began our take-off, the propellers sending two power hoses of rainwater past either window, and the chickens promptly fell on me. As the plane struggled to climb, we hit a miraculous wave of upward turbulence, which propelled us almost vertically into the sky, before a downward blast sent us plunging ninety feet. Net gain: ten feet. We were barely skimming the rooftops of Panama, before another gust sent us up another hundred feet, then we plummeted ninety. Net gain: another ten feet. By these stomach-churning increments, we hauled our way upwards. Every time we plummeted or soared, the stinking chicken cadavers would leap all over me like a horny teenage boy on a girl, claws and beaks everywhere, their leaking cloacae smearing me with their intimate juices.

We had reached a median height of around 5,000 feet – namely, oscillating between 4,500 feet and 5,500 feet – when the fat young woman beside Pedro decided she really had had enough, and started yanking feverishly at the door release beside her. When it didn't open, she rose to gain more leverage, so catching Pedro's attention. He wrestled her away from the door handle, in which noble struggle he was joined by another passenger. As the plane rose and fell, so too did this tussling threesome, as did the chickens about me. The birds might be dead, but their bowels were not, and with each visitation, I was freshly daubed in brightly coloured colonic effusions, rather like a Jackson Pollock canvas.

With the windscreen now as transparent as the Berlin Wall, the pilot, having donned some goggles, opened the side window and flew with his head sticking out of it. Desmond turned his lugubriously bearded face towards me, shook his head, and just like David Blundy a few years before, drew a finger across his throat. And rightly, for there was no way this plane wouldn't crash. The pilot could see nothing, the turbulence was like a rollercoaster on acid, in front of me was a madwoman who was fighting to open a door – and if she was successful, the slipstream would tear the aircraft in two. This ordeal didn't last a few seconds, but several centuries. Even now, I don't understand how we didn't all soil ourselves, though the chicken corpses festooning me were showing no such restraint. The pilot even took to flying his plane permanently at an angle, his wing lowered, so that, with his head still out of the window, he could see downwards, thereby thwarting all my attempts to keep the suppurating hens off me.

But then, amid my befowled, befouled misery, through a gap in the cloud, I glimpsed the green of jungle and a landing strip. The pilot promptly threw the Trislander on its back, and it dived vertically like a German dive-bomber, with the fat woman in front of me screaming like a Stuka siren. After only four bounces, each about 20 feet high, we came skidding to a halt, and those of us in the Gorta party instantly scrambled out. I assumed that the pilot would wait until the weather cleared, but he did not. With a roar of its engines, the Trislander instantly vanished into that cacophonous downpour, along – of course – with all our luggage.

Our appointment was with the Emberá Indians in the village of La Pulida, several hours up the Turquesa river. We tentatively lowered ourselves into two long and wobbly dug-out canoes, each crewed by three young men, naked but for loincloths. The rain was now – by Central American standards – quite cold, though I welcomed it, because it washed off the drying glaze of chicken spit and shit. Everyone was soaked except Smiley, who had prudently kept his bag with him on the plane. He was now cocooned within a huge, hooded waterproof cape.

The dugout rapidly filled with rain and water from the waves washing over the sides, and soon we were all baling out with our hands. The paddlers became visibly cold, their teeth chattering as they laboured against the current, their skin puckering like the necks of my beloved chickens.

'I don't know about you all, but I'm lovely and dry,' cackled Smiley happily.

The boats were making such slow progress against the steadily quickening current that all passengers except Smiley got out into the thigh-deep waters and began to push, while he remained on board, beaming regally. It was soon clear that the combination of the river flow and the rainfall was too much. Those who could would have to trek overland, carrying as much as possible to lighten the boats. Smiley, however, refused to get out.

'I am the guest of honour from Ireland. I must arrive by boat, dry and with dignity.'

So the rest of us began the slog through the steaming undergrowth. I took off my filthy shirt and threw it away. The rain continued to fall in warm torrents. We trekked for several hours. The Indian behind me saw a leech on my back, and neatly removed it, using a particularly acerbic jungle leaf which causes the leech to convulse, so that not even its mouth remained in my flesh. Finally, as we rounded a bend, we saw a welcoming committee of naked pubescent girls, with tiny rosebud breasts, doing a welcome dance for these important strangers. I happened to be in the front, and suddenly they abandoned their routine and came rushing towards me, three of them hurling their wet naked bodies on my equally wet naked torso, hugging me and shrieking with excitement. I write this frankly because it was not in any way a remotely sexually arousing experience, but sinlessly sensual and sublimely innocent.

They began to perform the humming-bird dance, exquisitely hovering around us, before encouraging us to join in, which we duly did, Aidan and I cumbrously capering alongside these angels, like steel-booted colliers from the Durham Miners' Gala pirouetting with the Bolshoi. Finally, exhausted, we sat down while the girls continued various exotic dances, in which they were joined by their mothers and aunts, all naked too, save for small coverings over their pudenda.

Then came a shout: boats!

The two dugouts were approaching with provisions for the Indians, and with just one passenger between them: his imperial majesty Ronnie Smiley, still in the marquee of his waterproofs. Seeing the people gathering on the water's edge and sustained by the delusion that he was a supremely welcome VIP, he rose to acknowledge his adulatory fans. As he stood, raising both arms over his head, the dugout's centre of gravity shifted well above the waterline and the canoe instantly swivelled like a driveshaft. One second Smiley was standing upright; the next he was invisible beneath the upturned hull. Three spluttering rowers rapidly emerged from the waters, but Smiley didn't, and no one moved to find him.

Finally, he rose from the deep, gagging and choking, and pushing his way through the waters that were so tragically shallow as to enable him to put his feet on the bottom. It was only when he reached the shore that he realised something was missing.

'Me spectacles. I've lost me blimming spectacles! Help! Help! Will nobody help me find me blimming spectacles?'

We all watched motionless while he returned to the capsized canoe, groping futilely under the water for the glasses. He then waded ashore, cold, sodden and nearly blind, an object of considerable diversion for all, with night falling and return not remotely possible. Was ever *Schadenfreude* so delicious? And God bless Germany for giving us such a word!

That night we had dinner in a community hut on stilts. The centrepiece of the banquet that followed was some sort of badger, or its Panamanian kin, which had finally expired after a long and harrowing illness. A lump of this poor beast had been hacked from its carcass, probably while it was still breathing, thrown onto a fire for a few seconds to remove excess body hair, put on a plate amid a pool of puckering grease, and presented to me with great ceremony.

I signed: 'What the fuck do I do with this?'

The Emberá all laughed uproariously and the chief obligingly imitated lifting the lump of meat with his hands, then gnawing on it, before putting a pretend-platter to his mouth and drinking the glorious broth within. I duly copied him. The meat was raw and rancid, and probably riddled with worms. I chewed and tried to swallow. My baffled stomach heaved in resistance at this lump of raw fat, sinew and gristle, which remained just above my oesophagus, simmering indignantly like a drunk not being allowed into a nightclub. Once I had forced the entire hunk past my Adam's apple, I faced the next challenge: the pool of grease on the plate, which was now growing a skin. In a single movement, I raised the dish and poured it down my gullet: instantly, it seemed that my entire interior was coated with tallow. I ran my tongue round my mouth, scraping off solidified grease like a snow plough, and concentrated very hard on not getting sick. Finally, I could feel my oesophagus opening and begrudgingly admitting the badger, while – upraised hand, like a discerning bouncer – saying *NO* to the solidified grease.

Mine host came before me, beaming proudly, signing: 'What did you think of that splendid example of our native cuisine?'

I beamed in unbridled ecstasy, rubbing my stomach in delight, whereupon he uttered a happy cry and clapped his hands. Another bowl was put before me, containing a visibly uncooked badger ear, plus another pint of puckering fat, which I welcomed with a cackle of gleeful despair. Once he had wandered off to attend to other guests, I managed to slip the ear into my pocket, next pouring the animal fat through a crack in the lattice floor, all the time willing my dinner southwards.

A woebegone, disregarded Smiley sat peering sourly and sightlessly around him, still in his absurd shorts from which a plucky testicle had broken free and was now perkily looking round. Speeches followed; first in Emberá, then translated into Spanish, then translated into English … *for two hours.* The chief spoke. 'We are here tonight to welcome the white man. Not all white man are bad, just most of them are. They raped us, they murdered us, they took our forests. We once governed this entire land from sea to sea. Now we are here, just a few of us, very poor. But as I say, not every white man is bad. The younger man, he is a good fellow. He eats everything. Yum yum. The other guest, the old wrinkled one who arrived late and stood up and then fell out of the boat and who ate nothing, not so good.'

The simultaneous translation was through an Indian into Spanish and into English via Desmond, who understandably faltered at times – he only gave me this unbowdlerised version later. Then to bed in a crowded hut, bodies every few feet. Half-naked, I lay on a palliasse, as various insects prospected across my body, pausing to bore deep into my flesh to drink my blood or to lay a Montessori of their young under an eyelid, while their winged, brain-eating cousins hummed an unbroken descant in my ears. We had been told nothing whatever about sanitary arrangements, so one thing that I really dreaded was having to take a crap, the vast social and personal implications of which would probably rank with having one in a space shuttle full of schoolgirls. However, the solidified grease of the banquet had apparently caused my alimentary canal to seize up from the tonsils downwards, so happily (what an odd word that can sometimes be) that proved not to be a problem.

Next morning, David, Aidan and I went for a dip in the river in our jeans, where I fondly bade farewell to the ear, and one by one the entire population of the village entered just upstream of us. We three were capering happily, whereas the Emberá people were strangely focused and silent, their eyes half-closed in pious concentration. A disconnected loincloth or two came floating downstream.

'Hush,' I admonished the others. 'Are they praying?'

David was studying the waters around him. 'Are they fuck!' he yelled, suddenly surging towards the shore. 'They're having their morning shit.'

My final night in Panama City was spent in a hotel with the Gorta team and several Indians. I went to bed early, leaving Desmond at the bar with some Panamanians. I came down at six to check out. All was quiet, save for the snoring sound of the party of Indians on the bar floor, and in their centre, legs akimbo, lay the naked figure of Desmond, showing his vast scrotum to considerable advantage – though perhaps less so his procreative acorn.

My journey back home was hell, and I swore, come what may, no more long plane journeys. During a day and a half in the stratosphere and sitting sleeplessly in terminals, I was able to consider my experiences. The Gorta-funded operation was designed to protect what remains of the Emberá people from the appalling impact of western civilisation. The only income they could get to fight the ruthless, predatory loggers – who were actually using the courts to acquire Emberá lands – was by cutting down and selling the trees themselves. There is hardly a more desolating equation. I cannot fault Gorta for giving them money as some protection against a future otherwise ordained by chainsaw and the brothel, where so many dispossessed forest girls end up. I don't say what follows to appease the more zealous feminists, who for the most part are either too ignorant to understand the complexity of life or are as unpropitiable as piranhas with rabies, syphilis and athlete's foot.

So here it is: man's cupidity and concupiscence have enslaved so many of the world's women and brought ruination on so much of its flora and its fauna. It is not women who have laid waste to rainforests or who have slaughtered entire species or who frequent brothels; only men. These deeds are the very obverse of those other male acts that have made human civilisation – its religions, its cultures and its organised kindnesses, along with all the philosophies that explain it. That they are two sides of the same coin suggests that this is a specie that is too costly for the world to endure. Might an entirely unwitnessed planet without a history or a recorded past not be a better place than the one that our civilisation was recording, even as we were destroying it? And do such speculations serve any purpose whatsoever? Questions have I many; answers have I none.

Nineteen

IN IRELAND, MEANWHILE, a strange cultural revolution was underway. Though it left little documentary evidence and was popular in origin rather than a result of top-down political leadership, it showed itself in an almost occult manner: tea leaves. Tea is Ireland's most important drink: our professional teabuyers cater for the most discerning market in the world. Until 1988, tea sales in the Republic were 80 per cent loose-leaf, 20 per cent teabag. The following year, the proportions reversed. Teabags are both barbaric and businesslike, whereas the more civilised loose tea is made in a pot, around which people stay chatting. T for tea and for tiger: for 1989 – symbolically, anyway – was the year that the Irish economic miracle was born. But culturally, one great breakthrough had occurred the year before.

Almost all acts of creation depend on the contingency of luck. By a miracle as inexplicable as that hole in a Beirut wall, Scotland's soccer team of portly pensioners managed an away victory over Bulgaria, the favourites to secure a place in the European finals in Germany. So, fortuitously, the Irish team, under Jackie Charlton, qualified. Conor Brady asked me to follow the team, doing day-to-day colour pieces.

In that innocent era, players and journalists stayed in the same hotel. Rather courteously, we would make ourselves known to the players, most of whom – being English, with faint molecular traces of Irishry that were evident only on a particularly sensitive gene-spectrometer – had no idea who we were. The brilliant Spurs winger Tony Galvin, who should really have been playing for England, had been taught by my brother David in Huddersfield. He had no idea that he had Irish blood, or where his name – originally Ó Gealbháin – had come from until some sharp-eyed genealogist in the Football Association of Ireland turned his electron-microscope on Galvin's paternal DNA.

Charlton's managerial message was simple: boot force. My room was next to his, and he would call in players for heart-to-heart conversations. These I could hear perfectly, and they usually sounded like a carotid-to-colon disembowelling.

'WHAT THE FOOK WOR YOU OOP TO OUT THERE YOU STUPID FOOKIN' COONT. IF I WANTED YOU TO PLAY FOOKIN' STRIKER, I WOULD FOOKIN' WELL HAVE PUT NUMBA FOOKIN' NINE ON YOUR FOOKIN' BACK, NOT FOOKIN' THREE, YOU STUPID FOOKIN' WANKAH. SO NEVAH NEVAH NEVAH DO THAT FOOKIN' AGAIN YOU DAFT FOOKIN' COONT, OR BY FUCK YOU'LL GET MY BOOT SO FAR UP YOUR FOOKIN' 'OLE YOU COULD UNTIE ITS BLOODY LACES WITH YOUR FOOKIN' TEETH.'

Though the Irish team won only one match, against England, the real victors were the fans, who made their mark internationally for the first time: friendly, boozy and happy. Ireland's reputation abroad had hitherto been largely created by the IRA, whereas the Irish people were now seen as what they actually were and remain: open, cheery and inexhaustibly social. They became the main story of the championship. Who were these charming people, who looked just like the English, whose speech – to most German ears anyway – sounded just like English speech, but who were so very different?

At home, a national unity was forged around the television sets, and later in the streets as people celebrated results that would barely have registered in Spain or Germany. A new sense of the possible was being born, but of course there was a limit to how far such a mediocre team could go, and we reached it in Gelsenkirchen, where we were finally defeated by the Dutch.

On that final night, droves of astoundingly beautiful young German women arrived at the team hotel in an unashamedly carnal quest for

Irish players. One by one, players were isolated like steers, lassoed and abducted for some unspeakable torment in their bedrooms, while I nursed a beer and wondered what on earth had happened to the soccer skills that had seemed so promising when, aged ten and three-quarters, I had played right-half for Christ the King Primary School, Leicester.

Two blonde girls aged about twenty entered the bar, which was now empty apart from the clearly despicable me.

'Where are all the Irish players, please?' asked Elke Sommer's younger, prettier great-niece.

'All gone.'

'That is terrible!' cried her companion, apparently Britt Ekland's even lovelier grand-daughter. 'We were hoping to meet a couple of nice Irish footballers. Are there none left? Is there none left? Which is correct, please?'

'Mmm, either will do. Actually, I think there might still be one left in the other bar.'

'Just the one?'

Their exquisitely pretty faces fell even more prettily, before they exchanged looks.

'This is a cultural question, which an older man like you could answer for us,' said Miss Ekland. 'Would he mind very much if we shared him? Two on one? Is that allowed in Ireland?'

Taking up rugby after leaving Christ the King now seemed like the greatest mistake of my entire life. On the plane to Dublin the next day, I saw the player that the two girls had corralled; he looked like the withered husk you occasionally see in the corner of a spider's web: an occasional twitch indicated that some last electrical pulses of life remained.

Some days later, I bumped into the newspaper's chairman, Thomas McDowell, who spoke the only words he would ever utter to me. 'Quite liked your stuff from Germany.' That was it. On the other hand, the Japanese ambassador to Ireland, Yoshinao Odake, wrote a beautiful letter to me to tell me how much he had enjoyed my reports from Germany. This was a quid pro quo, of a sort, for I had earlier written some complimentary words about his astute and honest observations about Irish life. Ambassadorial reflections are usually based on the universal diplomatic fiction that two disparate peoples – say, the Tibetans and the Masai – are bound indissolubly by deep cultural ties. The monogamous woollen-clad Tibetans endure six-month sub-zero winters, never eat meat and revere the sacred texts of Buddha; the naked Masai men are polygamous, survive by consuming vast amounts of cattle blood and, being illiterate, have no written texts. But in ambassador-speak, they are irrevocably bound by the deep cultural values that they have warmly and jointly cherished since the Mesolithic period.

Compliments thus exchanged, Yoshinao made me guest of honour at an embassy dinner. It was very pleasant, and he was free with the alcohol. As Grania and I left, Yoshinao remarked: 'You really must visit Japan one day.'

The alcohol in me spoke: 'Thank you. It is most kind of you to invite me.'

I had committed a terrible, terrible social sin: I had placed a Japanese under a public obligation, one he could not possibly evade.

'I shall be happy to ensure that it is so,' he murmured sibilantly.

What I had devoutly sworn during my return from Panama, another transcontinental flight, was what I had managed to negotiate for myself. Long before I left for Tokyo, the Japanese Foreign Ministry sent me a crowded itinerary, complete with many dense volumes of briefing notes. I paid little attention to either, saving them for the flight. Now, if you stand at the end of an east-facing runway at Heathrow, Japan is pretty much straight in front of you. Just head that way. It is not to your north. The North Pole is to your north. I have studied this on a globe. Going to the North Pole to get to Japan is like going from Ireland to Canada via Peru. But that was what I found myself having to do: flying due north for fifteen hours to Anchorage, Alaska, then flying south for another fifteen hours. If there is a more hellish route to Japan, it is probably behind the oar of a slave galley while the skipper does a spot of waterskiing in its wake.

At Anchorage, just four options awaited passengers: shit, sit, shop or stand. Item one, soon done. Two, no seats. Three, the main items for sale: exotic sadomasochistic pornography and $2,000 bottles of cognac. So the final option beckoned: I stood for four hours, my briefing notes unread at my feet, shuffling like an emperor penguin on the other pole.

Then a flight departure caused some seats to empty, and I grabbed one. But in my haste, I found that I had left the bag containing all my notes over *there*. I was *here*. Seat predators were prowling round us like hyaenas eyeing baby gnus, so, regardless of my pressing scholarly requirements, I stayed sitting in my seat for *ten hours*. After spending a sunlit arctic night drifting in and out of incontinence nightmares, I was finally allowed back onto the plane. I was in business class, so access to the onboard toilet was immediate. After imitating the Shannon at Ardnacrusha for about half an hour, I downed several large gins, devoured some unusually delightful airline food, with much wine, then slept. I woke enormously refreshed, breakfasted heartily, with several cups of coffee, before landing in Tokyo.

'It's still dark,' I remarked to the hostess.

'Not *still* dark; it's just *getting* dark.'

This was not morning. This was evening.

Before me stood the gateway to hell.

At the luggage carousel, a voice said, 'You're Kevin Myers, aren't you?' I turned. Two unmistakably Irish young fellows were smirking broadly at me. We talked, and I learnt they were staying at the same hotel as I was. I knew a government car would be waiting for me, and, *again* not thinking matters through, I suggested they travel with me.

A young woman translator with my name on a board was waiting as we walked into arrivals, and I introduced myself and my two new friends to her.

'There are three of you?' she whispered, dismayed. 'Ah ha ha, it says here one, Mistah Kevin My'ahs.'

(Like many Japanese, she avoided the palatal confusion between 'r' and 'l' by eliding them both.)

'Yes, but they're staying in the same hotel, and we're Irish.'

'But it says here, one passenger, Mistah Kevin My'ahs, to be collected, not three.'

'I asked them to join me.'

'Ah ah ah,' she whimpered in agony, 'my instructions are to collect one passenger, Mistah Kevin My'ahs.'

'And here I am, with my two friends.'

Her eyes were glazed with panic. 'Ah ah ah,' she gasped sadly, adding a forlorn 'Mistah Kevin My'ahs.'

We all got into the car, the poor young woman white with fear; all the protocols were being broken, and she had no idea how to cope with this crisis, or with its author, Mistah Kevin My'ahs. The journey that followed was long, and it was only when my companions broke into raucous song that I realised they were drunk. We arrived at the hotel, and the translator said, 'Mistah Kevin My'ahs, a car will collect you at 7.30 a.m. You bring these two also? Is this some Irish gay thing?'

This was deeply testing my liberal instincts. Obviously, her foreign ministry had briefed her on these strange western disorders. My companions weren't gay, nor was I, but to disavow either seemed intolerant, which was the worst possible thing in the new world order that even now was replacing Christianity.

'No, you're saying goodbye to them now. I'll see you in the morning.'

'No, Mister Kevin, not me. Someone else will look after you and your Irish gay friends.'

I needed a drink to sleep – body-time, it was about 11 a.m. in the morning. With my two ornaments of Irish civilisation still singing, I went to the bar and ordered three beers. At midnight, I repaired to bed; body-time, it was noon.

I vainly sought sleep. Acid droplets gathered slowly in the corners of my eyes, then a meniscus would break, and a corrosive tear would burn a streak into my cheek like aqua regia. Sleep finally and mercifully interposed its benedictions about three minutes before the hotel reception rang to declare that my government car had been waiting outside for the past ten minutes.

I scrambled out of bed and in the mirror caught a glimpse of a 75-year-old pervert with dark scythes under lurid sunset eyes. I showered frantically, dancing in and out the shower, the controls of which – like most hotel showers – resembled those of a lunar landing module, which, semi-asleep, you are expected to master without any NASA training. Half-frozen, half-scalded, and trailing shirt tails and an unknotted tie, I scampered down to the lobby, where a girl, apparently aged about fourteen, was holding up a card with my name.

'You're looking for me?' I called.

She gazed at me sternly.

'Mr Kevin Myers, yes? I have instructions from the Ministry. You are not to bring your gay friends with you any more on government business. We are late. We must go now.'

My child-translator strode out, me hopping, half-shoelessly, and stammering apologies in her wake as she led me to our chauffeured car. We did not speak as we drove to our first appointment of the day, in a university faculty office, where four members of staff were waiting. We were now very late. Stern words were addressed to the girl, and she hissed and bowed and hissed and dropped her pencil in irredeemable misery. I had caused her to lose face. We all knew it was my fault, but it was not diplomatically possible to say so.

My main host was Professor Takeshi Umehara, the director of the International Research Centre for Japanese Studies, in Kyoto, who had spent at least three hours travelling for this very meeting. The other three were a leading anthropologist, a social historian, and a research specialist, all professors of national distinction. They took turns talking to me, two of them in perfect English and the other two through my translator. However, nothing they said made sense, for they talked at great length about the German influence on Japan between 16,000 and 2,000 years ago. It was incredible: German this and German that – long before Germany as a political or cultural concept had actually existed. Was I hallucinating?

Tiredness was washing over me in evil, irresistible waves, as they continued to drone about German power over the Japanese, during the very period when Julius Caesar was laying waste to the Rhineland and the Romans had formed their northernmost colony, which – I recollected bizarrely – bore its name to this day, Köln or Cologne. Yet at the same time, the Germans were bringing civilisation to the Japanese? This was mad stuff. Finally, I had to ask a question, if only to end this weird LSD trip.

'I'm sorry, I had no idea that the Germans were so influential back then. I thought that relationship really began with the Axis in the 1930s.'

The silence that followed was like the very heart of marble. Had Henry Moore carved an abstract from it, any passing stranger would have instantly identified the work as 'Incredulity'.

'We are talking about the Jomon period, named after the cords in the prevailing pottery style of this period,' one of the professors said in a thin voice made taut as a high wire by a barely suppressed anger. 'As you will have seen in the notes that we sent you several weeks ago.'

Aaarrrghhh! The notes, the fucking notes, which I had never read! The Japanese habit of dropping the 'r' had caused me to mistake Jomon for German. I was in a snake pit, surrounded by hissing vipers. At that moment I fleetingly recalled the great Liam de Paor at UCD telling me about that particular cultural epoch.

'Forgive me. I am tired – no sleep – and the pronunciation threw me. The *Jomohn*, as we say in Ireland. We even spell it with an accent – a *fada* – over the second "o". Pray continue.'

They smiled obligingly, an alliance of disdain and disbelief warring with civility deep within their four sets of eyes. They talked at me for two hours about the Jomon era, while sleep rose within me like a terrible, irrepressible sea. Every time I jerked myself awake, I found a quartet of chrysanthemum wrinkles gazing at me in a facsimile of deadly politeness. Exhaustion was not the only force at work within me; so too were those sinister twins, shame and guilt, for which I was later to learn the Japanese have two especially powerful words: *tatemae* and *honne*.

We broke for coffee, and my translator tearfully declared that she was now facing professional disgrace. She would be held responsible for our lateness, and also for the fact that I clearly did not know anything about Jomon culture.

'Please do not be ignorant in our next meeting this afternoon.'

'Who's that with?'

'What? Surely you must know that we are meeting a Buddhist monk, the most important in Tokyo?'

'Of course, of course,' I lied. 'It's just that I'm so tired and jet-lagged.'

'Prease do not ret me down,' she pleaded, in her despair confusing those treacherous quasi-alveolars.

During the next session, my interlocutors would pause to allow me to ask intelligent, well-informed questions. When none came, they would resume talking. Studiously concealed contempt possesses a curious force, for though it exists without any visual expression, it is nonetheless as palpable as an inquisitor's thumbscrew. When lunchtime finally arrived, I felt as if I had passed through the very worst of the Middle Ages, all Black Death, leprosy, famine and the rack. Ahead of me lay the Buddhist sage, probably bringing with him the seventeenth century, with its religious wars, witch burnings and plagues, and possibly – no, almost certainly – the Great Fire of London.

Then a small miracle supervened. The interpreter scheduled to accompany a trade delegation from Mercedes had fallen ill, and as my young woman was also a German-speaker, she was instructed to leave me (thereby probably saving her career), while a fresh translator would take her place. Moreover, the meeting with the Buddhist prelate was not as catastrophic as the Iwo Jima of the morning. Firstly, I was able to spare the new translator, Hoshi, the consequences of my delinquencies. I simply told her to translate word for word what I said. Then I told the monk that she was new to the job and was not to blame for my failings, and that the notes that had been sent to me had been lost by the notoriously incompetent Irish postal service.

The monk made it plain that he didn't believe me. He frowned, he tutted, he coughed, why, he even scratched his groin incredulously. The Japanese have a reputation for being inscrutable; this monk was about as inscrutable as Mick Jagger. Admittedly, I could just as well have been talking to a designer of the Hadron collider for all that I knew about the subject of the interview. Moreover, His Holiness' capacity for withering sarcasm was both unexpectedly large and demonstrative; though our meeting lasted just an afternoon, in many respects its ferocity rather resembled the 1968 Tet offensive in Vietnam, which – it is often forgotten – was also by Buddhists, though of the communist variety.

Day one, and ten more to follow – oh, and nights, during which sleep became as much a stranger to me as steak and kidney pudding was to His Holiness. Hoshi was a plausible diplomat, and soon discovered my countless weaknesses. She prepared notes to cover interviews for which I was unprepared. Sometimes when I made what I thought were humorous quips, Hoshi didn't translate them. When I asked about this, she replied: 'You are quite funny, Kevin, but you do not always know when it is right to be humorous. You're not homosexual, are you?'

'No.'

'I didn't think so. The word in the ministry is that you are. Many Japanese think homosexuality is a western disease. I think just as many Japanese men are homosexuals. Women too – if only in their sexual fantasies – but of course they would never admit to it publicly.'

Hoshi was in her twenties, and lived with her father, who, she said, sometimes allowed her to stay away overnight – which might have been a hint of a kind. However, having already charged through the social delicacies of this complex society like Rasputin through a nunnery, I was determined not to make an even greater idiot of myself than I already was by making a pass at her. When I invited Hoshi to dinner on the penultimate night, she accepted – and added that that night she would be staying with a friend. Was that a code? It made no difference because she arrived at the hotel with news that plans had changed: I was to have dinner instead with a senior official from the Foreign Ministry, in a classical Japanese restaurant, sitting on cushions, eating in the traditional way. He spoke English fluently; her presence was not required.

'This is a compliment to you,' she said, but not happily. 'He is a most important man. If he cuts the dinner short, do not be surprised. This is how he is.'

'Not a compliment to me – but to you and your diplomatic skills.'

'You are most kind.'

I had dinner with the official. We spoke about the imminent collapse of the Soviet Union, and I warned of war on many fronts, especially in that most artificial of states, Yugoslavia. The official didn't leave early, and next morning Hoshi told me that the dinner had been a great success, and she had got the credit. With a lot of yen to spend, I offered to buy her a present. Together, we bought a particular watch she wanted, but I still had some yen, so I asked her if she wanted anything else. Yes, she replied, a vibrator, and we could buy it together.

We went to a department store, where there was an entire section for these devices. All the customers were women, though none seemed remotely abashed at the presence of a round-eyed male. Together, Hoshi and I chose a vibrator, and then we shook hands and very formally said goodbye outside the department store.

I was in the departure lounge at Tokyo Airport the next day, my eyes closed, when a voice beside me said, 'Did you think that was a proper way of saying farewell to a girl?'

It was Hoshi. She had travelled two hours by public transport from her home to see me off.

'I thought that it was a respectful way.'

'Really? You call that respect? What a strange man you are, Kevin Myers. Well, the good news is that last night's farewell gift number one told me how long farewell gift number two took to work. Not long actually. Less for the second, even less for the third and no time at all for the fourth. The bad news is that it wasn't you. Silly man. I left so many clues, and you didn't see any of them. Never mind. Kiss me.'

And there and then, in the very crowded departure lounge in Tokyo airport, she pressed her mouth on mine and unashamedly kissed me fully. Yes, I regret so many things that I did in Japan, but what I regret most of all is what I didn't do.

I wasn't particularly pleased with the Japanese articles I wrote on my return – and clearly the people at the Japanese embassy were even less pleased, for I never heard from them again.

Twenty

ONE FRIDAY AFTERNOON in late November 1989, I got a phone call from that fine gentleman Ken Gray, politely but non-negotiably asking me if I would leave at dawn the next morning for Prague, via Munich, to which Ryanair had just started a weekly flight. As I had foretold in Tokyo, communism was collapsing everywhere. I made a few hurried enquiries before setting out; amongst many other things, I would be unable to find toothpaste or toilet paper in Prague.

Snow was falling like an emptying eiderdown at 5 a.m. when my taxi collected me, causing me to hope that my flight would be cancelled and common sense would prevail. No such luck. As our Boeing 737 crossed Europe, it was clear that a huge Arctic storm had blanketed the entire continent. Our blizzard-landing at Munich airport required equal measures of skill and insanity from the pilot. I had fervently hoped that the autobahns would be closed and I would end up staying in a local hotel, drinking beer and improving on my deplorable record with German girls, but no; a gratuitously heroic snow plough had cleared a single lane all the way into Czechoslovakia, and it was safe to go. Or so said the bewitchingly beautiful woman at Hertz. And so, imitating a particularly gallant Antarctic explorer who didn't expect to return – but what did it matter, just so long as she simpered admiringly in my wake – I set off into a vast and all-consuming white-out. Outside the airport, I sat waiting for a break in the column of cars hurtling down the single lane. When a tiny gap finally came, I booted the accelerator and fishtailed wildly into the three-metre-wide road eastwards, between a pair of two-metre-high snow embankments. I was now in a single-track bobsleigh time trial, with visibility almost zero, trusting solely in the lights of the vehicle two metres in front of me, just as I was performing the same service for the car behind me, all of us driving at the involuntarily consensual lunacy of 150 kph. When people aver that all nationalities are basically alike, please, I beg you, remember German drivers.

Just about the last things that functioned in the collapsing state of Czechoslovakia were the border police, though few people were interested in entering their country. Those who did had to leave their cars, which were searched by police for firearms and propaganda, while individuals were processed in a bitterly freezing hut in which a coke stove kept only itself warm. The editor's secretary, the wonderful Eileen Lynam, had booked a hotel in Prague for me, and I had the fax acknowledging this. A waiting Englishman had apparently arrived at the checkpoint by bus, but, possessing no documentation, was not being allowed into the country. On hearing my voice, he cried out: 'Thank God. A fellow Englishman!'

'Irish,' I said, pointing to my passport.

'But you have an English accent.'

'Yes,' I said, with insane frankness. 'Born in Leicester.'

'Makes you English, what! We Brits must stick together. The name's Nigel, but you can call me Nige. I say, old fellow, you wouldn't give me a lift, would you? These ruddy blighters won't let me through without transport *and* a hotel-booking. I've got my hotel all right. All I need is a lift.'

He spoke as if he had undertaken a Gilliat and Saunders correspondence course on how an Englishman might have spoken in the 1930s, apart from the reference to 'Brits'. Perhaps disarmed by these clichés, I murmured a fatally imprecise negative.

'Thank you!' he yodelled, grabbing my hand warmly. 'Thank you so much! We Brits stick together!'

I was hoping for some resistance to such adhesive insularity from the border guards, but they were clearly grateful for any excuse to be rid of this utter perisher, as he might have said, and so they shooed him out of their hut. Without offering a word of assent or consent, but with a deadly lack of dissent, I now had a passenger, bound for Brno. As I listened to his noxious nonsense about the foul Czechs and the horrible Germans, I was soon indignantly wondering why the border guards simply hadn't shot him. Why else had Mr Kalashnikov so sedulously toiled, if not for such moments? Instead I was escorting him through this vast blizzard which, like his prattle, never once relented until we got to Brno. At the outskirts of the city, I halted at a tram stop, and told him to get out. I had to reach Prague before driving became impossible.

'But you can't do that to me! Dash it all, old man, you can't let a fellow Englishman down, not in the middle of ruddy nowhere. Just take me to the hotel. Please, I beg of you.'

Faced with this further onslaught of cheesy Englishness, my willpower failed me yet again. Driving through Brno proved horribly difficult, for the street signs meant nothing, cars were few and tram tracks plentiful, and I was exhausted. But by much trial and many errors, we finally found the hotel, and he hopped out of the car, my heart singing with joy at his departure.

Turning, he said to me: 'Don't go away, old fellow. You've still got my bag in the back.'

Now I could have done the sensible, selfish thing and simply driven away, or thrown his bag into the snow and abandoned him, but in my exhaustion, neither option occurred to me. No matter, for he emerged from the hotel, and as I reached for the bag, he got into the front.

'Hotel's full. I'll have to go with you to Prague.'

'*What?*'

'Yes, Prague. No choice.'

'But Nigel—'

'It's Nige. And look on the bright side – bit of luck for you, really, company on the road and me knowing the ropes and all that. Best start moving pronto, old chap, it's getting late.'

Bitterly shedding clutch-cogs like a past-it prizefighter's teeth, I gear-grated my way out of Brno and back to the straight-line ice track to Prague, my idiot companion complaining all the way. Once again, now close to midnight, I had to negotiate my way through a foreign city, in which the tramlines shimmering through the snow revealed the existence of an entirely different traffic culture, a place where no one spoke English and getting directions from a native was rather like hearing an explanation of simultaneous equations in Korean.

I finally found my hotel. I parked the car and went to reception, weak with hunger and tiredness and, most of all, a cold, impotent fury. I handed over my passport and a vast heap of deutschmarks, and in return was given my room key. I asked for a sandwich and a beer to be sent up after me, and then bade a final farewell to Nigel. As I closed the door of my room behind me, relief flooded through my soul like the choral explosion in the last movement of Beethoven's Ninth. A knock: room service!

I bounded over and opened the door. It was Nigel.

'Ruddy hotel's full! Blighters wouldn't give me a room. Oh I say – a spare bed!'

Another knock on the still-open door: this time it was room service.

'Pivo, sendvič?' inquired a little voice: *beer, sandwich*?

'Some grub,' chortled Nigel, slapping his thigh. 'Just the ticket.'

He raised two fingers. 'Same again, sweetheart. You go first, old chap.'

Next morning, a still-broken creature, I rose first, showered and fled downstairs for breakfast. Nigel joined me at my table.

'You'll spring for my breakfast, won't you, old duck? Just till Monday? I've only got American Express cheques, and the cashier won't honour them because I'm not a guest – well, not a listed one, that is.'

Feeling rather like Philip II of Spain on hearing news of the Armada, I nodded.

'What are you doing today?' he asked. 'Speaking for myself, I'm at a loose end – free to help you in any way.'

My brain contorted, as if a tourniquet was being applied to its larger lobes.

'Well, Nigel, there's a rally outside the Sparta Prague Stadium.'

'Sounds good! But please call me Nige. Maybe we should give that a look-see, what?'

Half a million people – or so it was reported, and I certainly said so in the consensually craven way of my trade – had gathered in the astonishing cold to hear the heroes of the anti-communist movement, including Dubček and Havel, denounce the dying regime. The police had already declared that they would not intervene, and they didn't, as speaker after speaker ridiculed the absurdities of Marxism and the state-controlled economy. With feet shaped from blocks of ice, plus a hatless head similarly composed, and wearing a raincoat that had been fine on a Friday evening in Dublin, but was now as useless as Brazilian gossamer, I fled back to the hotel, Nigel nattering in my wake.

He joined me for dinner and entertained me enormously with his conversational brio, his sparkling humour and his many scintillating anecdotes, though I do hope that even the sleepiest of readers will here sense the protective veneer of a thoroughly beaten man. The next morning, as various vertebrae about my person enquiringly contacted their neighbours with a view to forming a spine, I ventured: 'Nigel, I think you should go to American Express and get some money. I intend to look for a hat, gloves, shoes and an overcoat.'

'Nige,' he urged. 'It's Nige.'

It was only on this quest that I properly tasted the horrors of state-socialism: having exchanged my deutschmarks on the black market for *twenty times* the official rate, I was awash with Czech korunas. But I was unable to buy winter clothing, at any price, anywhere. In the deepest midwinter cold, not only did none of the laughably named 'department stores' have hats or boots or gloves or overcoats, they had had none since the previous winter. And the stores' real beauty lay not in the goods that they did or didn't sell, but in how they operated. You could only enter any single department within a store if you had a shopping basket, but each department had only four baskets at its entrance. This meant that the eight shop assistants therein had virtually nothing to do, while the four shoppers allowed in at any one time could view the unbuyable or the impractical – which on that particular day included a tennis racket and a bottle of suntan lotion. Meanwhile, a queue of dementedly optimistic potential shoppers waited to receive one of the returned four magic baskets.

I then went for lunch – an even more salutary experience. The only meat available, at any price, was a vaguely familiar animal knuckle, all gristle and sinew, swimming in grease – the Slavic cousin of my dinner in Panama, only now it was accompanied by the luxury of turnip composed solely of roof beam. This was not in a jungle in Darien, but a foremost restaurant in one of the great cities of the world, where I was paying top prices. How did ordinary people survive? How was life possible?

I was re-entering my hotel when I met Nigel coming out.

'I've decided to move on, squire. Communism's done and I'm off. Nice meeting you. I've settled my share of the bill and left some cash to cover the loan. If you're ever in London, old chap, don't be a stranger. Pip pip!'

With that farewell, marked by a complete absence of 'thanks' or any useful tips about how not to be a stranger, namely an address or a phone number – though not even if I was on fire and being eaten by wild dogs on his welcome mat would I ring his doorbell – he slipped into a taxi and disappeared. When I got to my room, I found that my toothpaste and toilet paper were gone.

In time, I met a few Irish people who lived in Prague simply because it was the most beautiful city in Europe, possibly the world, and the Czechs are strangely accommodating and likeable, though nonetheless unpredictable. The Good Soldier Švejk was made flesh in their company. Most Czechs I met had an odd view of Ireland, created by delegates of the Workers' Party, who had been regular guests of the Communist Party. These officially hosted visitors would exultantly extol the virtues of socialism to the paupers who had to endure its chronic privations and its grotesque unfreedoms, before returning to the horrors of capitalist Ireland, with lashings of toilet paper and oodles of toothpaste.

Prague has a grievous and unhealable open wound, as testified to by the Old Jewish Cemetery. There are almost no Jews remaining in the city. Most of them vanished in the chain gangs of Theresienstadt or the furnaces of Auschwitz. The once 'oppressive' traditional laws that confined Jews to the Prague ghetto and their dead to a small Hebraic cemetery turned out to be far more tolerant than the twentieth century was disposed to be. The densely populated burial ground is raised well above the surrounding streets, elevated by layers of corpse and clay, as the bulging outer walls struggle to retain their subterranean secrets. Densely and chaotically packed gravestones on the surface honour the memory of all those buried deep below. The true beating heart of *Mitteleuropa* was Jewish; it perished in the *Endlösung*. Not merely is Prague probably the most beautiful city in Europe, it is also the quintessence of all that is toxic about the continent's competing national identities. This was once the brotherhood of Abel, and here it was that Cain triumphed.

Having completed my pilgrimage to the cemetery, there was no further reason to stay in the city. I went to settle the bill. My guest had not paid for his room or anything he'd eaten and had left nothing as a repayment of my loan. Game, set and match to Nige. I have sometimes wondered whether this buffoon was actually MI6, and used me to get into the collapsing Soviet empire. But how to explain his caricature English, as if he were a KGB agent who had been trained using a 1930s' manual? Either way, my last shrivelled attachment to socialism perished amid the gristle and grease of a Prague restaurant and the frost of a Bohemian winter. In the great liberal view of Irish history, the hostility of the Irish Catholic Church to communism is seen to be anachronistic, reactionary and small-minded. Good. But history has shown that the Catholic Church was right all along.

The following summer my mother paid her annual visit to Ireland. She is such an important person in my life that I cannot do her justice in these pages, and I hope in due course to do so under another cover. But, in brief, she acted and talked strangely. On her return to Leicester, she was diagnosed with brain cancer, to which, after a truly horrifying two months' illness, she finally succumbed. Death brought peace to her, and an astonishing amount of grief to her children.

After the funeral, we all gathered to hear her will being read out by her lawyer, to whom complete power of attorney had been assigned. He undertook to sell the house and to divide the proceeds between the six of us; meanwhile, all presents to my mother were to be returned to the respective donors.

'But I would suggest that it might make sense, and accord with your mother's kindly nature, that you leave as much as possible of those presents to be allocated to deserving charities that were close to your mother's generous heart. As executor, I would of course administer the estate and the attendant charitable bequests.'

We duly agreed, and he made off with it all – house, furniture, the lot.

Twenty-One

MY REPORTS FROM PRAGUE in *The Irish Times* had been rewarded by some complimentary letters from the greatest and bravest intellectual Irish critic of totalitarianism, Hubert Butler, whom I had occasionally met during trips to Kilkenny. The founder of the local archaeological society, which later anathematised him for his fierce criticisms of the pro-Nazi Croat Catholic hierarchy, Hubert was for much of his life an outsider within his own country. His great personal project was to create a larger and more open interpretation of both Irish history and culture than that provided by the conventional nationalist narrative. This dovetailed neatly with my own ambitions.

Hubert Butler was unique, in every sense, not least because he was both an intellectual and a member of the gentry. I share Claude Chavasse's dislike of the term 'Anglo-Irish' to describe that caste. It is one of those hyphenated and lesser forms of Irishness concocted by pseudo-republican racists, who also invented other subordinate categories such as West Brit, Castle Catholic, unionist, horse-Protestant, shoneen, and so on. That republican bully and minor writer Brendan Behan encapsulated all the sneering condescension of this nomenclatural apartheid when he described an Anglo-Irishman as 'a Protestant on a horse'. No one divides Irishness as keenly as those who insist on its inherent indivisibility.

Paradoxically, members of the Irish ascendancy, of which Hubert was an intellectual jewel, had been part-midwife to the victory of the set of ideas that would do so much damage to Ireland. The great essayist from the start of the twentieth century, Michael J.F. McCarthy, still speaks to us about the toxic mysteries of the forces that that idiot savant Yeats would later revere. His *Five Years in Ireland 1895–1900* studied two murders in rural areas that could have occurred only with the complicity of the local communities. McCarthy's heroes, the revolutionary force of modernism opposing the mysterious forces of pre-Catholic heathenism that still flourished amid the outward practices of Rome, were the men of the Royal Irish Constabulary.

A fictionalised version of the murder McCarthy described would soon form the heart of the most prescient drama in Irish history, Synge's *The Playboy of the Western World*. This play is largely seen today as a comedy rather than what it is: a terrifying dissection of Irish rural attitudes to violence. Yet it was not the values of the modernising RIC that triumphed in twentieth-century Ireland, but the counter-revolutionary alliance of peasants and lower-middle-class, ancestor-worshipping fantasists. Having destroyed the RIC by boycott, intimidation and murder, they then created a perverse state creed that attempted to fuse Iron Age mythology with a ferociously authoritarian Irish Catholicism. Almost nothing of artistic or intellectual merit could survive, never mind thrive, in the nutrient-free lava bed that resulted.

The Celtic Revival – the bogus creation of those who simply did not comprehend the deep and ferocious angers of a post-Famine peasantry – actually produced very little of literary merit, aside from the great works of two of its instigators, Synge and Yeats. However, it helped to unleash forces that would effectively destroy both caste and castle of the old Ascendancy. The woes of the Irish gentry have largely been forgotten, though this class endured a ferocious firestorm in the first thirty years of the twentieth century. The Land Acts – the larger justice of which is indisputable – not merely devastated many of their estates, but also served to undermine their right to exist. The wave of house burnings – some 250 in all – and generalised terror between 1919 and 1923, combined with a healthy dose of murder, further reduced their status within what transpired to be a thoroughly austere and culturally philistine state.

The so-called Irish revolution, which owed its origins to some silly Great House musings, rapidly metamorphosed into a reactionary exercise in 'rediscovering' and then inhabiting an imagined and wholly contradictory past, one that was both Catholic and pre-Catholic Celtic. In this strange fusion, outsiders – Protestants, gentry, non-believers – might just be tolerated if they remained silent, as Henry McAdoo had told me, but otherwise, woe betide active dissenters – and none was more visible than Hubert Butler. Yet notwithstanding his boycotted isolation, which lasted for years, he was lucky: his neighbours the Desarts, less so. Lord Desart had publicly warned of the dangerous forces that Yeats was encouraging, declaring that the people whom the poet was romanticising were 'backward'. This was probably a fair but politically imprudent description of a peasantry who still believed in fairies, curses and witchcraft. For non-Irish readers, these 'fairies' are not the epicene elves of Victorian literature, but the fearsome lesser gods of the woodland, whose existence was probably 'empirically' confirmed by schizophrenic delusions – and we now know that multi-generational schizophrenia is a genetic consequence of famine. In McCarthy's textbook example, the wife-burning in Ballyvadlea, County Tipperary, in the mid-1890s, the killer was almost certainly a mentally deranged man who, with the assistance of the victim's father, killed his wife over an open fire while trying to exorcise her of the fairies. The most ominous aspect of that terrible case was that the local community sided with the murderer, and even refused to assist in the burial of the poor woman's body. Between 1919 and 1923, the same posthumous boycott awaited so many rural victims of the IRA.

The Desarts were good landlords, freely surrendering their lands to their tenants after the first Land Acts, though maintaining the tradition of giving out hampers at Christmas. In 1922, Lord Desart accepted a seat in the Senate. His Palladian home, Desart Court outside Callan, County Kilkenny, was one of the most exquisite in Ireland. Two storeys over basement, its centre block had four superimposed Doric and Ionic columns, and even by the elaborate standards of eighteenth-century Irish houses, its marvellous interiors were spectacularly enriched with ornate plasterwork rococo ceilings, which in turn were flanked by a pair of staircases with carved oaken scroll balustrades. Bookcases with fluted pilasters lined the walls, and a beautiful inlaid mahogany cabinet graced the main drawing room, while the adjoining boudoir contained a Georgian mantel in Siena and white marble.

Readers will have gathered that I would not have given such a description had the house not been burnt by the anti-Treaty IRA as punishment for Senator Desart's participation in the new state. A lorry driven by a family loyalist managed to get away with a thousand pounds' worth of precious paintings and books, but this was soon intercepted by a party of heroic republicans and the contents rather pluckily set on fire. Yet to say that the 'IRA' destroyed Desart Castle is almost meaningless: it was the insensate forces that Yeats – and that silly, posturing crew around him – had helped conjure from the genie's lamp of the Celtic Twilight which did so much murder and mayhem, and in this case destroyed one of the finest houses in Ireland.

Desart Court was valued at £53,000 – or about €8 million in today's money – and the cost of compensating the family was borne by the ratepayers of County Kilkenny. Heartbroken, Desart never returned to his homeland. His daughter rebuilt the house, but the spirit was gone; the new house was demolished in the 1940s, and the ground ploughed over. In droughts, the outline of the foundations can be seen in the grassland, rather like the Turin shroud. Nothing was gained and so much was lost by this deed, and so many others, then and in the decades to come.

What is usually forgotten is that Irish culture – music especially – certainly did not benefit in the aftermath of this bloody turmoil, because so many of the founding fathers and their heirs were paramilitary boors. That great wonder of modern Irish life, Comhaltas Ceoltóirí Éireann, was founded only in 1951 in a desperate attempt to arrest what had become a precipitate decline of Irish culture. Moreover, no Irish music whatever was recorded in Ireland from the foundation of the state until Claddagh Records was formed in 1959 by Garech Browne – and he was of the same caste as the Desarts and Hubert Butler, but financially fortified through his mother by Guinness money, which made Claddagh Records possible. Hubert had stood four-square against the heathenry that had accompanied the creation of the Irish state. It was my great honour that he confided in me that he saw me in the same tradition to which he belonged.

'It's not just that you oppose violence; you also oppose the entire so-called republican mentality that makes it possible. You are like me. Not quite in the house, not quite outside it, but on the sill, peering in, gazing out.'

On that sill, over time, I formulated a semi-coherent set of precepts. Underlying almost every perverse attitude in nationalist life was the Famine. This was not just a demographic and moral catastrophe, but a trauma nearly as deep and as shattering as the Holocaust has been for the Jews. The degree to which the Famine was an intentional act of British policy is in one sense largely irrelevant. That it even *seemed* purposeful is sufficient, for it is surely not unreasonable to ask: would such a calamity have been permitted in Sussex? If not, then the issue of 'purpose' is already decided; thereafter, it is a matter of detail.

The political sect that triumphed in Ireland not only saw the Famine as the fault of the British government, but also viewed it as the abysmal benchmark against which its own efforts should be judged. Since it was impossible for that nadir to be reached again, anything the state did must by comparison be successful. Moreover, this new 'Ireland' was to become, as in any state where totalitarian ideology ruled, an abstract ideological concept, whose living inhabitants were simply a disposable means of attaining the later goal of the perfect society. But unlike despotic totalitarianisms, Ireland didn't imprison or enslave its inconvenient citizens – it merely exiled them to the Birmingham and Kilburn Gulags. And thereafter, as is usual anywhere, an interim expedient rapidly became a standard practice by all parties. The system could give reasonable guarantees of employment to the sons of the *nomenclatura*, and the daughters could stay at home.

As I have already reported, the legacy of 1913–23 was dire. In the first year of peace, with school absenteeism at around 40 per cent, over 200,000 pupils were playing truant. Thus, already uneducated and undemanding parents were generationally replicating themselves, producing semi-literate, unskilled offspring who were of limited economic utility at home, and only useful as labouring, often drink-dependent, drudges abroad. The 'No Irish' signs in British boarding house windows, which appeared over the coming decades, might in part be explained by some of the ruined men whom I used to meet when working on the building sites of Leicester: filthy, improvident, alcoholic wretches at the very bottom of the social ladder. Who would freely have allowed such unfortunates in any bed they owned or upon any toilet they had to keep clean?

A folklore was created to explain how dire conditions had been in Ireland before the April putsch of 1916: one fabrication was that the Irish people as a whole had been undereducated. In fact, as the historian Joe Lee has pointed out, Ireland at independence had proportionately the same number of graduates as Britain and more than the Dutch, the Danish and the Norwegians. One of the 'heroes' from this period, whose reputation has extraordinarily survived the revelations about his life, was the demagogue and architect of the so-called Lock-out of 1913, James Larkin. I wrote several columns pointing out that he had embezzled union funds before fleeing to the U.S. With a pleasing symmetry, after he returned to Ireland, he settled in the house in Ranelagh where the similarly canonised Douglas Gageby had been born, both men being able to enjoy the pleasurably lifelong sanctity that results when fiscal sleight of hand is accompanied by protestations of selfless virtue.

Another generally accepted falsehood that is still repeated as gospel is that the death rate in Dublin slums matched that of Calcutta. So just who was the intrepid, indefatigable coroner in that Indian city who so faithfully assigned causes of death in a city the size of Dublin and Belfast combined? The origin of this comparison is easily ascertained: Dublin's chief sanitary engineer was Sir Francis McCabe, whose own son happened to be a sanitary engineer in Calcutta. McCabe senior had publicly declared that the 'condensation' – a technical word meaning 'population density' – of Dublin's slums compared with that of Calcutta. This term seems to have mutated into 'consumption', or tuberculosis, then an invariably fatal condition, and thereafter gave Dublin its enviably Indian-scale victimhood.

But far from Dublin's mortality rates matching Calcutta's, they were even less than those of Sligo, Kilkenny and Ballymena, while some eighty towns and cities in Britain had higher infant mortality rates. But perhaps McCabe was an apologist for the last remnants of the Protestant Ascendancy? Perhaps indeed, but this would surely have been a rather unusual avocation for a man whose middle name was Xavier. Still, he serves as a useful marker for the rise of Catholics within the administration of Ireland. By the outbreak of the Great War, the Lord Chancellor, the Master of the Rolls, two Justices of Appeal, the Solicitor General and ten of the fifteen senior judges were Catholics. The schools most responsible for producing the judiciary were Catholic: Clongowes, Blackrock, Castleknock and Belvedere. The only state positions that remained beyond a Catholic's reach were the heads of the Dublin Metropolitan Police and the Royal Irish Constabulary, historically absurd anachronisms that would come to serve as 'proof' of how the majority community were disbarred from high office in their own country. Even this exclusion did not survive the turmoil of 1916, after which the head of the RIC until 1920 was General James Aloysius Byrne from County Derry. He was probably the last Catholic from the future Northern Ireland to achieve general rank in the British Army. The head of the Royal Army Medical Corps during the Great War was Lieutenant General Sir Alfred Keogh, a Catholic from Roscommon. Field Marshal Haig's personal physician was another Irish Catholic, Colonel Eugene 'Micky' Ryan. General Bulfin, who liberated Jerusalem, was a Catholic from Rathfarnham, and the last of the 120 British generals to die in the Great War was Major General Louis Lipsett, the son of an ordinary Ballyshannon shop-owner.

The follies of those who reshaped Irish history around their own delusions were in time to be matched by the comparably mistaken beliefs of those who wrote it, so that the success of Catholics within a union that was *finally* bringing unprecedented prosperity to Ireland was to be occluded both from the official record and from popular mythology. And after the monstrousness of the Famine, is it surprising that counter-factual fantasies should prosper? Such profound factual misconceptions are not so much 'Irish' as simply human.

The Irish and the English are divided by many characteristics, but none as defining as memory. The English largely forget their past, while the Irish 'remember' theirs with a ferocious devotion – and I'm not sure which is healthier. Irish memory has so often dwelt on a few choice bits of victimhood to caress and exult over, whereas the English seem to have opted for memorial nihilism to cope with a history that really has been dreadful. The Norman conquest cast the Anglo-Saxons into two and a half centuries – say, ten full generations – of economic, linguistic and cultural oppression. Ireland's full penal laws lasted less than one hundred years. South African apartheid lasted thirty.

The great Norman cathedrals of England were built by Anglo-Saxon slave labour. All court, church, political, legal and trade transactions were conducted in French: *bouchiers* controlled the sale of meat – which when off the hoof was *boeuf, mouton* and *porc*. It was *grossiers* who sold wholesale food and *drapiers* who sold clothes. The building industry was controlled by French speakers, hence *maçon* (mason) and *plommier* (plumber). An apprentice – *apprenti* – would travel to his work, which was of course *travail*, as the French for a working day, *journée*, became English for 'movement'. French words are still esteemed over English ones, as quilt was recently replaced by its exact French equivalent, duvet, 'first' elbowed rudely aside by 'premier' and that pretentious 'faux' has displaced its own earlier derivative of 'false' – when English already has fake, bogus, phoney, mock and pseudo. Prawn has recently been sidelined amongst the pretentious and the vapid by *langoustine*. And so on.

Consider those other English catastrophes: the Black Death, the Hundred Years' War, the Wars of the Roses, Henry VIII, the English Reformation, the English Civil Wars, the Enclosures, the Industrial Revolution and two world wars. There is so much to forget, while the Irish memory not only has cherished authentic injustices, but has even invented others, such as the £5 that Queen Victoria allegedly gave for Famine Relief, to match the £5 she had given to a dogs' home, whereas she actually gave £5,000 for victims of the Famine. Another cherished fiction is that the Duke of Wellington said of his Irish birth, 'Because one is born in a stable does not make one a horse.' As a young soldier attending Military College in Angers in France, Wellington unashamedly described himself as 'un officier irlandais', and he certainly would not have understood the loathsome term 'Anglo-Irish'. Absent from the public memory – and from almost all Irish history books – is the title 'the greatest living Irishman' that was bestowed upon Wellington by the Catholic hierarchy in gratitude for Catholic Emancipation and his defeat of Napoleon. This so enraged Daniel O'Connell that he created the stable calumny, and this lie thrives still, while the truth about Wellington's greatness is forgotten. The foggy amnesia of the English is generally kindlier than the acidulously selective memory of the Irish.

Hubert Butler was fully aware of the din of rival myths amid the deafening clamour of forgetfulness, and he interrogated them all with impartial thoroughness. However, being a gallant dissident from the prevailing cultural norms was a perilous business, and for a long time he paid a high price, with local exclusion and national disdain. Only in his later years were his eminence and courage fully acclaimed. The last time I saw him was by his invitation in 1990. He welcomed me with the jest: 'On the sill still I see.'

Though still spritely, death was clearly staking a claim on him: the slowing of physical response, the unfocused eye, the palsied, liver-spotted hand, the conversational non sequiturs and the baffled silences with which they finished. The final silence was not long away, and soon it arrived. I am proud to have known, to have been moderately well regarded by, one of the greatest Irishmen or women of the twentieth century. He died just as the land where he had staked his claim to greatness, Yugoslavia, was about to reveal the emptiness and pusillanimity of Europe's many airs and pomps.

Twenty-Two

BY THIS TIME, Grania and I had bought a house on Royal Canal Bank, on the northside of the city centre, overlooking Dublin's original reservoir. I had fallen in love with the little Georgian terraced property the moment I had seen it, and since the owner was out, I shoved a letter under the door offering to buy it at its asking price, never having been inside – we Myers are put on this earth to bring orgasmic joy to the vending classes. One clinching feature for me – as I was soon to discover – was that it had once been owned by a family called Ledwidge, which was also the name of the poet killed in action in 1917. Estate agency takes on a whole new dimension when I am in the market.

No sooner had we closed the deal and moved in than we discovered that the house was an artful combination of both wet and dry rot, a soup of decay that required us to move back to my 'condominium' in Mountjoy Square while builders gutted and rebuilt at ruinous cost. Little wonder that I am still haunted by recurring dreams that I cannot escape that freezing garret. Nonetheless, once I had moved back, I loved Royal Canal Bank. Besides being charming, it was handy for work, and close to two places close to my heart, Phoenix Park and Islandbridge. The latter was now being restored under the horticultural wizardry of John McCullen, one of the unsung heroes of Irish life. With great pride, I attended the official opening of the Memorial Park there, feeling sure that history was now on my side.

With a home of my own, I grew more settled, and my drinking eased. But not always. So, one morning, I was lying in bed, hungover after a midsummer's eve party, studiously ignoring the phone's repeated imprecations. Next, there was a hammering on the door. The postman, presumably. I tottered downstairs, but, instead of the postman, I found a messenger bearing orders from *The Irish Times*: I was to proceed immediately to Bosnia to report on the war there, about which – had anyone bothered to ask me – I could have proclaimed an unassailable ignorance.

So, armed with no maps or historical knowledge or language or any preparation whatever, that same afternoon I headed off to the front lines. First, I flew to Frankfurt, then to the new state of Slovenia. Thereafter, I travelled by bus over the foothills and mountain passes of the Dinaric Alps, a jagged landscape of endlessly recycled massacre, migration and rapidly forgotten peace settlement, followed by ...

And yes, I have brought you to this point abruptly, pretty much as I experienced the transition: hangover one morning, war the next. On the coach towards Split on the Dalmatian coast, the woman sitting beside me turned and said conversationally: 'Are you aware that the great tragedy of the female sex is that women's breasts are at their very best when girls are just seventeen?'

'I, ah ...'

'I speak as a doctor, you understand. Yes, they are still too young to appreciate their beauty, and their own libidos are so small – that is, compared to what will follow. I speak from bitter personal experience. Do you know that just as my breasts began to droop and I became less attractive to men, my libido began to soar? Isn't that unfair? I'm sure, looking at someone as plain as me, that you'd never guess that I have to have an orgasm at least once a day. Tell me – do you like Serbs?'

In this uninhibited dam burst of query, enquiry and disclosure I swiftly settled for the Serbs, declaring stoutly that I knew none.

'That is good. They are rather like my breasts. Of no real use to anyone else. What Serbs do to Croats is unbelievable. They remove their eyes and make them eat them before killing them. I have spoken to a fellow doctor who has done the autopsies on the bodies. He found the eyes in the alimentary canals.'

She was a Croat doctor living in New York and was returning to her country in its time of need. She was the kind of creature who divides most of the human race from its contemptible subspecies, journalists: such ranting would make a normal person smash the bus window with their firstborn in order to escape, but a journalist-on-assignment considers it pure gold. So, I listened raptly, aural joy filling my squalid heart.

'And pregnant women have had their bellies cut open and their babies torn out, and living cats stitched back inside them instead.'

Yes! She actually said that! Such bliss!

'Some fellow doctors and I were discussing why the Serbs could behave so evilly – genes, of course! After centuries of Turkish rule, killing is nothing to them. The Serbian Orthodox Church is the only church anywhere that doesn't say Thou Shalt Not Kill. Serbian priests encourage the killings.'

Having done some thorough research – namely scanning a discarded *Newsweek* at Frankfurt airport – I pointed out that the Orthodox Patriarch of Belgrade had declared of Serbian atrocities: 'The devil himself would be ashamed of us.'

'Propaganda designed to hide the truth that he is secretly blessing the killers! It's a scientific fact that the Serbs' DNA is inferior to ours. Even their doctors are imbeciles, murderous apes, their language – babble babble babble. The sheer beauty of Croat poetry is beyond them. Their animal instincts are more basic, more uncontrollable. A Serb man cannot content himself as I can content myself. No, he has to rape. That is what Serbs do. It's in their genes. It explains a lot.'

After I arrived in Split, with eyes swimming with warm tears of gratitude, I made a story of this doctor's gibbering – minus the sex stuff – not having the least idea whether what she had said was representative of what I would find. Actually, her words proved to be almost an essay in Methodist even-handedness. When I managed to contact that great Irish hero of Bosnia, Commandant Colm Doyle, the already legendary aide-de-camp to the European Community's interlocuter, Lord Carrington, he gave me the first and best advice I was ever to receive in the region: never believe *anything* anyone here ever says to you. Falsehood is as much part of the landscape as the Dinaric Alps, and since everyone had incorporated exotic and often violent fictions into their own egos, it was literally impossible for them to distinguish between fantasy and fact.

There were two inescapable burdens for any journalist in the field in those days. The first was communication: how do you contact your newspaper from the front line where there were no landlines and the mobile phone was still a twinkle in a Finnish woodcutter's eye? The second was the news desk at home, which, as all journalists on foreign assignment (no matter who they work for) will agree, would invariably misunderstand anything you said to it. *The Irish Times* generally did not use surnames, but the exception was during the twice-daily conferences. So many journalists had been culturally imprinted by *All the President's Men*, and the afternoon conference had become a celebration of greyback chest-beating, .shape-throwing and last-name-calling, where even the knitting correspondent would assume the strutting, sword-bearing majesty of a toreador. The lesson was: never commit to anything just before it.

But I had forgotten that Croatia is ahead of Irish time, just as I began to give the news desk an immensely scholarly overview of the region, every detail of which, including commas, I had plagiarised from a report on the BBC World Service (in those days a reliable organisation). The names – Zagreb, Belgrade, Sarajevo, Mostar – authoritatively tripped off my deceitful tongue with saurian ease, before I mentioned the siege of Dubrovnik, which, I said airily, had been under land and coastal bombardment for weeks.

'Dubrovnik?' yelped the news desk, erectile tissue suddenly alert and questing. 'Is it possible to get there?'

'Possible? Well, all the approach roads are still under fire, and the Yugoslav navy is bombarding it from the sea, but, theoretically, it *might* be possible.'

The desk went briefly silent before I heard across a thousand miles of telephone line the yodelled declaration:

'MYERS SAYS HE'S GOING INTO DUBROVNIK!!!!'

Nothing becomes a certain fact quite like a half-ventured casual idea that is suddenly turned into capitals and festooned with exclamation marks and then thrown into the concrete mixer of the conference. Next, a few grey-backs add some gravel of approval, and others throw in the cement of enthusiasm, and then everyone jumps up and down beating their chests and going *whoo whoo whoo.* However, not even those babbling simians were so deranged as to think I could get into Dubrovnik that very night. Nonetheless, the idea was now fixed on the agenda, from which not a JCB on Olympian steroids could have shifted it.

I asked around the hotel if anyone was prepared to share the costs and the risks of the journey, along with the high price of my company, but no one was interested. You'll never make it was the consensus. Why risk that danger for so little return?

'It came up in conference,' I explained.

'Oh fuck,' was the sympathetic reply, as if I had just admitted to buboes in both armpits, beriberi and purple discharges. I hired a Fiat Punto, the only colour left being an almost luminous white, causing hilarity back at the hotel. Perfect for nocturnal target practice, mused one English journalist wryly, how very thoughtful of you. Next morning, miserable, morose and mapless – not even the UN had maps – I set out for Dubrovnik. Road signs had been removed, but all I had to do was head towards the sound of the guns, with the sea on the right, hills on the left, along the most staggeringly beautiful coastline I had ever seen. The Ring of Kerry is like Luton Airport in comparison.

Initially, some signs of civilian life remain – even roadside traders selling fruit, but soon the landscape becomes one of war. Bouncing towards me from the front comes an improvised ambulance – a car with its windscreen removed, the patient, a soldier with his legs strapped onto the bonnet, his bandaged, bloodied head lolling in the passenger compartment, held there by a blood-soaked young woman. The Yugoslav Army had given all its weaponry to the Serbs, and the Croats improvised: hence the next vehicle, a furniture lorry with armour plate welded onto its side, rumbling in the opposite direction, towards the war.

Over there lie the wondrous islands of Dalmatia, thousands of them, set in glitteringly cerulean waters beneath the azure of the

Adriatic sky. In the distant sea mist, grey as wolves in a fog, Serbian naval vessels are firing into Dubrovnik, while from the highlands above the city, Montenegrin gunners are bombarding all the approach roads into it. This is Europe, forty-seven years after the Second World War ended. Wonderful.

I'm alone, ignorant and terrified as I pause at a junction. Just as my nerve is failing and I'm about to turn back, a cacophony of horns warns that I am about to be overtaken by a self-importantly hurtling convoy of white cars. Each is marked EU, and they are being led by a Croat armoured vehicle. Chance, contingency, coincidence explain so much in this world when intent cannot. I instantly attach myself as a tail-end Charlie to this cavalcade, and we are waved through the various Croat Army check points, soldiers duly saluting me. My once laughably white car has suddenly turned me into a VIP. The passengers in the final EU car keep looking indignantly back at me, as we draw closer to Dubrovnik, the siege of which, the BBC had that morning reported, was over. Not remotely true, as the cannon fire ahead testifies.

Then comes the point when the EU convoy disappointingly turns left, off the road to Dubrovnik, and away into the highlands, leaving me alone. I am now near the outer suburbs of the city. Guns are firing from the hills above me to my left, and all present – myself, the gunners and their targets – can effortlessly observe their efforts and their outcome. *Boom* ... one, two, three, four ... *BLAST*.

It's an odd thing about war. Sometimes you feel immortal, and sometimes you don't. Having sailed through those saluting roadblocks like a general at a victory parade, I feel giddily and gloriously immune. I stop and get out of my car. The hillside is scorched and smoking. What had been houses are now smouldering funeral pyres of brick. I approach a trench containing some soldiers with rosaries around their Kalashnikovs. Between them, they manage to assemble some cooperative sentences in English. The hillside fires were caused by napalm attacks from Serb MiG-29s. There are bodies nearby, they warn. Also, the MiGs might come back.

I walk on a hundred yards. The hideous stench of burnt and decaying flesh greets me, and then I see a column of flies rising and falling in the air above a rotting mound: once a human, and now a putrefying part of the lifecycle of wanton maggotry, for whom we are all merely passing hosts.

Tingling sensors in my pineal body cause me to look round. Yes, I can feel it, someone has me in their sights. Slowly, I return to my car. The soldiers cry out something like 'Pazi Snayper Chetnik' – *Beware Serb snipers*. I feel it all now: my gut, my brain, my heart. This is dangerous, very dangerous. Briefly, I pause. Should I? Shouldn't I? Shall I? Shan't I? Will I? Won't I?

Fuck it. I get in and drive on. As I near the city itself, a car lies at an angle across the road. Its windows are smashed; the tarmac round it is burnt. Cartridge cases are strewn everywhere. There are rattles of automatic fire very, very close. By this time, I know a front line when I see one. I stop. Some soldiers run diagonally across the road, crouching, zig-zagging, in open-skirmish order. Two soldiers to my right put down covering fire. This, yes, right here, is the final combat zone; beyond, just up the hill, are the Serbs. I don't and didn't speak Serbo-Croat, but sometimes one can translate.

'What the fuck are you doing here?' cries a Croat soldier. 'How the fuck did you get this far? There are roadblocks for the past ten miles which should have stopped you! Are you fucking mad?'

Or something on those lines. Another soldier runs over and gets into the car, then, pointing his Kalashnikov, gestures back down the road. I am a little relieved: the curse of the conference has been thwarted by a still greater force: zealous Croats with rosaries and AK rifles.

He starts speaking Serbo-Croatian, and I shake my head. 'Speak English?'

'I see you not Chetnik, so what are you?' he barks, looking at me in a puzzled, angry way.

'Irish.'

'Irish,' he smiles. 'Good. Catholic. Bobby Sands.'

My escort tells me a lot about himself as we head away from the battle. He is an ardent Catholic who is not bound by several of the middle-ranking and lesser commandments – those concerning sex and human life. He has fucked many women and killed many Chetniks.

He is a good Catholic: see here, the rosary beads on his rifle. I serve God, the Blessed Mother, Croatia. He dedicates his life to the Virgin at Medjugorje; every Serb he kills, he offers to her.

'Irish,' he repeats approvingly. 'You Catholic?'

'Yes,' I lie. (Was.)

'Ireland good. IRA good. Fight British like we fight Serbs. Bobby Sands. Hero. I have cousin in Ireland.'

He says his name. Incredibly, I have met and interviewed his cousin. I tell him this.

'This is God's will. Good country, Ireland. Catholic country.'

'Yes.'

I tell him I am staying in Split, and I name the hotel.

'Ees okay.'

We drive on. We see a vehicle stopped at a roadblock. A man has been taken out of his car by Croatian Military Police. He is trembling. He clearly is in dire trouble.

'Chetnik,' spits my soldier: the mysterious alchemy of tribal identification, common to Ardoyne, Alsace and Anderlecht, has exposed him. The MP unholsters his pistol, cocks it, pointing it upwards, presses the trigger. It misfires. He lowers the pistol, pulls back the slide to get rid of the dud round, and then chambers another one. The man, weeping, is forced downwards, a rough hand on the shoulder, his knees buckling.

My companion turns his rifle on me and cocks it. 'Do not look.'

Out of the corner of my eye, I see the pistol is presented to the nape of the man's neck, and we drive by. I watch through the rear-view mirror as the man's head goes down, like Anne Boleyn's on the block, and next my soldier hits the mirror with the top of the barrel, so I do not see what happens next.

But I know what happens next.

The single *crack* tells me what happens next.

We drive on.

'Do not write about this,' says my soldier. 'I know your hotel. I kill you. Or my cousin will.'

So I didn't write about it. Until now. I was part-afraid, and part-ashamed. You hear about survivors' guilt, though I have never felt 'guilt' about any people dying near me. But shame at not having done more to help those in need – ah, that is a different thing. At least two British soldiers in Belfast were shot when I might have acted to save them, though such acts might have endangered me. No simple choices then, and no easy conscience thereafter, *ever*.

That Sunday, I file a bowdlerised story, in which I cannot be sure that the Serb was shot. Later the news desk offers pointedly insincere commiserations about my not actually getting into Dubrovnik – though I could well have died on that road.

'Maybe you'll have better luck getting into Sarajevo.'

'I'm sure I will.' The auxiliary verb (main verb assumed) is deliberately aspirational, not the futural 'I shall'.

'Myers says he's going into Sarajevo!'

Twenty-Three

THE INEXORABLE, INSANE logic of conference decisions is now exercising its hold over me like a powerful magnet over brain-damaged iron filings. In the press centre, I ask fellow journalists about the Sarajevo option.

'Why do you ask?'

'It came up in conference.'

'Oh fuck,' but now with serious sympathy, as if the buboes have started weeping and my brain is dribbling through my ears. Everyone agrees it's a non-starter. There are no maps, most roads are closed, and Bosnia is a patchwork quilt of armed factions whose locations and front lines are unknown to everyone, including the UN, so even if I had a map, it would be of little use.

All true. *But it came up in conference.*

In the hotel lobby, I meet an Irish Army officer: like almost all such officers, a credit to Ireland – genial, efficient and tireless. He tells me that a UN convoy is heading out for Sarajevo the next morning. But no one can join them; the vehicles are UN only and in UN livery. However, I have already been in an EU convoy, in a white car that just about passed muster. So, at first light the next morning, I introduce myself to the convoy captain, a cheery Canadian major called Molloy, who tells me that so long as he doesn't know what's going on at the back of the convoy, and I haven't got any guns, and I am Irish, I may tag along. You any guns, hey?

No, no guns.

Headlights on, we drive north into the mountains, me at the rear, and, as the sun rises, darkness falls on my soul, for we are going into its very heart. Metaphors are meaningless; language falls mute; words become empty husks. I remember Colm Doyle's warning: everyone speaks untruth here. Everyone. I have been to Beirut and Belfast, where the different sides speak variants of the truth, with many lies. But in the Balkans everyone creates believable and wholly exclusive falsehoods that might even develop into chemically verifiable formations within their brains. A thought occurs: *is Charles Manson really Karlo Mansonović?*

Soon we leave the road and follow logging tracks through the forest. This is worrying. I had assumed we would stick to main thoroughfares. My vehicle is the only car – the rest are lorries or four-by-fours – and the little Fiat struggles on the unmade pathways, slipping and sliding in the mud, often howling in pain on some of the steeper slopes. But for hour after hour this gallant daughter of Turin gamely stays the course. I have brought with me a sandwich and a bottle of water. I am not hungry, so I just sip water on this long, long journey through a long, long day.

The convoy halts. My Canadian friend comes back and breaks the sickening news that they have just been told that it is too dangerous to proceed to Sarajevo, so instead they have been ordered to head for a UN-only encampment nearby, to which I may not follow them. I must make my own arrangements, but he adds that there is a compound housing units from the HVO/HOS (Hrvatsko Vijeće Obrane/Hrvatske Obrambene Snage) nearby. He wishes me good luck.

I am friendless, mapless and clueless in the Bosnian highlands. I drive as directed. I know little about the HVO/HOS, except that the former is the Croat Army, the latter a locally recruited and fairly lawless Croat militia. This being the Balkans, they detest one another.

As night falls, I see the 'compound'. It is a collection of vehicles, with sentries guarding the approach roads, and with at least two different flags and many kinds of uniform. UN officers had warned me: in this place, when you see more than one kind of uniform, beware.

But I have no choice.

I make myself known by name and nationality to a sentry, who says 'Bobby Sands'. I am told to report to the compound commandant, which I do. He is curt, and tells me I must show no lights, ordering me to disconnect the light bulbs inside the car. He points out an area of broken ground between the demarcated lines separating the HVO and the HOS, where I am to park.

I am exhausted. Yugoslav hire cars come with a little kit, so I obediently unscrew the interior light, eat my sandwich, drink some water, and curl up in the back seat of the Fiat. All around me, men are drinking slivovitz, the evil plum brandy that surely explains so much about this madness. Sleep of a sort follows.

I am awoken by shouting and then gunfire. Long automatic bursts, very, very close, and screaming – much screaming – at first abuse, then the screams of men being shot. The encampment has turned into a Croat-on-Croat gun battle.

I slip lightlessly out of the car door and lie on the ground, feeling around for cover. Because the car is on a slight incline with hollows, I can work my way under it. The shooting continues. Long, demonic, insane bursts this way and that; screams everywhere. I try to hunker deep into the ground. Will someone put a precautionary burst under this strange white car?

At length, lights come on around me, engines are started. The encampment is decamping. I stay where I am. Within half an hour, I am alone in the dark on a hillside in Bosnia, a Fiat on my back, a Torino tortoise; nonetheless, I sleep restlessly for a while. I wake as grey dawn seeps in beneath the sill of the door, and I ease my way out of this sanctuary, metal underparts clawing strips of skin from my shoulder blades.

I stand and look round. A soft rain is washing away the dark puddles of blood on the lush grass. Whatever bodies there might have been are gone. Ahead lies a logging track through a forested slope, and from the light of the rising sun to the east, I guess that it must lead north towards Sarajevo. I am as alone as Robinson Crusoe at Man Friday's funeral.

I get into my car and head off, up logging tracks through the mountain forests, for maybe four hours. At length, I come to an army checkpoint. Whose? No idea. I don't recognise their insignia. How could I?

I don't know the difference between Serb, Bosniak or Croat. I have no idea where I am or what I am doing, only that I am here. That's it.

I show my ID and say nothing.

'Bobby Sands,' says the soldier, waving me through.

And on I go, through other checkpoints, with different pennants, and different headgear. Artillery fire echoes across these alps.

'Sarajevo?' I ask, pointing.

'Sarajevo,' they agree, exchanging glances.

And then, miracles of miracles, after many miles, amid a green upland meadow, I come across a rustic inn. A brook babbles playfully, and people are breakfasting beside it. Most are journalists, all speaking English. I introduce myself, and they explain that they came up in a UN convoy a couple of days before. But this is as far as they can get. It's not possible to enter Sarajevo; the fighting from here on is too intense.

Grateful to be liberated from any undertakings to distant news desks, I decide to stay here indefinitely. I buy breakfast – salami and eggs and olives – and drink three cups of coffee and down two litres of water. A dog sidles up to me. Its legs are uncoordinated. Its head hangs on one side. Its mouth is open. I don't like this one bit. I pour some water into my saucer and put it in front of the dog. It yelps, recoils and lollops away.

I turn to the journalists at the next table.

'This dog is rabid. You're in danger.'

They laugh, and return to their coffees, visibly thinking *madman*. Maybe – but the dog has that faltering *To Kill a Mockingbird* waddle that bespeaks a central nervous system being destroyed by the deadliest virus known to science.

I go to the manager. I say the dog is rabid. *La rage*. Bizarrely, I know the German for rabies – *Tollwütig*. He laughs.

I decide. I'm not staying anywhere near a mad dog. I get into my car, but I will not return the way I came. Too dangerous. I will go onwards, to wherever onwards leads. I leave the idyll of the inn in the sunlight, relaxed journalists chatting in the sunshine. At a little service station, I fill the Fiat's tank, and pay in deutschmarks.

A few miles on, the road is closed by a barricade and I continue along logging tracks, upwards through woodlands for mile after mile.

Finally, I leave the forest and enter a clearing, now a desolate wasteland after another battle – an ambush of some kind. Burning vehicles are on the side of the road. In the hills just above me, a gunfight is taking place; automatic fire is hose-piping this way and that. I know I made a terrible fatigue-driven error in leaving the safety of the inn. But I cannot go back. I must continue. The hills around me thunder to the sound of war. Artillery reverberates, pulsing through the air. Nearby, men are shooting at one another, so I keep going away from them. I finally leave this contested space, and move higher still, meeting another roadblock, more pennants, more uniforms, regarding all of which I am illiterate.

An officer is on the road. I indicate ahead: 'Sarajevo?'

'Da,' he says, looking at me curiously.

'Thank you,' I say.

'It is dangerous.'

'Yes, I know.'

He smiles, and says: 'Good luck.'

Then he does something really, really terrible. He puts his heels together and salutes me. Yes, a soldier saluting a civilian: this can only mean serious trouble, but I am too scared to go back. What is ahead surely cannot possibly be worse than what I have come through. Almost immediately I arrive at a crossroads which has been disputed, and the debris of war is everywhere: two busted T-54 tanks and a burning half-track, and alongside them the scattered pink liquids of crewmen, mere smears on the road, like crushed raspberries. Nearby, there are bodies, the angle of their booted feet declaring that their tendons are posthumously mimicking military symmetry. Rifle fire is so ear-shatteringly loud that the shooters seemed to be just yards away.

I have to get out of there *immediately*, and I accelerate away, the hairs on the back of my neck bristling with primeval terror, my backbone tingling with the expectation of bullets. *Not the spine, dear Jesus, head or heart, fine, but not the spine.* Within a minute, I am clear of the immediate battle zone, and into a sandy clearing in the trees, almost like a beach, and free of gunfire. I can relax. That's the odd thing about war. Stunning violence in one place; a hundred yards away, the delusions of peace.

I assume that the battle I have just come through was the reason why the officer had shown me so much respect, but I am mistaken. For suddenly around me I see the reason, and my heart stops and the silence of a corpse's lungs reigns in my breast cage. A breeze has cleared the surface sand to reveal that I am driving through a minefield. Mine detonators protrude like the clenched feet of dead spiders; and the imprints of the explosive discs just underneath make ominous circles on the surface. Someone has scrawled on a board *Achtung Minen*. Yes, it sounds better in German. (Now I finally understand that officer: the only civilians that soldiers may salute are the dead ones.) By chance, I am on two parallel winding tracks that run through this sandbar. Someone with a mine detector made these tracks. Mines are beneath me and alongside me, and, though I assume the tracks are a sort of guarantee of safety, I know that mines are often re-laid from the side, underneath existing tracks, to catch the trusting. I proceed as if I am threading a needle with the bonnet of the car. After several minutes of focused, purposeful driving – slow, slow, slow – yes, resisting the temptation to put my foot down and get the hell out of this abominable place – finally, I leave the minefield.

But I am not yet through, in any sense of that word, for within a couple of miles I am in a village, in the aftermath of another recent battle. Two or three tanks are burning, as are half-a-dozen upturned vehicles. Houses are on fire. The road is littered with many hundreds of used rifle-calibre cartridge cases, plus a few large shell casings. Sprawled nearby are a couple of slack-jawed corpses. The battle has moved on, and I am not in immediate danger, though I can hear unseen men trying very hard to kill one another. Single shots, short bursts, the long *brrrrrr* of a belt-fed Šarac machine gun, a copy of the German MG42. I would go back, if I possibly could – ah, but *possibly* expired long ago.

At the end of the village, the road forks. Which fork do I take? I am staring round, paralysed and fearful, when I see, bizarrely, inexplicably, a man sitting in his front garden, drinking a cup of coffee. He is unkempt and has a broken arm in plaster, and yes, I am not hallucinating, he is having a cup of coffee in his garden in the middle of a gun battle. This is from Magritte, whose death I heard of the last time I was in Yugoslavia in

1967, the summer of love. I understand now. No events are unconnected. In all chaos, there is contingent unity. You must seek that unity and exploit it.

I call out of my open window: 'Sarajevo?'

His eyes turn towards me, then narrow warningly. Suddenly I am aware that we are being watched. I can see it in his face. He is clearly scared – not for himself, but for me. He looks hard at me, covertly signalling with his eyes – darting this way and that – that we are surrounded.

'*Nicht gut*,' he whispers in German. '*Nicht gut.*'

Below the level of the table, invisible to any watchers, he makes a small sweeping gesture with his good hand: *go away*, it says, *now!*

The day before I left Dublin, I had read the obituary of a Canadian Army officer who in Normandy in 1944 had come to a bridge beyond which he knew the Germans were waiting. He realised the only way he had of persuading them to hold their fire was by making them think he had a right to be there. So he deliberately sauntered across the bridge, while, out of sight of the Germans, his riflemen crawled alongside his feet. Back and forth he went, escorting his entire platoon, while the watching Germans wondered who this madman was. Was he one of theirs?

This is my contingency: from his grave a Canadian is now advising me. I lazily get out of the car and smile at my host. 'Sarajevo links oder rechts?'

'Links,' he whispers, still making small, below-the-table, get-out-of-here gestures. Instead, I stroll over to the middle of the road, and putting my hands in my pockets, admire the scenery. The Canadian had survived; so could I. This is not courage, oh absolutely not, for of that brainless commodity I have long since run out, but simply a desperate, abject desire to stay alive.

I stroll back to the car door, and pause, while he looks at me beseechingly, still making tiny thigh-high gestures with his hand, as if shooing over-familiar mice away from his feet. Finally, I get back into the car, pausing for a final chat. I babble meaningless words through the open window, while he gazes incredulously. Waving him goodbye, I slowly drive off, and as I approach the fork, I begin to take the right turn, away from Sarajevo, and even – in the middle of a battle – courteously using my indicator; and then at the last second, I swivel the steering wheel hard left, put the foot down on the accelerator, and with tyres and engine screaming, I head for Sarajevo.

It takes a second or two for my unseen watcher to react, and to judge from what happens next, he is behind me and obliquely above me. A car is not such an easy target as you might imagine, especially if the shooter's angle is wrong. His first burst of fire hits the ground before me, and I intuitively turn into it, assuming that next he would rake the road ahead of my original path, which he does, his burst hitting where I would have been. I then turn into that, but at this point I am now running out of road, so I have to head back to the centre, where he now will surely get me, and, against my will, I look in the mirror to see where he's firing from, but I can't, because I have just driven into the shelter of a bluff, and am now out of his line of fire. When I emerge from the bluff a second or two later, his next burst is wild, and then I round a bend, and am safe from his fire.

I slow down. I am still in the Serb-held area outside Sarajevo, and there's no shooting here in the town of Pale. I see a uniformed man, a Thompson submachine gun balanced on one arm, ambling along the road with a moll on each arm, both of them in flouncy party dresses, hips swaying, 1950s' style. The Thompson is an obsolete trench-clearing weapon with no other purpose here apart from moll-pleasing or murder. Pure Magritte.

Soon I am clear of Pale, and in the outskirts of Sarajevo, near a resolute Bosniak enclave that I later learn is called Dobrinja, and at a front door of a house, I see a mother kissing her armed and uniformed teenage boy goodbye – at most he is fourteen, and he wears a military hat with a tassel as he sets about God knows what purpose …

Then I am back in the front line again, as gunfire rakes the road around me, but without even hitting the car, so I get through that unharmed. I am on the main dual carriageway into Sarajevo, going about 100 kph, and I see a car in front me, marked *TV.* I overtake it on the inside, lowering my window and sounding my horn as I do. The driver opens his window.

'I'm a new kid on the block,' I bellow. 'What the fuck do I do?'

'Follow us, and DO NOT FUCKING STOP FOR ANYTHING!'

He leads the way at terrifying speed towards what I can see is the Holiday Inn. Then down the looping road behind, towards the underground car park, in howling third gear, tyres screeching for mercy, their treads being pulled out by their roots, and at the final bend I come under intense and very nasty fire – only now it feels *personal* because I'm nearly safe, and the shooter clearly doesn't want me that way. Suddenly I am in the underground carpark, and unwounded, and am nearly weeping with relief and trauma.

The CBS newsman gets out of his car and offers a hand.

'Welcome to the Sarajevo Holiday Inn, sir. I do hope you had a pleasant journey.'

Twenty-Four

I GO UPSTAIRS, shaking badly. Near reception, a muscular, radiantly handsome man in a T-shirt smiles at me in greeting. He looks American.

'You got a warm welcome there,' he says drily. Ah. English. 'It can get warmer. Wherever you've been in life before, this is worse. Believe me, this is far worse.' He sticks out a hand. 'Paul Douglas.'

I introduce myself. He escorts me to the receptionist, who looks through her books and at length offers me a room, but when he hears its number, Paul tries to get me another one.

'There's nothing else available,' says the receptionist. She warns me that it's on the fifth floor, its windows have no glass and, because it is facing sniper-infested mountains, the curtains have been nailed shut. There is no electricity – and oh yes, there's a dead body in the room above, so I might notice a certain smell.

Paul is about to escort me upstairs when a huge blast nearby rocks the hotel, and he races off to get his camera equipment.

I must ascend five storeys with connecting landings, that is, ten flights of stairs right in the centre of the enclosed core of the building. Light is seeping in from windows on each floor; the stairs themselves are unlit. I finally reach my level and go along the corridor to my room. I open the door. The room smells like a Cairo butcher's shop in late afternoon, while flies on the ceiling are investigating a Bisto bloodstain. I plonk myself on the bare mattress covering the bed. Night is now falling and soon the gravy browning above me disappears as liquid dark pours through the glassless window.

I need food. I grope my way outside, into an unlit corridor, which is like stepping into a coalmine, and I finger-feel my way towards the lightless stairwell, and then feet-tap my way to the steps. I take these one at a time, seeing nothing, knowing that if I fall, I do so alone and unheard. It takes me many minutes to get down the stairwell into the reception area, which is illuminated by a single gas lamp. I am directed to the dining room: several half-lit tables, no water, a plate with a slice of tinned meat, and some tinned peas. That's my evening meal. Price: ten dollars, paid in advance.

To go to bed is a major undertaking, for the stairwell is in total darkness. I must count the steps to know when I have reached my floor. Exhausted, I lose track of where I am, so I have to go downstairs and start again. When I get to the right floor, I grope my way to the corridor, and feel my way along the walls to the doors, on which, by divine providence, the room numbers are both raised and in separate digits: Yugoslavian corridor braille, in the event of war.

Then into the room. I have no torch. I find my mattress. I lie down, and reach for my Sony radio, already tuned into the BBC World Service. In that complete dark, the soothing civilities of the English Home Counties are murmured into my ears. I have just caught the start of the final of the *Brain of Britain* quiz, and the contestants are introduced. The last one turns out to be a solicitor from Leicester, he who made off with all the Myers money after my mother's death. Now he is famous in Britain, and I am marooned beneath a stinking corpse in this total dark. Can it get any worse?

It can. He wins.

Somehow, I sleep. I feel flies negotiating their way across my face like blind men, *tap tap tap*. I doze. Back and forth. At some time in the desperate dark of early morning, I am woken by the sound of human screaming. The shrieks are blood-curdling. I can feel my veins and arteries pause about their liquid duty to listen. These are the worst noises I have ever heard or shall ever hear. They are what results when a trench raid is done with cold steel, the final cries of men being stabbed to death not far away. I lie there and listen as distant ribcages are broken open and I think I can hear someone gagging on his own blood.

In the half-light of morning, journalists gather for breakfast, looking ancient, haggard, filthy. There is a small bottle of water to drink, and none to wash in or flush our lavatories. I have no memory of what breakfast consists of. Later, those with cars assemble in the basement, preparing to make the pell-mell journey up the ramp, past the hundred yards of snipers' alley, and into the cover of Sarajevo's buildings. Paul sees me and asks me if I know what to do next.

Not a clue.

He tells me, slowly.

I get my Fiat warmed up. When it is my turn, with the car in gear, put the foot on the clutch, rev the engine once, then take the right foot off the throttle and left off the clutch, and hit the throttle. *But not too much. Do not stall as you leave.*

Forty-four journalists have already been killed covering this war, and scores maimed. More will follow; we just don't know who or how many. Atheist and Anglican, Roman and Jew, Methodist and Muslim, ecumenically unite around a single supplication: not me, God, not me, but if me, heart or head, dear God, but not the spine. One American camera crew behave as if they are at a gospel-meeting, psyching themselves up, their fists clenched, their eyes shut. Their producer shouts, 'Okay guys, one, two, three, let's go!'

They high-five one another and scramble into their vehicle as if they are escaping danger rather than driving into it. The driver revs up the engine in neutral, next double-clutch first gear, then up and out, the gunfire erupting as they vanish from sight. Soon it is my turn. From beside his car, Paul nods at me.

I rev, clutch, then declutch, and I rocket up, skidding wildly as I round the bend and emerge into daylight, a huge blast of automatic fire hitting the concrete balustrade around me, and I hurtle, weaving left and right, to make it to that final cover, where a wall contingently obstructs their line of fire.

It is breathtakingly terrifying.

In the city, I find a safe place to park my car, protected in all directions from sniper fire, and I wander around, hoping to speak to people who are out taking the air. Vox pop, it's called, but the pop has no vox, for the few people around don't want to talk. The shops are all closed. The city has no power. It has no fuel. It has no batteries. It has no water. It has no lavatory paper. What need have they for that when there is no food?

I ask a passer-by to show me the place where Gavrilo Princip assassinated the archduke. He walks with me up a side street to a quay alongside the River Miljacka, and points. There are, grotesquely, footprints on the pavement to mark where Princip stood, opposite the Latin Bridge. My companion gestures with his hand: stay low, stay low. Snipers, of course.

This is it. This is where our world began with the ultimate contingency. The Archduke Franz Ferdinand decides that he and Sophie would not drive down Franz Joseph Street but would instead continue driving along Appel Quay. But the driver is not told, and when he takes the wrong turn towards Franz Joseph Street, the head of security, Oskar Potiorek, in the front passenger seat scolds him. Panicking, unfamiliar with the car, the driver brakes and as the Gräf & Stift limousine stalls, the clutch seizes. The driver cannot find reverse, thereby giving Princip plenty of time to move from Moritz Schiller's café and close in on his target, as the driver wrestles with the stuck gear stick and the jammed clutch plates. The archduke is wearing a green ostrich feather in his hat, useful for would-be assassins.

Seconds elapse. The heir to the Habsburg throne should now be one hundred metres away. Princip approaches and opens fire, badly, because he is young and inept, and manages to shoot Sophie, the very person he is trying not to hurt, hitting her in the abdomen. His bullet severs the main artery just below her heart, and her lifeblood falls out of her as if from a barrel sawn in half. He shifts aim, going for a headshot, but only manages to put a bullet into Franz Ferdinand's neck, severing his femoral artery. Yes, just like the shot that killed the girl in purple in Beirut. In his dying seconds, the archduke implores Sophie, 'Don't die, darling. Live for our children.'

Two wretchedly inaccurate shots: two lives forfeited. More will follow.

I return to my own car, which has a good reverse gear, and then drive back to the Holiday Inn, repeating the same dreadful gunfire-accompanied corkscrew down the chicane, and into the underground carpark. With nightfall comes the routine of the night before. And the next. The only communications I have with *The Irish Times* are through Reuters. I file my copy by phone while lying on the broken glass of the floor of the Reuters' room. Snipers will shoot anything that appears at the window. Then 'dinner'. Then bed, and the smell of putrefaction oozing from the ceiling just above me, and flies wandering over me through the night. Being awoken at 4 a.m. by the screams of men. Sleep over. Breakfast. Then the underground carpark, with Paul watching me, minding me. Revving the engine, balancing the clutch and throttle, with the final plea: *Jesus, don't stall.* Into the city. Then back, having learnt nothing. That evening, queuing for the phone in Reuters, only to learn that it has gone kaput. The other working phone is at reception, with a two-hour queue, meaning I shall miss dinner. I join it, with nothing to file except a vague account of fighting and fear. An hour waiting, and dinner has come and gone, and suddenly there's a huge *BOOOM!* and the plywood sheeting across one of the windows is blown apart, as a Bosnian runs in from outside, shrieking *TANK TANK TANK.*

The queue in front of me scatters. I am too stunned to move. Through the shattered plywood, I can see the gun barrel of the tank gazing at me. Then it fires. *BOOOM!* I do not know what happened to the shell. Maybe it was a dud, maybe an armour-piercing solid shot that kept on going. Still paralysed and standing at reception, I see the tank reversing. It has been settling scores, and now it is leaving. It stops, and fires its 105 mm cannon upwards, possibly at a sniper: *BOOOM!* Then it's gone. So too is the queue. Thank God for small mercies.

I ring the news desk.

'Sorry,' someone says, 'we're rather busy here. Can you phone back later?'

For two days, I am deaf. I do not know it then, but I have suffered irreparable ear damage. I had already noticed that the shooting seems to die down before dawn. There's a sniper on duty immediately outside the hotel through all the daylight hours – a gallant soul indeed – but the more general cacophony begins at 11 a.m. Presumably most of the soldiers are snoring through their slivovitz hangovers. I have decided to leave, but I will never make that journey alone again. I suggest to Paul that a three-car breakout would give any ambush party too many targets to hit. I tell him of the minefield: it cannot be crossed at speed or at night. Paul tells me he must stay with his crew, but he knows some journalists who can go, and he plots an alternative route for us.

We gather at five, as haggard as centennials in a famine city, waiting for first light. Since I am the only one of the party to have made my way into the city unaccompanied, and it is my idea, I must go first. Later, another car with a map reader will navigate Paul's route. In those final moments, I am nearly vomiting with terror. Paul comes up to me and puts his hand through my open window and whispers: 'Good luck, my friend.'

I start my Fiat and sit there, wondering if these are the very last moments of my life; these now, these few seconds, inhaling petrol fumes and surrounded by the thrum of warming engines. I gaze up the ramp as grey displaces dark, yes, 'But look, the morn in russet mantle clad' (Horatio, *Hamlet*), touch the concrete balustrade above me. Paul, our starter, is peering out through the basement doorway, then he turns and nods.

Clutch pedal down, foot down on accelerator, full rev, then engage first gear, foot off clutch and *vroom* up the rampart to where the first blast of fire should greet me, but there's none whatever and I race round that deadly chicane, tyres screaming as the car slides towards the concrete rim. I steer into the skid to control it, with the balustrade a mere coat of paint away from the car, and I am onto the slip road, and then on the main drag out of Sarajevo, foot to the boards, heading for freedom, not a shot to be heard, oh fuck, not one, such joy, such fucking undiluted joy, 100 yards, 200 yards, still not a shot. Jubilantly, I look in my mirror.

The chase cars have not followed. *FUCK FUCK FUCK.*

I instantly know what's happened. The second car has stalled. And then, as I race past the UNPROFOR Telecom building, I see ahead of me

– oh, holy fucking hell – something even worse. Overnight a makeshift barricade has been erected to block the road out of Sarajevo. There is no way past it. None.

Jesus Christ. Jesus Christ alive.

If I stop, I become a target.

If I do a U-turn, I become a target.

If I get out to shift the fucking thing, I become a target.

I skid to a halt to do a three-point turn that becomes a panic-stricken five-pointer, bouncing off kerbs and nearly ramming a lamp post, expecting the ground around me to erupt in a fusillade of 7.62 rounds, oh, *any* second …

But the advantage of the second car stalling in a three-car convoy is that it and the third car can see other options, and those cars behind me are already flying down the wrong side of the dual carriageway, sounding their horns. Forty-five years of communism have made even Serb terrorists plan their ambushes according to the rules of the road. I hurtle across the central reservation with a criminal disregard for Yugoslav traffic laws, and follow the other cars at top speed, me now at the tail and waiting to be riddled by that familiar cascade of bullets out of nowhere, into my head or my heart, oh dear sweet Christ, but not my spine, not my fucking spine.

As we leave the city, a few desultory shots are fired. One Sarajevo stall doomed the archduke, but another saved me. We drive on and on until we reach the upland meadows of the Dinaric Alps, an evil Eden of gorgeous wildflowers and giddy birdsong, and we stop our cars and get out and tearfully embrace one another. As far as we can see lies a fragrant banquet of blossom, to the horizon and beyond.

I am alive. Yes. I am alive.

I step through the flowers – orchids, hay rattle, corn marigold, Alpine hawkbit, sawtooth sunflowers – up onto a bank of rosemary and thyme, and the roast-lamb fragrance of their sap fills the air. Across these meadows vast shoals of butterfly dance and hover, waves of colour borne on the invisible, sea-less sine-waves that sweep over this paradise, this garden, this Gehenna.

Then we all head south, the other two cars for Split, and I – because my deadline is drawing near – search for somewhere I can file my escape story from. Finally, near Mostar, I see a café, and it even has a working phone. Lord above. I hammer out a story, ring the news desk, and tell them I am alive, having managed to escape from Sarajevo.

'Without consulting the news desk first? You had no right to do that. You'd better turn around and go back in this second.'

I laugh the laugh of the free. I am alive. I don't bother filing my story. Fuck 'em. I'm going home.

Twenty-Five

IN THE LAST DECADE of the twentieth century, it became clear that doctrinaire liberal-feminist-egalitarianism was *the* coming force within western civilisation. In its most acute form, the western synthesis presumed that no values were inherently superior to others, and that Europe, which had invented most of the political, economic and cultural systems that had swept the world, had actually created nothing of transcendent merit. In this new moral order, 'equality' became the Apollo of virtues, a deity-dogma that was undefined and undefinable, and therefore loved by lawyers, who alone could untangle this weave of undefinability, usually with the assistance of the Divine Oracle of Asymmetry. This was the cerebral machinery that enabled tennis associations to declare that a women's tennis match of three sets was equal to a men's match of five sets. And naturally, journalists were soon proclaiming the virtues of equality, though they were as capable of explaining it as they were of photosynthesis.

The word 'sex' rapidly lost its primary meaning as a defining noun for the male–female division, a duty that was now assumed by the newly recruited word 'gender'. This had traditionally functioned as a grammatical term to attribute maleness or femaleness to French or Latin nouns. As such, 'gender' was historically both arbitrary and negotiable: over time, a word could change gender according to circumstance. And, according to the new rules that spread their authority over all matters with the zeal of the armed missionaries of the Conquistadors, so could human beings.

The vast differences between men and women, in their hormones, their nature, their chromosomes and their physique, were turned into minor cultural characteristics that could be altered with suitably enlightened education.

Very soon, anyone in our trade who dissented and tried to question the great conjoined falsehoods of feminism and asymmetric equality, as my colleague John Waters so often did, would be routinely portrayed as a 'misogynist'. This is one of the most exhausting words in the English language: it means a hater of women. That is half the human race. That's a lot of hating. Of course, it was now routinely deployed against any critic of the new feminism. It took its place alongside those old familiars from earlier creeds, 'class enemy' and 'heretic', and showed how ordinary language had been weaponised, as words were anagrammed into a sword.

A woman colleague gleefully showed me a newspaper report of a man named Lascille Carruthers who had fainted after his wife ripped off one of his testicles and then waved it in front of him. When I challenged her on her amusement over this violent castration, she told me that he must have been asking for it. Another case involved a garda, whom I named at the time but whom I'll now call Tom. He went on a pub crawl with an American policeman, before the two men retired to drink more in a flat the American had rented. The American's two adult nieces were asleep upstairs. As the American slipped into a drunken coma, Tom erupted in a drunken rage, punching the walls with his bare fists, and crying 'Where is he, where is he?' He then hit the American's wife, before running upstairs and searching the bedrooms. He found one of the girls, tore her T-shirt, wiped his blood on her back, and then ran downstairs, opening wardrobes and cupboards, still repeatedly crying 'Where is he?'

It took a dozen truncheon-wielding gardaí to subdue him. At the insistence of the American embassy, he was charged not with common assault, but with sexual assault, though of course there was no specific sexual content to his actions. It transpired that Tom had been raped nightly from the age of seven to the age of twelve by his American uncle. His aunt told the court that his history became known only after he had erupted in a comparable rage in her presence. He was sentenced to six years' jail, with all but eight months suspended, and was placed on the sex offenders' list.

After I wrote a sympathetic column about this unfortunate, a colleague, Kathy Sheridan, penned a column in which she actually congratulated the judge for imprisoning the man, and regretted that the sentence wasn't longer. I duly replied, asking what male journalist would even dream of congratulating a judge for imprisoning a woman who had been buggered throughout her childhood? She then returned to the fray, wondering precisely just who were the vengeful, politically correct females that were so often the butt of my eloquence.

I checked back. I found that over the previous three months, I had not written a *single* criticism of the women's movement. However, I had written two columns on related issues. One, following an analysis of fatal car crashes, had proposed more stringent driving tests for young men. The other, after another analysis of court cases concerning violence, concluded: 'What a harvest of human misery is contained in those few headlines, and all of it caused by men.'

Those words had been forgotten. The gamma rays of earlier words still burnt in the feminist memory. However, the most zealous ideologue of the new values was male. Fintan O'Toole's first attack on me was over a column of mine on the fallacy of 'equality'. He seemed to think that it was a reply to something he had written – which I had not even seen, for I had been enjoying the delights of Bosnia, where forty years of mandatory equality under Tito had proved such a splendid success. I had said in my column that Carl Lewis was not Mother Teresa, who was not Germaine Greer, who was not the comedian Brendan Grace. There was an intentional circularity to these comparisons, covering race, vocation and sex. However, O'Toole cited only the first two – the runner and the nun – as if they were the sole examples mentioned in my argument, sniffing that to compare the two was 'frankly inane'. He accused me of Social Darwinism, whatever that might be; perhaps he was referring to the concept of 'the survival of the fittest', a common undergraduate mistake, since the term was invented by Herbert Spencer, not by Darwin, who disliked its human implications, as I do. O'Toole concluded with a triumphant incoherence: 'just think of the implications for people with disabilities.'

Well, I suppose you can't lose an argument if you push a wheelchair into its bleeding heart. Nonetheless, O'Toole's crude attack on me proved an early example of how public criticism of me would henceforth be carried out.

One column from that time remains relevant today: it was my homage (and when did people pretentiously start saying '*ommahj*'?) to the sex-worker Belinda Pereira who was murdered in her Dublin flat. I noted then – as I do now – how little feminists cared for working 'prostitutes' (as opposed to former prostitutes who campaigned against the business). What does a woman's right to choose mean if the real choice is to be imposed by feminists and law-makers? Since then, between them, they have made the purchase of sexual favours illegal; that is, punish the man – or – a Swedish solution to an Irish problem. Any male journalist who dissents on this issue is vulnerable to implications that he consorts with prostitutes, as another journalist, June Levine, quite disgracefully hinted that I did.

I dislike saying what follows, because it might seem like I am courting the approval of those I despise, who would never give their approval anyway. But I detest prostitution. It is a violation of what sexual relations between men and women should be, for why would a man want to have sex with a woman who had nothing but contempt for him? Nonetheless, I see no reason to incorporate my feelings into law. The adherents of the new moral order have shown no such reticence, in their great pursuit of the goal of asymmetric equality.

In any mature, tolerant society, commentators differ, and then get on with life. At around this time, I wrote a review of a television programme in which we saw close-up footage of men being shot dead, and a Japanese soldier being burnt alive by a flamethrower. These were amongst the worst things ever shown on television, but in the course of the programme, a British soldier's use of the word 'cunt' was bleeped out, and when I criticised this editorial decision, the same word was deleted from my column. Man being fried alive, okay: a four-letter word meaning pudenda, censored! My criticisms of the underlying feminist agenda at work in television were then denounced as 'misogynistic bluster' by the Belfast journalist Fionola Meredith. This was about the only occasion over several decades when I was accused of anything relating to the m-word. Fionola was later to argue against the criminalisation of the clients of prostitutes, and in 2017 emailed me when the lynching was at its height 'as a small gesture of solidarity'. We subsequently had a champagne lunch, and I now think of her as a friend.

My repeated forays into road-death statistics provided evidence of the profound biological differences between men and women, yet feminists were determined to ignore these simple raw experiments into animal conduct – but only when it suited them. So, for example, lighter insurance premiums for women drivers (which I agree with) were somehow acceptable to the new feminists, even though they are clearly sexist. As I said in another column: 'show me a farmer that thinks that cows are the same as bulls, and you're showing me his headstone.'

Our lawmakers certainly knew the difference between a bull and a cow when they passed the Sexual Offences Act 2006, a little masterpiece of asymmetric equality. This declared that if two underage teenagers had sex, the boy could be prosecuted and the girl *could not*. This implicit contradiction was another version of the Sacred Heart on the tricolour. Even Judge Mella Carroll – whom I had otherwise admired so much – later justified this asymmetry on the grounds that girls can get pregnant.

One group of women excluded from the new dispensation were nuns, one of whom, Nora Wall, had been convicted of rape. The lurid account of how she had held a girl's legs apart to enable her co-accused Pablo McCabe to force himself on her, was both fanciful and anatomically improbable. I denounced the verdict and the life sentences that she and Pablo were given, while so many feminists appeared to stay silent. They continued to do so even after it became public knowledge that the two women who had instigated the complaint had a record of making such false accusations, and, of course, they were not charged with perverting the course of justice. Nora Wall was freed, but poor Pablo McCabe was soon forgotten, and died relatively young, without any public contrition or state regret. In the Irish folklore of injustice, the Birmingham Six and the Guildford Four live on; like the Birmingham Twenty-One and the Guildford Five, Pablo McCabe is forgotten.

Professionally, my life had already moved in a new direction with the television quiz show *Challenging Times*, which, as the title suggests, was sponsored by the newspaper. Even though I had a first-rate producer, Aidan Maguire, a thoroughly professional and charming man, I largely disliked recorded television, which takes so much time and effort and then vanishes forever like light from the far side of a star. But for a decade or so, the programme gave me a certain imprecise celebrity with the occasional request for an autograph, but, rather more usually, an imprecise belief as to who I was, as in that excited whisper I overheard in a supermarket: 'There's Mike Myers!'

These were extraordinary times, as the rising tides of feminism, liberalism and libertarianism – different and often opposing forces – met the residual power of the old Catholic Ireland. This was exemplified by the undercover garda sting operation against Virgin Megastore in Dublin for selling condoms without a prescription, even while the AIDS virus continued to kill. Intrepid plain-clothes officers – who, with the IRA campaign continuing, *clearly* had nothing better to do – bought condoms over the counter, before crying 'Gottcha!' Virgin Megastore was duly fined £400 – around €5,000 today – and threatened with a £5,000 fine, plus an extra £250 daily levy every time it repeated the offence. On appeal, the fine was *increased* to £500.

A letter to *The Irish Times* speaks for itself: 'As a mother, if I had to choose, I would rather my sons died of AIDS, provided that they were aware of God's love for them and asked for His mercy confident of his forgiveness, rather than that they should live to a ripe old age and die of natural causes with hearts and minds centred on themselves and their own comfort. Young people need truth, not condoms.'

Possibly the letter writer lived to regret her words. Certainly, I sometimes wonder when reviewing my columns – *did I really write that?* I have often been moved by the emotions of one day to pen thoughts that would be entirely alien to me on another. It is a boring soul, or a very sanctimonious one, who is consistently consistent, though on one subject I have remained unwavering. Over the decades, I have written scores of columns about the horrors of the Third Reich, in part because so many people in Ireland for so long lacked any real grasp of their sheer magnitude. This ignorance was apparently an offshoot of the official state creed of neutralism, which – despite Ireland having at this point rejected de Valera's economic isolationism – had remained a powerful moral force within Irish political culture. Hence the reverence still accorded to the writer Francis Stuart, who in 1940 had raced to Berlin to throw in his lot with the Nazis. It pains me still that in 1999 *The Irish Times* had to pay him around £100,000 libel damages because of a column of mine that rightly accused him of anti-Semitism. Unfortunately, a line in a television documentary in which he is heard to say 'The Jew is the worm in the bud' was in fact a quote from a letter to him, something the programme-makers did not disclose. Even more painful was the later discovery of material in which his anti-Semitism was made plain and which would have prevented the settlement (this sorry affair is dealt with in the final chapter).

The legendary Christabel Bielenberg and her husband Peter often wrote to thank me for reminding people of the Holocaust, of which they were true witnesses, and I wrote this of her funeral:

Christabel Mary Harmsworth Bielenberg, the last great witness to Hitler Germany, paid her final visit to St Columba's Church in Tullow on Wednesday, and the Bielenberg tribe, tall as oak trees, gathered as a grove in the front pews to bid her farewell. Christabel was truly a daughter of Ireland's middle kingdom; the Ireland of Goldsmith and of Yeats, of Shackleton and of French, an Ireland that most of us recognise as being validly Irish as the Ireland of the Gael. She was herself an exemplar of the virtues of the Middle Kingdom, both martial and literary. There was always something of the general's wife about her, always a hint of a soldier-servant loitering just within earshot ... On her mother's side, she was connected with the three great Irish newspaper magnates, Lord Harmsworth, Lord Rothermere and Lord Northcliffe, people of enormous drive and single-minded ambition ... Such similar steel glittered in Christabel; it showed in her eyes, in the unbending and unflinching manner in which she faced adversity, but it was always tempered with a grave courtesy and a quite bewitching charm. For she was, above all else, utterly adorable. You could see this as her grove of oak trees, some no longer so young, were visibly grief-stricken ... though she had passed her 94th birthday last June, her hearing and her sight were gone and had for some while marking time before she went the way of her beloved Peter. So even though the call of death was due, and it was in its own way welcome, her passing has left a huge void in their lives; in that redoubtable Bielenberg woodland, there will always be a clearing where the noble oak of Christabel once stood.

Of her great book, *The Past is Myself,* I added: 'We needed, we need, that testament, as does Germany. In the darkest days in the history of the world, there were brave Germans who were prepared to risk all; as we now know, that risk they took and that all they gave. And not just that their country might be free, but that if it were to perish amongst the nations of the earth, at least it would not do so with complete dishonour.'

Whenever I visited them, their habits were unchanging. Each would sit on an easy chair alongside a little table bearing a nice stack of cigarette packets. They spent the day in a single-match cycle of chain-smoking, with each expiring cigarette lighting its successor as their guests did not just get secondary smoking, but primary, secondary, tertiary, quaternary, the lot, until the angle of the sun suggested that it was finally time to add some whiskey to the glorious, life-enhancing toxins of tobacco. Amid the blue spumes of burning Virginia, they would speak of their friends who had ended their days on Hitler's meat hooks, but they could hardly bring themselves to mention de Valera's condolences on the death of Hitler, uttered after he would have learnt of the death camps.

I'm proud to have had the approval of the Bielenbergs, survivors of the foulest regime in European history. Something in Europe perished in the fires, the death pits and the slave yards of the Final Solution – and not just millions of innocent lives, for a great existential curse has also been placed on European identities. After the ABCD of the Third Reich – Auschwitz, Belsen, Chelmno, Dachau – any attempt to associate the basic human quality of '*ethnos*' – which had been central to most organised societies since the Greek city states – came to be seen as a revival of Hitler's deadly alphabet. This was the Führer's last poisoned gift to Europe: a taboo on discussing the role of kinship and identity within society which might one day spell the death knell for an entire civilisation.

Twenty-Six

MEANWHILE, GRANIA had left me. She did us both a favour. She was to embark upon two successful careers, firstly as a mountaineer and secondly in international equestrian management. I was to settle with the woman I would later marry. Rachel Nolan had originally contacted me looking for publicity: a budding musician, she was seeking sponsorship to defray the £8,000 cost of her new bassoon. One thing led to another, and a few months later, Rachel moved in with me. She has asked me to keep references to her to a minimum, so this it. Three years later we married – by far the wisest and best decision of my life.

Other preoccupations remained. I felt that armed republicanism had deeply corrupted Ireland's moral fabric, with even the courts making degrading compromises to accommodate it. Two known English sex offenders, Shaw and Evans, had even come to Ireland from England in 1971 because they thought it was an easy place to rape and murder young women. So, although they were arrested on English extradition warrants, a court let them walk free, because if they were extradited, might not IRA terrorists suffer a similar fate? Soon after their release, the two men abducted, serially raped and then murdered two poor country girls – Elizabeth Plunkett and Mary Duffy – yet there was no outcry over their fate. Later, the Supreme Court would rule that republican terrorists who killed people with handguns in pursuit of the constitutional objective of a united Ireland could not be extradited. Such feebleness was not the monopoly of a Fianna Fáil culture; a Fine Gael-led coalition chose not to protest formally to the regime of that barking, bemedalled despot Gaddafi, over his supplying weapons to the IRA, lest it damage Ireland's commercial relations with Tripoli. The result: more Libyan arms to the IRA, resulting in hundreds of deaths.

Such corruption was also educational. Irish children were not taught that peaceful, constitutional means had brought Ireland the Land Acts, democratised local government, extended the franchise to include most adult men, and led to a huge government programme to build labourers' cottages, all culminating in the Home Rule Act. So one of my journalistic objectives was to correct that, but also to tell some of the darker, untold truths about 'republican' violence, such as the murders of ex-servicemen and Protestants between 1919 and 1923. My investigations were vitally helped by a young student at Trinity, Jane Leonard. She was working under the guidance of the splendid David Fitzpatrick, whom she later married, and who died while this book was being finished. Their huge contributions to these conjoined themes have been grievously overlooked. Naturally, this project earned me the implacable hostility of the republicans, their support groups on the left, and the perfectly loathsome, Pravda-like *Phoenix* magazine. This was a pro-Haughey satirical publication, itself a concept beyond all satire. Enmity from such detritus is of course a badge of honour.

I began a weekly series of profiles/interviews with unpraised but important figures in Irish life, especially women, such as the political ecumenist Barbara FitzGerald, the feminist and trade unionist Sylvia Meehan, the publisher Ann Reihill, the poet Nuala Ní Dhomhnaill, the equestrian Iris Kellett, the businesswoman Margaret Downes, the choral director Ite O'Donovan, the director of the National Library Pat Donlon and the German scholar Eda Sagarra. Yet, even though I was extraordinarily busy, for some now unanalysable reason, I agreed to return to Bosnia. At least this time I was able to prepare properly. I spoke to Bosnians, usefully, and to semi-pacifist support groups for Bosnia, uselessly. At one meeting, a speaker denounced Milošević and his 'henchpersons', and then apologised for the 'gender imbalance' of the all-male platform party.

'That's all right: I'm gay, so I count as an honorary woman,' one of his colleagues brayed. For these cool, right-on folk, the calamity of Bosnia was just another opportunity to display how much they *cared*. Pacifists too often give peace a bad name. Even the term 'henchpersons' goes to the nub of the matter, for it was not women doing these terrible deeds, but men. What were needed was men of a different kidney, the kind that pacifists usually despise – professional soldiers willing to kill and, if need be, die in order to save Bosnia. Such a man was Commandant Mick Beary, former town major (or military administrator) of Srebrenica, whom I interviewed as part of my brief. Off the record, he told me he was sure that without a major intervention by American-led NATO forces against Serbia, Bosnia generally, and Srebrenica in particular, were heading for genocidal calamity. Indeed, I had said as much after the deputy prime minister of Bosnia and Herzegovina, Hakija Turajlić, was shot and murdered in a UN vehicle at point-blank range by a Serb soldier in 1993, though the victim was under the 'protection' of French troops, who did not even return fire. The only option now, I had said, long before the Srebrenica massacre, was to close down Belgrade as a trading entity by aerial bombardment.

This was a long way from happening (and when it did, it was the Americans, not Europeans, who chose to act) when I took my first trip to the Krajina/Knin front in southern Croatia. Here an ancient lodgement of Serbs, strategically planted by the Habsburgs as a barrier to Ottoman encroachment, remained in an otherwise overwhelmingly Croat region. These Orthodox Christians retained the warrior ethos of a frontier people, which, together with the dark mysteries of *ethnos*, had made the vernacular of ritualised atrocities common parlance; hence the 'Serbian necktie', created by cutting a man's throat just below his chin, and pulling out the tongue over the top of his sternum – *posthumously*, if he was lucky; if not, not.

In Zagreb, I found a translator, a chirpy young woman called Vesna. She introduced me to her friends, whose own stories demolished the simple myths of the region. One had two uncles, twin brothers, who were separately forcibly conscripted into rival militias during the Second World War, one into the communist partisans, the other into the fascist Ustaše, though these labels meant nothing to either man. One was later hailed as a hero of the communist revolution, the other was executed as a traitor. As usual, contingency remained the lord of all.

One afternoon, Vesna and I set out for Zadar. She warned me that since night attacks on roads by Chetniks – as the Croats then called all Serbs – were frequent, we must be in Zadar by dusk. However, we were delayed at a security checkpoint outside Zagreb, and evening was fading as we headed south towards the stomach-churning sound of artillery. By nightfall, we were already deep into Chetnik country, a single car driving through a black night, with no other vehicles on this post-apocalyptic road, towards the boom of cannon rolling down from the hills. Should we go back? It was really up to Vesna.

'We go on,' she said decisively. 'Knin is so close.'

Soon the guns stopped, and the dreadful silence that followed on this lightless, carless road was far more frightening than the sound of artillery. At length, we saw lights flickering within the wooded hills above us.

'Chetniks,' she whispered. 'Keep going, please.'

I obeyed. She looked back.

'Fuck. They've just blocked the road behind us.'

Then lights ahead, waving at us.

'Jesus,' I muttered, 'what do I do?'

'Bluff,' she said. 'If we turn around, it'll look as if we're escaping, and we are in trouble. You are you. I am your girlfriend. We met in a hotel. If they start to rape me, you must leave me, run.'

'Run where?'

'If they rape me, believe me, they'll give you the necktie.'

The torchlight ahead danced hither and thither, in glow-worm slow-down gestures.

'God help us,' whispered Vesna.

I turned off my headlights, leaving just my sidelights on, and slowed down, gradually, authoritatively. The Canadian rose from his grave and spoke: *Always make it look as if you have the right to be there, and the other fellow is the intruder.* I lowered my window.

A masked man stood at my car door, AK in hand.

'Dobar dan,' I said, casually.

A torrent of Serbo-Croat followed. He too had mistaken me for a local. Vesna spoke up, apparently telling the Chetnik that I was an Irish idiot who couldn't be trusted to take a drive to Knin without night falling. He took my passport and Vesna's ID and went away. He and his colleagues had a brief chat.

He came back, passed us our documents, and spoke to Vesna, then waved us on.

'Lucky,' she said. 'A good Chetnik.'

'What did he say?'

'That I am a young fool to be out with an even bigger fool like you, that's all.'

'Are you okay?'

'Of course. I've just shit myself, but otherwise fine.'

We sat in a café outside Knin. A fierce two-way artillery barrage was underway in the nearby hills, yet the café lights remained on. The few customers swapped stories about recent Chetnik depredations, and forty years before, and eighty years before, and one hundred years before, a seamless, timeless garment in which ancient history and yesterday's events become one. I could have been in the Fews of south Armagh.

'You are unusual for a foreign journalist,' said Vesna. 'You seem to understand us.'

'No, it's not that I understand you. But I do understand why I don't understand.'

'That's very good. You should write that.'

I didn't then. I do now.

The next morning, she took me to the ruins of the great Maslenica Bridge that had linked the tail of southern Croatia with the body of the tadpole that is the rest of the country. When the bridge had been destroyed two years earlier, the Chetniks had massacred scores of Croats. Now, two elderly Americans were studying the landscape. They told me, rather implausibly, that they worked for a magazine specialising in military uniforms. This was so obviously a cover story that Vesna and I kept our distance thereafter. I looked at the terrain where the Chetniks were holed up: rugged defiles, broken mountains, thorn clinging to steep hillsides – just like Gallipoli.

'Your Army will never drive the Serbs out of there,' I said.

'Not if those old idiots are our allies,' she agreed.

(Three years later, the Croat invaders – presumably with the assistance of those old idiots – took Krajina and expelled the Serbs from lands they had inhabited for 500 years. I was wrong, yet again.)

'We are not like Serbs,' said Vesna on the journey back to Zagreb. 'We lie. Croats lie. Serbs are crude, self-pitying loudmouths, but they speak the truth. We lie. Never believe what a Croat says.'

'That include you?'

'It was me I was talking about.'

She smiled wryly, which meant that it wasn't.

Twenty-Seven

I REALLY NEEDED to meet Serbs, meaning I had to fly firstly to Budapest and then travel by bus to Belgrade. Once there, I found a game, outgoing, and furious chain-smoker whose name was – improbably – Anne. She introduced me to some Serb friends. When I asked one young women about the allegations that Serbs had mass-raped Muslim women, she replied: 'They deserved it. Serbian men have strong libidos and Muslim men are not men at all. Little Arab penises. It'll do those Muslim whores good to know what it is to have a strong Serbian man between their thighs.'

'How can you possibly say they deserve to be raped?'

'Individually, maybe they don't. But as a people, considering what their ancestors did to us, they definitely do. When I hear about them being raped, I cheer.'

In my report, I didn't quote the lines about rape. Journalism is often about what you may not say, for I was sure that those words would be misinterpreted as if I was somehow endorsing what is a uniquely detestable crime. I had already expressed much disdain for doctrinal political feminism, and this – as we have seen – was returned with much personal vitriol, which I didn't feel like transubstantiating into *aqua regia*. Cowardice is the primary cement of consensus.

Anne and I entered Bosnia from the north, encountering checkpoints manned by the homicidal thugs of Arkan's Tigers and Šešelj's White Eagles. These had performed unspeakable atrocities that matched or even exceeded anything done by the SS, for the latter *generally* did not rape, whereas the Tigers and the Eagles exulted in sexual crime. Like the SS, both favoured black battle dress, but with masks, even on scorching midsummer days. We saw them at their roadblocks, arrogant and disdainful, and observed their handiwork along the northern Bosnian corridor: hundreds of burnt-out houses, their populations slain, violated and exiled. This was the unapologetic face of criminal, murderous fascism, which Europe had thought it had rid itself of in 1945. All the evils that men – not women – are capable of were distilled in these creatures. At checkpoints, Anne faithfully translated their conversations to me. At one, the masked paramilitaries openly discussed her.

'One said I was too ugly to fuck,' she said, as we drove away. 'His friend said if I asked nicely, he might do me up the ass, so he wouldn't have to look at my face.'

I said nothing.

'Serbs are animals. No one else speaks like that. Croats don't, Bosniaks don't. You Irish don't, do you, ever?'

We found a vile little hotel near Pale – not far from where the man with the broken arm had waved me away, and where I had seen the Thompson gunner with his two molls. I never had any doubt about the nature of this region: it was far worse than Belfast or Beirut, because it was all so casual, and open, and yes, *enjoyable* for the perpetrators. All the filth of different empires, religions and cultures had gathered in this juncture of Roman, Cyrillic and Arab alphabets, endlessly seeking a lowest common denominator, in vain, for the moral nadir that had been created by these abysmal fusions was bottomless.

Next morning, Anne told me that she had just heard of a recent massacre nearby, and we should check it out. That was fine. That was what I was there for, but, as in Beirut, I was determined not to be mistaken for a participant, so I put on a white shirt. At a checkpoint, upon Anne's enquiry, a policeman directed us towards a logging track into the hills. We took that, up through the rising woods, until we reached what resembled the film set for *The Sound of Music*, our car swishing through the long grass of bright green meadowlands, a pastoral paradise set on glorious mountainsides.

Finally, we come to some army Land Cruisers. We stop. Serb soldiers are deploying line abreast, with a tall blond machine-gunner holding the left flank, his weapon over his shoulder like a street sweeper's broom. An officer who initially gazed at me in evident disdain suddenly comes over and suggests that we join them.

We join their advance across these sun-kissed grasslands. Slowly I realise why I was invited to take part: my white shirt will probably draw the first sniper bullet. I have been sunbathing in Belgrade, so my tanned skin is now almost khaki. I remove my shirt, and walk on, hearing the steady clink-clink of the machine-gunner's ammunition belt.

Hovering skylarks are singing their giddy chorus; cuckoos are chanting on the hillsides. Butterflies rise in small waves before our feet. A thin wisp of smoke is coiling up from some distant buildings. We keep going, sensing in the pit of our stomachs that we are being watched. This is an instinct shaped in the Palaeolithic and husbanded in our genes for days like this. We don't hurry, we don't dawdle, but keep our line straight to make sure that a flank doesn't become exposed. The machine-gunner takes his belt-fed Šarac from his shoulder and carries it at port, across his body.

Pop pop pop.

Distant rifle fire. Who at? Don't know. A scan along our line. Nobody down. But the machine-gunner now cocks his Šarac, and having test-fired it *brrrrr* into the air, walks with it pointing towards the distant buildings. What follows is like an old Yugoslav film about the partisan war. The sun. The heat. The rifles. The thirst. The tense human silence amid the birdsong. It normally takes about fifteen minutes to walk a mile; multiply that by ten to get a sense of what Anne and I are feeling on that long, long trek through that abominable sunlit Elysium, until we reach the village of Povatek.

Anne learns the background story. Three Serb women have been murdered while the village was undefended. A Serb shepherd had gone missing a couple of days before. Presumably, before they killed him, his Muslim captors had discovered from him that the men of the village were fighting elsewhere, leaving easy killings for the Bosniaks. The attack is easy to analyse from the evidence in the houses. The killers – boys, I guess, though boyhood does not last long in this place – arrived at the front door, hammered on it, and when the woman wouldn't open it, sensing where she stood, perhaps knowing her and the house well – were they once regular guests here? – they shot her through the door. The first splattering of her abdominal blood is across the hallway, with smears of skin and tissue on the wall and the floor. See – she turns and runs along the hall, leaving her wide bloodied toe prints – she is barefoot on this, the last day of her life. She runs up the stairs to the safety of her bedroom. Look, foot by bloody footprint, with their splayed fat toes, trailing volumes of bright-red, newly oxygenated blood fresh from her heart, gushing from the open wound in her stomach. She opens the sanctuary of her bedroom door, but another attacker is already there, standing on the balcony, perhaps smiling at her, having climbed up while his colleague was hammering on the front door. He opens fire and rips her apart with his 7.62 rounds, the cartridge cases of which are now scattered across the floor. Blood everywhere. I mean everywhere: the floor, the ceiling, the walls, the bedclothes. Does he rape her amid her still warm corpuscles in these, the final seconds of her life? Does it matter that in these last atrocious moments she has been so deeply violated?

Yes. Yes, it does. The act that she had so often done for pleasure and love is the final hate-filled violation of her life, of her bodily integrity, and now she is gone.

What a species we men so often are.

The three dead bodies are lying alongside one another outside the church, the wrinkled skin of their naked feet washed and as bloodless as drained veal, yet their gnarled toenails remain yellow and uncleanable, like very old ivory. Few things are so pathetically moving and so thoroughly dead as the feet of a corpse. Two of the women, Linka Milanka and Mira, are middle-aged. Linka's mother-in-law Zorka is eighty-five. She was all of six when the archduke's car stalled just outside Moritz Schiller's delicatessen, and the twentieth century began.

The villagers come and share their story with us, muttering about the 'Turks', which is how they refer to Bosniaks. A Bosnian-Serb soldier listens to the litany, and then murmurs to a colleague: 'Is this any worse than what we have done?'

227

His friend emits a small, knowing laugh. Anne whispers the translation. Overhead, the larks sing their lyrical hymns.

In due course, the bodies – in this celestial heat already smelling like discarded offal – are buried in the cemetery, with a *clump clump clump* as the Bosnian soil is shovelled onto the Bosnian wood of their rude coffins, and birdsong antiphons are rained down from above. Anne and I are invited to join in the funeral supper: boiled mutton, potatoes and sweetmeats, followed by slivovitz. We learn that, in revenge, a nearby Muslim village has already been destroyed and everyone in it killed. However, it is too dangerous to go there, because there are other Muslims in the hills nearby: wild, armed and vengeful.

Quite so: that *pop pop pop* on our journey to this Nirvana.

And now the people of Povatek sit in the shade and drink coffee and slivovitz and dreamily talk. A policeman on secondment from Serbia says that these are not true Serbs, but Bosnians. They are like the animals of these mountains, the lynx, the bears, the wolves, he says; they are at one with death. They take it for granted.

As we leave, we come across Luvić, Zorka's son, Linka's husband, who returned to his village to find that his wife and his mother had been hunted down and murdered in their home. Now his cow has gone missing, an almost comparable tragedy, and so he is looking for it. He waves cheerfully as we drive away, and actually smiles at us in farewell.

Life and death in Bosnia.

We drive through those film sets from *The Sound of Music* again, only now we know that Julie Andrews' part is being played by Myra Hindley, until we get to a burnt-out village far from the front line. It is deserted. I type up my story sitting on a veranda, and get Anne to read it for any mistakes.

'This is good,' she says. 'You seem to understand us.'

I don't repeat the line I gave Vesna, for I understand nothing. I am sick with grief and anger. She and I wander through the ruined houses, looking for a phone. She finds what look like a phone socket. I connect it to my computer, which crackles! Incredibly, it is live. I cannot phone anyone, but I can file my story directly into the *Irish Times* computer, and I do so, immensely proud of myself.

That evening the foreign desk doesn't bother looking at their computer in-tray, so the story isn't used. I learn about this the next day and make a furious phone call to the editor's office. The despatch is used the following day, but someone in Dublin inexcusably – but in a way predictably – changes 'Turks' to 'chetniks', which is of course the slang for Serbs, and which is rather like confusing the IRA with the SAS. This makes nonsense of the whole thing, and yet manages to make unintentional sense. This is the Balkans. The forces here cannot be captured by mere words. And *The Irish Times* is *The Irish Times*.

The next day, I returned to Sarajevo – this time, the Serb-occupied parts. Unexpectedly, it was nearly as dangerous as the Bosnian sector, sniper bullets pinging everywhere. The soldiers talked the usual deranged stuff about 'the other side' – that is, what animals they were; they must surely have different genes. The woman doctor on the bus to Split had been a mere foretaste of an entire smorgasbord of non-racial racist stupidity.

Civil war is, of course, the original war, the foundation deed of all that followed, as Cain killed Abel, and Slobodan killed Alija, and, between 1941 and 1945, Tito killed almost everyone. The arithmetic that he was prepared to accept defies all morality: the Germans promised to murder one hundred civilians for every German soldier killed. The 'Chetnik' (then meaning just the royalist resistance) baulked at such a contract, but Tito revelled in it. He knew that in the longer term, such an exchange rate, with the ferocious Balkan mentality towards life and death, favoured him. Was he wrong? Consider, Luvić, looking for his cow, smiling, waving farewell.

I drove with Anne to an artillery position overlooking the Bosniak part of the city. We found a group of men eating around a mound of soil. The stench was perfectly vile. It slid into my nostrils and filled my sinuses like cholera diarrhoea in a sewer. I looked down. Huge flies, black and glossy, were emerging slowly from the soil, their strong, spade-like front legs pushing aside the surface loam.

'What are they?' I asked, fearing the truth.

'They're gravedigger flies,' declared the resident lieutenant-colonel. 'They're following the smell. They're looking for the bodies of the Turks we killed last week.'

I paused. 'They're here?'

He proudly, almost proprietorially, tapped his foot on the ground. 'Of course.'

'And you're eating over their graves?'

'It's the best spot. Safe to dig and safe to sit.'

It had been a night attack. Thirty Bosniak soldiers had come up the slopes on a blind Serbian flank. They got as far as the first picket, but they were already exhausted; they had climbed the almost vertical slope far too quickly. One of them made a noise, and the Serb defenders were able to put down defilading fire before they got any farther.

'Many prisoners?'

'Some, initially' – a boys-will-be-boys smile – 'but now, none. They're all here.' He again tapped the mound with his foot, as fresh fat black flies waddled away from the soil, their ascent up this particular slope meeting with much approval.

The colonel took us to the edge of the ridge. Down below, well beyond the range of any defending sniper, Sarajevo lay before us: prostrate, helpless, a human sacrifice upon a Balkan altar.

'You see there?' he pointed to a P & T sign outside a house with a green roof. 'My sister lives there. The traitor. One day she will get her just deserts. The angle is very difficult to get a clean shot at it. Maybe one day we'll be lucky.'

An affable man, happy in his work, we left him to his business, his sister and his fat and contented flies.

'Why are they eating right on top of the bodies?' I later asked Anne. 'It can't simply be that it's safer here.'

'This is Bosnia.'

Forget it, Jake. It's Chinatown.

When we were returning north, we got stuck in a long and immobile line of traffic. Ten minutes went by. Twenty. Nothing moved. The last thing I wanted was to be benighted in Bosnia *again*.

'What is it?' I asked Anne.

'A railway crossing. It'll be clear soon.'

'"Soon" has come and gone,' I said, getting out.

'Do not cause trouble.'

'I'm not causing trouble. I just want to see what the fuck is going on.'

'Don't,' she whispered, scuttling after me.

I got to the gates and looked down the track. One hundred metres away, the stationmaster was talking to the engine driver beside the train.

'Anne, please, follow me.'

'No, Kevin, they are government officials. Please don't.'

But I stalked up to the two men. They were uniformed, and in what was still a communist Serb culture, the uniformed will has its uniformed way.

'Would you translate, please?' I said to Anne.

'No.'

I turned to the men, pointing at the crossing.

'Open those fucking gates *immediately*.'

The stationmaster wordlessly went into his office, and a moment later the gates opened. I walked back towards the traffic jam, and was greeted by applause from drivers who, despite the open gates, had waited for my return. I wondered aloud to Anne that maybe these Bosnian Serbs were actually more like murderous sheep than wolves.

'Maybe. But they might have lynched you if the stationmaster had turned on you. Is that what sheep do?'

'Bosnian sheep, possibly.'

Once again, we drove through the Bosnian night, the bark of artillery following us for many miles in the dark. But this time I was heading in a sensible direction, away from the shooting, to a hotel room, an airport, home and safety.

Twenty-Eight

BEFORE MY FINAL TRIP to Bosnia, I interviewed many Bosnians in Ireland. Always charming, and desperately pleased, they gave me letters and money to pass on to families in Sarajevo. I bought maps, and the newspaper gave me a brand-new laptop. I went to Belfast, to be fitted with body armour and a steel helmet, which was, finally, standard equipment for journalists covering the war.

In the UN press centre at Split, I happened to befriend an ABC cameraman, Tim Brabourne. He was a hardened soldier – a veteran of Rhodesian Light Infantry – of the Zimbabwe war, and, as I was to discover, a very useful chap to be near in a scrap. Our Hercules from Split landed at Sarajevo airport while a ceasefire was supposedly taking place. However, the pilot told us that a sniper had just shot dead a UN soldier – a Ukrainian sunbathing on the airport roof – and that we were to leave the plane quickly. One by one, we lumbered across the tarmac like deep-sea divers on the ocean bed trying to escape a shark, our body armour flapping uselessly.

We were driven to the Holiday Inn in a UN Armoured Personnel Carrier, while the merry rattle of machine-gun fire outside reminded us of why we were there. I went to reception and heard someone call my name. I turned. It was Paul Douglas. Of course, I would have recognised him immediately – the only black man in the hotel – but I was touched and flattered that he instantly remembered me from a year before.

He spoke to the receptionist. 'This is my friend Kevin Myers. Would you do me a favour? Would you give him a room without a dead body on the floor above?'

The receptionist, smiling, turned to me.

'Certainly, Mr Myers,' she said chirpily. 'Would you like one in your bath instead?'

Of course, that's all there ever would be in Sarajevo – certainly no water. Once in my room, I opened my bag, looking for the vital letters and money for distribution in Sarajevo. They weren't there. Nor were any of the maps. Then, in my mind's eye, I travelled back to my bedroom at home where I had packed. I had put all the things I needed for the journey into a shoulder bag, leaving the letters and the money until last. But then I had left them there. Just as I had fucked up my last journey to Beirut, I had fucked up this journey to Sarajevo. My subconscious was doing its best to sabotage this trip. When I tried to file my first report, my laptop declined to transmit. Someone in the hotel with more technological knowledge than I had tested it: my laptop had no internal modem. And then I remembered that *The Irish Times* had bought two visually identical kinds of laptop, some with an internal modem, the rest with an external modem that was attached to the connecting flex. I had got one of the external-modem variety, but with the wrong kind of flex and so with no modem attached. It was idiocy of a high degree for any organisation to buy two different kinds of visually indistinguishable laptops, but it was even greater lunacy for me not to have checked carefully before going into a war zone.

I had to throw myself on the communicative skills of two resident correspondents, Kurt Schork of UPI and John Burns of *The New York Times*, both of whom were intellectually, morally and psychologically equipped to cover this war. Kurt was taciturn, aloof, preoccupied; a latecomer to journalism, he had the peculiar reticence that such men often had – perhaps an inner belief that he wasn't the real thing. But he was the real thing: a gallant journalist and a stalwart colleague. John Burns was an altogether more gregarious man, easy-going, affable, erudite in half-a-dozen languages, including Mandarin and Russian. His speech was peppered with long sentences that clearly knew where they were going from the very first word, and always ended up at their intended destination, like a Japanese train drawing up precisely alongside its station markings. His mastery of the details of Bosnia was almost complete; he assured me that as bad as things were in Sarajevo, Srebrenica promised to be much worse, and he was proved hideously right. John had survived cancer and looked on his post-lymphoma life as a kind of rebirth. His single vanity was his hair, which he cultivated upwards in vast abundance, as do many vigorously unbald middle-aged men.

My strategy of bewitching locals into a professionally rewarding friendship with gifts and letters from abroad was now useless. All I could do was get their addresses from Rachel over the UPI phone, for which there was often a two-hour wait. Then I would make my way on foot through sniper alley, where the ceasefire had never taken hold, darting from cover to cover like a deranged and unarmed infantryman, in order to find their houses and so give them some of my own money, plus apologies for the forgotten letters. The cash helped; but the absent letters broke their hearts.

I got a translator and guide, a student named Elma Abadžić. Her father was an officer in the Bosnian Army. I also attached myself to Tim Brabourne: 6 foot 4 inches, always in short shorts, with legs that went on for ever; in other words, the sort of man a sniper would invariably choose over little me. The lessons from that white shirt on that long walk to Povatek were not wholly in vain.

Better still, Tim had a soldier's eyes for action.

One afternoon, on a hillside on the outskirts of the city, to which we have driven in his network's armoured vehicle, we watch as a concealed Serbian mortar crew play havoc with downtown Sarajevo. They are invisible to their targets, as they methodically drop their bombs. Tim locates their spotter, a couple of hundred yards away, radioing in the fall of their mortar shells.

'Oh, for a Mark Four Lee-Enfield with a sniper scope,' he whispers savagely as we watch these men about their systematic business of murder. Mortars into the tube: one, *thud* as the percussion spike detonates the propellant in the base of the bomb, which leaves the mortar moments before the next bomb is dropped, *thud*, then a third, *thud*, as our eyes follow the line of the first bomb in its upwards arc over the city, then it falls towards earth, followed by its two siblings – three tiny specks. They hit the target, puffs of smoke as they explode, and a second later we hear the *BOOM BOOM BOOM*.

The spotter radios corrections. The mortar man adjusts the angle of his tube. More bombs are lobbed at the distant target.

'Enough,' says Tim, turning off his camera. He is ashen with anger as we head towards his vehicle.

We never heard the outcome of those attacks. Too many people had been killed that afternoon to know how and where they died. But after night had fallen, the dead were buried in Koševo, at the Lion cemetery. I ask Elma to escort me there and she agrees to take me the next Saturday afternoon.

We walk, skirting junctions marked *Pazi, Snajper* (Beware, sniper) as I muse – *What an evil journey the snipe, that innocent little wader, has taken in translation, from its blameless moors and lakes, firstly to honour those who slaughter it, and next to grace those who practise those recondite skills on their fellow human beings, who are as unarmed as the little bird itself, so neatly completing this charming cycle.* It is clearly a safe day, for we stroll openly through the grand entrance, guarded by the leonine eponyms. Single, empty graves have been dug here and there around the cemetery, presumably awaiting the next bodily harvest. Elma walks among the mounds of earth above the recently buried bodies and pauses. 'This is the grave of a 13-year-old girl who was killed by a sniper down by the river. And here,' she gestures at the next mound, 'is the communal grave of her family, who were caught in a mortar blast while they were burying her. The Chetnik mortar crew saw the freshly dug grave and so knew exactly where the girl was to be buried. They had their mortars already zeroed in when the family gathered. No ranging rounds. They got them all. Now graves are dug in different parts, so the Chetniks never know where the next funeral is to be.'

'But the dead are always buried in ready-dug graves?'

'Generally speaking. But when the gravedigger's daughter was shot, he dug a fresh grave for her. It was only decent.'

A question rises in my mind that I should have asked earlier.

'If the Serbs were able to snipe and mortar people right here before, what's to stop them doing it to us now?'

'Nothing. You just said you wanted to come here, so here we are.'

'Isn't this a little dangerous?'

'Of course it is. Life in Sarajevo always is. It's a matter of chance. Inshallah.'

She speaks the Arabic word for *the will of Allah* almost by rote; she is not religious, nor are any of the Muslim women I have met in Sarajevo.

'Can we go now?' I ask, the chilling liquids of apprehension bubbling through my lower abdomen.

'Of course, but slowly. People who hurry attract attention. They're probably looking at us now, wondering whether or not to shoot us.'

I look at her. She is serious.

We saunter out of the cemetery, my spine tingling in terror. We leave behind us all those unfilled graves with their welcoming, red-clay smiles. I return to the hotel to tap out my copy.

'Most of Koševic's dead come here singly, killed by snipers even yet in this city, in this ceasefire … Eighteen months of this moral filth, and weariness is the sniper's friend: why take the long way round when that inviting short cut awaits, where nobody has been shot in ages? But the spider on its web can sit stationary for a year, awaiting its prey: the snipers of Sarajevo are made of similar mettle. Five dead on Friday, six on Thursday, eight on Wednesday, six on Tuesday, seven on Monday.'

I file the story from John Burns' room, my day and duty done. That evening, shortly before nightfall, a half-dozen Bosnian woodcutters creep through the cemetery to the trees beyond to collect fuel, as they have secretly been doing on recent evenings. But they had been spotted the night before, and this time the Serbs are waiting. As the woodcutters approach – unarmed, of course, because they must carry back all that they fell – they are ambushed and methodically cut to pieces. There is a reason why the Serbs did not kill Elma and me; they had a far more profitable target in mind. Why, they even got the bonus of the woodcutter's axes.

Of all the many crimes committed by the Serb besiegers of Sarajevo, the deed that constituted a formal application for membership of the genocide club was the destruction of the capital's library. Of the

2.5 million documents there, just 900 were saved, and Elma had been one of the few to brave the flames to help retrieve them. Lost in the holocaust were 5,000 handwritten books that predated the printing press, plus the first great census of Bosnia, which, like the census of 1842 in Ireland, had gathered too much information for existing methods of processing to cope with.

What do motives mean when deeds of such cultural vandalism are deliberately perpetrated? And maybe that is where absolutes come together and warm their hands before the comforting bonfire of insanities. In Ireland, the destruction of our national records in 1922 was wrought by 'patriots' who felt they had no need of yesterday because they were building a new tomorrow; and for Bosnian Serbs, including two professors from Sarajevo University, by destroying the title deeds of Islamic Bosnia, they were invalidating Bosnia's right to exist.

However, Sarajevo's museum had not been destroyed, and the curator met me in her damp, electricity-free office. The air was full of the fragrance of decay, as – rather less ruthlessly than the Serbs, though of course time was on their side – armies of bacteria and yeasts devoured the pages of the ancient volumes around her. 'At least the museum library is intact,' she said, gesturing. 'We can use that to show that Bosnia is not just for Muslims but for Croats, Serbs and Jews also.'

The curator had no batteries at home, and thus no radio, and so did not know that the last of Sarajevo's Jews had left the day before. Serbian fascists had turned the city into a *Judenfrei* zone – something not even the Nazis had managed. However, the much-publicised arrival of the photographer Susan Sontag added a certain burlesque element to the siege. Safe as she was from snipers wherever she went, she did not walk before the many cameras that followed her, but visibly *stepped*, as celebrities are wont to do. Although not a theatre director, she would be directing *Waiting for Godot*, and for the besieged people of the city she was a Name, with the city authorities being pitifully anxious to generate as much propaganda as possible. To most of the media, she was just a self-regarding wanker.

I arrived deliberately late for the production, so I could be near the little hall's exit – a lifelong precaution whenever attending am-dram – but

I was instantly pushed not merely to the very front, but up onto the stage. Latecomers in a siege city do not get the benefits of their unpunctuality. We soon learnt that all five roles in *Godot* were to be played by three different actors, each speaking exactly the same lines one after the other, thereby replicating the fiction that the peoples of the region have three languages. However, this production was not just three times longer than usual, for under Sontag's direction it entered another space-time dimension of sublimely vacuous pretentiousness. Much of the first act focuses on Vladimir's need to urinate: and all three Vladimirs – the Croat one, the Bosniak one, the Serbian one – finally depart for that purpose, so leaving a fourth full bladder on the stage, mine, simmering with ferocious hydraulic purpose. Moreover, sitting cross-legged on the bare boards had disconnected the blood supply to my feet, where cramps were being succeeded by gas gangrene. My testicles weren't exactly ecstatic either.

When not dwelling on the three fictive languages of Bosnia, at archaeological length, Sontag's production was heavy on the use of meaningful silences. Not just one shared ecumenical silence, rather like Catholic, Anglican and Orthodox priests at the moment of a shared consecration, but each language representative was allocated his very own chunk of solemn, purposeful speechlessness, during which the only sound that could be heard throughout the hall was that of Atlantic breakers crashing against the seawalls of my bladder. I think my bowels also had an opinion on theatrical matters, but we'll skip that for the moment.

The point about *Godot* is that there is no point: life is a puzzle, a riddle to which there is no answer. But under Sontag's infirm and laborious guidance, the plight of Lucky, the slave, became a metaphor for Bosnia as subtle as open-heart surgery with a pickaxe, while the greater play was a dramatic representation of Sarajevo's trials and tribulations. And if Sontag wanted to convey the discomfort, the boredom, the hunger, the dirt, the encrusted anal filth and the crushing sameness of life in a besieged city without heat or water or toilet paper, for month after tedious month, all compressed into a couple of hours of the direst tedium known in the history of stage, she succeeded triumphantly.

The military reality beyond that *opéra bouffe* was that the Serbs were using that 'ceasefire' to conduct a scorched earth policy. Just as the purpose of the destruction of Sarajevo's library had been to exterminate Bosnia's past, so the Serbs' comparable annihilation by arson that week of the $100 million Olympic complex on Mount Igman was a comparable curse on its future. On Igman, Tim Brabourne and I encountered Serb forces whose commissariats were stocked with tinned foods marked 'UN'. The besiegers of a starving city were being re-provisioned by the United Nations. It was on these slopes that my loathing of the pomposities and vacuities of the EU began. Mick Beary was right: only the US had the muscle and will to end the catastrophic plight of Bosnia's Muslims, meaning that the siege of Sarajevo would last much longer.

Tim had heard about a girl named Zlata Filipović who had been writing a siege diary, and we drove to see her. Through the front door came the sound of a piano being played with elegant perfection – by a parent, I assumed. No, it was Zlata, aged twelve: a remarkable girl, perfectly composed, with almost flawless English. She recited the absurd cost of food in the city: one egg was five deutschmarks – probably about €20 in today's money, and a packet of coffee 120 deutschmarks. Her parents were as delightful as she was. This was a sophisticated, modern, open-minded, twentieth-century, European Muslim family, under siege from the Middle Ages.

After interviewing Zlata, I asked Tim if we could cross the Serb lines to buy food for the family. Tim sighed. Tim *always* sighed when he was about to accede to anyone's requests to do something really, really stupid. He drove me in his armoured vehicle via the backroads winding round the outskirts of the airport, through two Serb checkpoints, and into that parallel Bosnia where food was plentiful and eventide woodcutters were not casually slaughtered. I bought a dozen eggs there for the price of a mere *glimpse* of an egg in Bosniak Sarajevo. Sadly, no coffee was available. The journey back was largely uneventful; the occasional *ping ping ping* of snipers plying their trade. I gave the eggs to Zlata's mother at her front door, then left. I never saw the Filipović family again. They were smuggled out of Sarajevo that autumn, later settling in Dublin, and Zlata's diary became an international bestseller. For these memoirs, I downloaded it. Sure enough, for that week she writes about meeting and liking a journalist called Kevin. Touched by this modest sliver of global celebrity, I duly tracked her down.

She is now a successful filmmaker, but alas, she remembered neither me, nor any 'Kevin', and – most tragically of all – not even my eggs.

Many journalists who went to Bosnia endured infinitely worse times and saw scenes far more harrowing than I did. For the most part, we usually helped one another. John Burns and Kurt Schork were typical, while Paul Douglas was a universal source of kindness to all, resourceful, energetic and always smiling. My time for departure from Sarajevo was well overdue, and I told Dublin I was getting out. Paul Douglas came to reception to bid me farewell. We promised to stay in touch. I felt like kissing him. Instead, our hands just touched, our eyes met: friends for ever.

I consider my flight from Sarajevo to Split one of the most joyous events of my life. I was *alive*. I took a taxi to Strožanac, a small and pretty resort, where I bathed in the most beautiful sea God ever created. The warm, crystalline waters of the Adriatic cleansed my skin of the vile residues left on it by the muck and fear of Bosnia and my nostrils of the lingering aromas of rape, genocide and cultural holocaust. Later, at my hotel, I dined on the terrace overlooking the Adriatic, almost weeping with ecstasy and relief, as I drank my wine and ate my food, composed of what ingredients I cannot say, but all covered with the irresistibly delicious sauce of survival.

Nearby, a table for about fourteen had been laid, with bottles of wine down the centre, and a bottle of cognac or whisky at each place setting. The party finally arrived: French air force officers in high-octane good form. They waded into the drink as exuberantly as a party of psalm-singing, born-again Christians undergoing full-immersion baptisms. As I went to bed, I paused to toast them and France, and they did likewise to me and Ireland. Through the long night I heard them carousing. On other occasions, I would have objected, but not now. As I journeyed back and forth between sleep and wakefulness, the happy din of drunken Frenchmen deep in revelry repeatedly drew me smiling from my dreams. Shortly before dawn, I heard them end their carousing, and with bottles shattering and chairs falling over, they staggered off to bed. My alarm went, and I rose, went downstairs, trod carefully around the upended tables and broken glass on the terrace, then caught my pre-booked taxi to Split Airport for my flight to Zagreb.

I was sitting at the departure gate, when the crew for my plane to Zagreb tottered past me. They were my French air force companions from the terrace, baffled, weaving and whey-faced, with eyes like half-digested stoats peering grimly through a cat's arsehole, confusedly helping one another up the steps of their Transall.

By God, I swore, if I survived this flight, I was never going back to war.

I did, and I didn't.

People are often critical of journalists, of the low standards that govern our trade, of our indifference to truth, of the cynical use of 'facts' to sustain questionable arguments. Much of this is justified. But Bosnia saw journalism at its best, for we all knew the perils there, and each of us had privately said goodbye to life. Over 70,000 European Muslims were murdered while the EU/UN dithered, prevaricated and posed. They were butchered, hacked to death, raped and slaughtered in the greatest killing sprees since the Jewish genocide, and as then, the vast majority of the culprits got off scot-free.

But for me, all wars were over; I would never go into action again. There was, however, a personal toll in these matters. Here it is.

Paul Douglas was killed in action in Iraq. So too was Kurt Schork. Clark Todd was killed in Lebanon. John Hoagland was killed in El Salvador, wearing camouflage. David Blundy got one through the spine in El Salvador, as he'd always feared, but died before medics could rescue him for a life of paralysis and impotence and shit.

I honour their memory. Rest in peace, my comrades in war.

Twenty-Nine

WITH NORTHERN IRELAND once again briefly loitering in that pathologically inconstant organ, the London mind, Dominic Lawson, editor of the *Spectator*, rang and asked me to write a piece about the province. The subject was my choice. I went for the so-called 'disappeared', who had been abducted, murdered and secretly buried by the IRA. They had vanished twice over, for, at that point, they featured in no existing perception of the Troubles. My list of the disappeared – though incomplete – was the first of its kind to appear in a British publication. Moreover, I put the column in the context in which I am convinced that all accounts of the Troubles should be put: in the past. It is from that depraved hinterland that the IRA ethos takes its certainties, its culture and its precedents; and though Irish historians might at that point – though no longer – have studiously neglected the disappeared of 1920–23, such abductions, and the moral validation behind them, were part of the secret lore of the IRA. What they had done during their 'victorious' war of 1919–21 could surely be repeated by a later generation – for would not historical narratives both accept the teleological necessity for such deeds and the subsequent need to conceal them?

So I began my piece not in contemporary Northern Ireland, but in the troubles of the 1920s, which I had often visited in my *Irish Times* columns, with the abduction, probable torture, murder and secret burial of Captain Herbert Woods, Protestant and ex-soldier – winner of the Military Cross and the Military Medal – along with his two uncles, the

Hornibrook brothers in Cork. Not merely had these men vanished, they were mentioned in no history books of the time – a manifold abduction, whose dark gravitational pull must surely have influenced the orbit of paramilitary conduct thereafter. If such disappearances were possible in 1922, with no historians holding those responsible to account, would more of the same not be done subsequently, and be similarly ignored?

I believe that my *Spectator* piece helped to put the most recently disappeared into the agenda of the peace process. Over the years that followed, anger and disgust over the abductions of the 1970s – most spectacularly and wickedly the abduction of the widowed mother of ten, Jean McConville – became central to the machinery of historical redress. Unless the bodies of the dead were recovered, and their loved ones allowed to give them funerals, no settlement was morally possible. I think I helped to create that agenda.

I freely confess that the 'republican' spirit that animates so much Irish nationalism is not merely alien to me but incomprehensible. This was no doubt what motivated the Taoiseach Bertie Ahern to give state funerals to twelve men executed by the British in 1920/21 (though no state funerals have so far been given to the nearly eighty anti-Treaty men, such as poor Charles Healy, executed by the Free State government). Presumably, comparable motives were at work for the celebrations for the ninetieth anniversary of an IRA ambush in Clare in which six RIC men – four of them Irish – were surrounded by thirty-seven IRA men and slaughtered. Here is the official timetable.

1.00pm Remembrance Mass
in St Senan's Church, Kilkishen, celebrated by
Fr. Hugh O'Dowd and Fr. Harry Bohan
2.00pm Assembly at Glenwood Site.

2.15pm Welcome address
Unveiling of Memorial
Wreath-laying ceremony
Address by Minister Tony Killeen, TD
Military salute

3.00pm Blessing of Site

Fr Bohan's address

Beautiful Vale of Belvoir sung by J P Guinane

3.15pm Mock Ambush by K McCormack Re-Enactment Group

3.45pm Safe exit from Site

4.00pm Refreshments in Donnellan's pub Kilkishen

I cannot vouchsafe the accuracy with which the butchery of six men at point-blank range in the beautiful Vale of Belvoir by over three dozen ambushers was portrayed by the K. McCormack Re-Enactment Group, though no doubt it was done in the best possible taste. However, in a prudent departure from the historical record, the programme guaranteed a safe exit for all, followed by – no doubt delightful – refreshments in Donnellan's pub.

When Dominic Lawson moved on to the editorship of *The Sunday Telegraph*, he took me with him. I was able to speak to his readership not merely about the evils of the IRA (about which they needed little persuading), but also about some of the follies of British security policy – most especially the murderous latitude allowed to the Parachute Regiment, whose three battalions had been responsible for around 80 per cent of the deaths of innocent civilians shot by the British Army.

By this time, Rachel and I had sold our house in Dublin and had moved to County Kildare. The man who had so brilliantly conducted the auction, the estate agent, Paul Newman, rang me shortly after the move. He was thinking of moving to Ballymore Eustace, as I had done. Would I recommend it? Of course!

My new life gave me new horizons away from the metropolitan provincialism that characterises most capitals, and I was moved to write about the nearby Barretstown Castle Hole in the Wall holiday camp for sick children. Some weeks later, Rachel came in with a letter for me. I looked at the back of the envelope: it was from Paul Newman.

'Him again,' I sighed.

'No, not him,' she said. 'The other one.'

It was from *the* Paul Newman, congratulating me on my article about the Barretstown Camp, which he had founded. He said many people had written about his project for dangerously ill children before, but none had moved him so much as my column. We stayed in touch. Some months later, he took Rachel and me out for dinner. He proved to be a delightful and courteous companion.

Another man whom I had admired since I was in my twenties was the writer Patrick O'Brian. I had no idea that his Irishness was as much a work of art as his books; and though he had initially rebuffed my attempts to befriend him, in time he melted. Rachel and I once drove him to Cork to check on some geographical details, and in gratitude he named a character in one his novels after my uncle, Captain Kevin Teevan RAMC. Max Hastings invited Rachel and me over to a banquet in Patrick's honour in the Painted Hall at Greenwich, attended, it seemed, by half of MI6 and the US Naval Academy at Annapolis. However, what seemed like his hour of triumph rapidly proved to be his downfall. Celebrity soon prompted investigation, and it transpired that Patrick O'Brian was in fact Richard Russ, who in the 1940s had abandoned his Welsh wife with a handicapped daughter to run off with Mary Tolstoy.

'I feel like everyone is pointing at me and laughing,' he said the last time he stayed with us, shortly before his death. 'Fame is worth nothing if this is what it brings.'

Meanwhile, within *The Irish Times*, I had shifted the nature of 'An Irishman's Diary' from being a largely social column to a more varied and often more serious one, with no opposition from the newspaper's management. So I regularly expressed an unequivocal hostility towards the IRA, and Gerry Adams, whom I regard as a narcissistic egomaniac. I felt no more warmly about Martin McGuinness, whom I accused in one column of arranging the murder of his fellow Derryman Patsy Gillespie, who was blown up by a bomb he was forced to drive to a British Army checkpoint, also killing five soldiers. McGuinness had driven through the checkpoint earlier in the day, making a scene, which required the calling out of the guard, thus enabling him to count the number of soldiers there. The beauty of this stunt lay in McGuinness' official status: because of the peace process propitiations, he was on a no-arrest list, meaning he could brazenly plot mass murder with impunity.

The vehemence of my opposition to the IRA was acknowledged by the security forces, north and south. The British military attaché, Colonel

John Wilson, and his wife Val had become good friends of mine. I would regularly give talks to the Irish Army's Command and Staff course, and upon meeting me at the firing range in the Glen of Imaal, that very great soldier Major General Dermot Earley remarked: 'At last: a journalist I can trust.'

'There's no such thing, general,' I replied, not inaccurately. Soldiers, to my mind, live on a far higher moral plane than do civilians, and as for those poor wights, *journalists* …

Meanwhile, I had come to know the GOC Northern Ireland, General Alistair Irwin, who had first arrived in Derry on the very day that I had foolishly rescued a churlish Conor Cruise O'Brien. I gave a talk to Alistair's staff at his invitation, and later I was approached by a middle-ranking officer.

'Do you ever think you're in danger from the IRA, or some breakaway faction?' he asked.

'Sometimes. But what would they gain from killing me?'

'Possibly a lot. *Pour encourager les autres.* You do irritate them, you must know that, and no one else in the Republic seems to challenge them the way you do. Have you ever thought of getting a firearm?'

I had long known that I was a possible target, as the ex-IRA-man-turned-informer Seán O'Callaghan had once warned me. He broke his usual security procedures to let me know that his minders had told him that the IRA Army Council had twice discussed the advantages of killing me. They were apparently confident that the political requirements of the peace process would mean that there would be no irreversible consequences if they did.

However, getting a gun would mean *always* having it on me, never drinking, and rigorously rehearsing the skills that alone make the possession of a firearm useful. Very boring and very dangerous.

'Thought about it, yes, but decided, no,' I told the Army officer.

'Well, they mustn't take you alive. Here's a tip. The first man who takes hold of you, don't push him away, but pull him towards you. Then bite into his Adam's apple, hard, like a piece of steak, and then tear it out. This will incapacitate him, and the shock will probably paralyse his companions.'

246

'Really? And what the fuck will it do to me?'

'Keep you alive. Or get you killed on the spot – which is far better than being kidnapped, like poor old Tom Oliver.'

In 1991, that unfortunate Louth man had been taken alive by the IRA, beaten to a pulp and then finished off with a horse-vet's headshot. The people of his county subsequently expressed their passionate revulsion over that barbarity by electing the convicted IRA man Arthur Morgan as TD. This is the kind of thing that happens when governments do not draw clear boundaries between violence and peaceful means. Because of the deep moral equivocation and confusion engendered by the peace process, I was now completely against further propitiation of the IRA. Possibly this was why I was put beside a senior MI5 officer at a British Army dinner in Derry.

'I've read your stuff,' he said in an amused tone. 'All very righteous and moralising. You haven't got a clue what's going on, have you?'

He was right. In due course, the price of this endless appeasement would be paid by the two centrist political parties in the North, the SDLP and the Ulster Unionists, both of which went to their electoral doom. Meanwhile, the two groups that had caused a blood tide of woe – republican and loyalist fundamentalists – would, as I had predicted, scoop the political jackpot. There was a historic, constitutional price for this cosseting of extremes: twenty years later, in 2018, the DUP held the balance of power at Westminster, and was effectively able to decide the future of the United Kingdom, Ireland and the EU. Betray democrats systematically, as happened in Northern Ireland, and whoever remains will take a leaf from your play book, with general woe resulting.

Two killings in 1989 perturbed me most: these were the killings of the senior RUC officers Harry Breen and Bob Buchanan, who were murdered after leaving a meeting at Dundalk Garda Station. As they crossed the Border, they were flagged down at what looked like a British Army checkpoint, but was in fact an IRA ambush, set in 'dead ground', invisible from army watchtowers. Then, at point-blank range, they were ritually slaughtered. I was sure that this would have required garda collusion, and I began to make further enquiries. Very soon, I got a double confirmation that an IRA mole was working in Dundalk station, and had set them up.

I wrote a column revealing that the two RUC officers had been murdered with assistance from at least one rogue garda. There was, of course, instant denial by the garda authorities, but after the issue was taken up by unionists in the House of Commons, and later raised in the Dáil, Judge Peter Smithwick was appointed to conduct an enquiry. Two senior garda officers questioned me at my home, and the Chief Superintendent warned me that I was now in danger from the IRA.

'If you want to get a gun, and I think you should, I'll back your application.'

Gun ownership, as I've said, is tedious and even then your would-be killer *always* has the drop on you. Add to this the certainty that while I was trying to disentangle my pistol from my pants, my assassin would have turned my heart into a colander.

The Smithwick Tribunal spent several years gathering evidence, during which my assertions were condemned by senior garda officers, which put me in a very special position indeed: that of being condemned by both terrorists and the security forces. On the day the tribunal published its findings, rumours spread through Dublin that it had found against me. I was asked onto several radio and television programmes to defend myself, but I declined them all until I learnt what the judge's conclusions were. In fact, his report praised me and supported almost all my assertions about treachery in the station, whereupon, *quite amazingly*, the media lost all interest, and even excluded Smithwick's findings from the evening news bulletins. Indeed, to this day, Wikipedia makes no mention of me in its account of Smithwick, even though it was my allegations alone that had caused the enquiry to be formed.

Others did not forget. Having got two flat tyres on a trip to Belfast, Rachel and I were taken by an AA man to a depot near Forkhill in south Armagh. A customer there stared at me closely, then did a rapid assessment of the full shop, which included Rachel, the AA man, and some other strangers.

'You that Kevin Myers fellow?' he finally asked.

I looked at him. His eyes were as expressionless as those of a corpse, of which I guessed he had seen a few. Electrons in my spine began to form into icicles. This was serious.

'Who's asking?'

He searched my face with those lifeless pupils.

'A man who would have organised a reception committee for you if we'd known you were coming,' he purred in the strange tongue of the drumlins. 'Next time, I'll be prepared, and believe me, you won't be leaving in a hurry – if at all.'

I recognised him only later, when I saw his photograph in a file about the IRA's primary killers in south Armagh. He had been responsible for many murders, including those of Breen and Buchanan. Perhaps at this advanced stage in his killing career, his memory didn't recollect them all, but his inner eyes most certainly did.

Long before this, I had largely succeeded in my quest to honour the memory of the Irish of the Great War. Nonetheless, I had declined an invitation from Paddy Harte TD to join a working group to raise a memorial to the Irish who had fought at the Battle of Messines in 1917. As well as not being a committee man, I strongly disapproved of the presence of Glenn Barr, an unrepentant Protestant paramilitary leader and, like most of his ilk, a congenital thief. I warned Paddy that he would steal from the funds, and dear old Glenn, he didn't let me down, vanishing over the horizon, his back pocket weighed down with a hefty wad of Irish taxpayers' money. However, what I was most unhappy about was that the focus of the memorial should be a battle in which some 10,000 German soldiers had been killed by huge mines in its opening seconds – until Hiroshima, the greatest deliberate mass extinction of human life in history.

Though Paddy would often ring me seeking historical details about the war, one falsehood that I was unable to remove was that the Irish losses amounted to 49,400 dead. I had deconstructed this fictional figure in my first *Irish Times* article in 1980, but it nonetheless possessed an irreducible and almost Vedic quality. That aside, Paddy was a mover. The old workhouse in Mullingar, a protected building, was demolished so that its granite walls could be cannibalised to make the round-tower memorial at Messen (Messines), for a joint opening by President McAleese, Queen Elizabeth and King Albert II.

Thus, the great project which I had begun journalistically in November 1979 was, nineteen years later, resulting in a tangible outcome; although, through some no doubt unintended oversight, I was not invited to the ceremony. However, an Army friend, Colonel Tom Hodson, arranged for me and the rest of The Chaps to be present. Both the Defence Forces and the two Irish infantry battalions of the British Army, the Irish Guards and the Royal Irish Regiment, participated. The profoundly moving ceremony was broadcast live on RTÉ radio and television, with a variety of panel discussions, but happily, with expertise on this subject now apparently so widespread, RTÉ felt no need to invite me to participate in any of them.

Notwithstanding these little attacks of amnesia by the national broadcaster, the historian Keith Jeffery in the preface to his book *Ireland and the Great War* freely acknowledged the success of my campaign. 'Above all,' he wrote, 'we are indebted to Kevin Myers of *The Irish Times* who (almost single-handedly, it seems) created and sustained a lively public interest in Ireland's engagement in the Great War.'

The Taoiseach, Bertie Ahern, who was launching the book, agreed. 'Notwithstanding some inevitable disagreements with one of the country's foremost polemicists, I think it would be appropriate to join Keith Jeffery in paying tribute to Kevin Myers in creating and sustaining a lively public interest in Ireland's engagement with the Great War.' He then put down his script and repeated the words.

Now I have to confess at this point that, despite our many differences, I rather like Bertie, perhaps because we are both idiots. My claim to my title has already been staked in these pages, with more to come; his came from his spectacular achievement in being scuppered by the very tribunal that he had himself founded, the Mahon Tribunal. The self-sealing fate of HMS *Amphion* is not just emblematic of the Great War; is it also emblematic of life.

Thirty

SEPTEMBER 11, 2001, and at a purely journalistic level, I felt – and still feel – deeply for Conor O'Clery, at that point the newspaper's North America correspondent, who was present in New York for the attacks on the Twin Towers and witnessed close-up the falling, burning bodies. These are companions who will, I suspect, remain with him for ever. But at a global level, as I would write in *The Sunday Telegraph*, we had now entered a realm of chaos from which there was no exit. Any response would be counter-productive, while any inactivity would be as dynamic as any action. There was no neutral deed in this hall of inverted mirrors: inertia was kinetic, centripetal was centrifugal, defence was attack. Furthermore, with the meridians of oil and Islam intersecting – a melancholy coincidence to some, a divine confluence to others – the diabolical House of Saud had been able to funnel bottomless resources into their twin wars against the west – one, cultural subversion, the other, proxy-terrorism. We were now faced with an existential and cultural threat that would not disappear in the lifetimes of the grandchildren of a baby born that morning.

The Twin Towers attack finally ended the Bosnian epoch and inaugurated the Islamist one. I had wrongly thought, like so many people, that the confection of Yugoslavia was the primary long-term consequence of the Great War and had written a novel based on my experiences there. My publishers emphatically rejected my original title, *News at Last from Sarajevo*, so I settled for the makeshift *Banks of Green Willow*. I got a very good review in *The Irish Times*, but that Saturday the linking machinery connecting the literary supplement with the main body of the newspaper broke down, and so that edition was sold without it. I had done a successful interview with Ciara Dwyer of the *Sunday Independent*, who loved the book. That Saturday night, the linking machinery connecting the two parts of the newspaper similarly broke down, with comparable consequences. The novel soon vanished, rather like the mini-epoch to which it belonged.

Like most of my peers, I had long been a critic of Israel. But even before 9/11, I had begun to reassess the evidence. It became clear to me that it was not Israeli but Palestinian intransigence that was now prolonging the conflict, and the Second Intifada showed that I was right, for jihadism, even as a threat withheld, is incompatible with either civilisation or any putative treaty. Moreover, I felt that much anti-Israeli sentiment was lupine anti-Semitism in the dissembling fleece of anti-Zionism. I regard anti-Semitism as the foulest of all bigotries, simply because the Final Solution came so very close to accomplishment. Any equivocation on that issue is unacceptable. Indeed, my very first published article as a professional journalist was about the Mayor of Limerick, Stevie Coughlan, who – almost unbelievably – had reached back to 1903 to extol the anti-Semitism of that time. So I now combined a loathing of anti-Semitism with a philosophical support for the Jewish state, not least because logic told me then what it even more urgently repeats to me today: Israel is now Europe's front line.

In 2002, in the middle of the economic boom, *The Irish Times* ran into deep financial trouble, having been over-spending like a drunken sailor on shore-leave. The editor, Conor Brady, resigned and retired to enjoy €100,000 a year from the newspaper's coffers while waiting for his pension to arrive a dozen years on. Brady was replaced by Geraldine Kennedy, a brilliant political reporter whose extraordinary revelations about Haughey had so infuriated the Taoiseach that he ordered her phone to be tapped by the security forces – an action worthy of a central American mini-despot. She had been an old-fashioned shoe-leather journalist, and not usually given to philosophical abstractions, though like the men in the editor's chair before her, financially speaking she did not underestimate her importance. When news of her income, and the equal sum being paid to the managing director, Maeve Donovan, was leaked, a group of journalists asked me to sign a petition condemning their salaries. I flatly refused: 'If I didn't publicly condemn the level of pay being paid to their male predecessors, why should I condemn the similar income being given to women?'

Fintan O'Toole showed no such compunction and soon became the visible leader of the dissidents. Speaking to the rival Independent newspaper group – an especially grave offence in the journalistic world – he denounced the women's income: 'We as a paper are not shy about preaching about corporate pay and fat-cats but with this there is a sense of excess. Some of the sums mentioned are disturbing. This is not an attack on Ms Kennedy, it is an attack on the executive level of pay. There is a double standard in seeking more job cuts while paying these vast salaries.'

Quite so: but it is interesting to note that he had never condemned the pay of the male predecessors of these women. Moreover, he did not denounce Conor Brady's absurdly generous pre-pension pension and did not even refer to it the following October in his long and eulogistic book review of Brady's account of his time as *Irish Times* editor. Brady had of course brought him into the newspaper.

By this time, I had written some deeply unpopular columns supporting the American invasion of Iraq in 2003. My reasoning was simple. Saddam had persistently violated UN resolutions. He had fired ballistic missiles against four neighbouring countries and had gassed thousands of his own subjects, while sanctions had both impoverished the Iraqi people and enabled him to intensify his control over them. The arguments against intervention were and are obvious; however, Iraq was not a country enjoying peace, but one suffering from perpetual and violent oppression. That Blair and Bush might actually lie to justify an invasion, as they clearly did, and that the former might even revel in the prospect of leading his country into a war for which his army was not remotely prepared, were depravities quite beyond my predictive powers. However, not doing anything about an irredeemable psychotic like Saddam would also have had terrible but wholly unforeseeable consequences. That is the nature of all true historical dilemmas: the jury of history awaits regardless.

But at least the calamities that befell the people of Iraq, and later Syria, and soon much of the Arab world, nonetheless revealed the asymmetrical values of liberal-left opinion across the western world. For whereas there were repeated mass demonstrations against Israeli policies towards Gaza and the West Bank, there were no comparable protests about the conduct of the governments of the Arab world, from Aden to Algeria. The atrocious euphemism 'honour killing' in relation to women is actually incorporated in the legal codes of most Arab states. The fate of hundreds, perhaps thousands, of Yazidi women in Iraq, who were gang-raped by their captors before having their throats cut, apparently aroused little anger outside Iraq and none at all in comparison to the rage evinced at Israel's policies.

The Jewish state lay outside the general benefactions conferred by the new authorised religion of Political Correctness. That such an irrational dispensation can have deluded the intelligentsia should surprise no one; there was never an idea so barren of wisdom and lacking in common sense that was not prized by that self-esteeming caste. Communism one day, doctrinaire feminist-egalitarianism the next, gender-plasticity the day after. These are the sort of people who would argue that a stone is more intelligent than a dog, because – as the social psychologist Zenon Pylyshyn suggested – if you kick a stone, it stays away. What made the PC creed in Ireland particularly powerful was that it filled the empty spaces left in the minds of the country's political classes by the death of the belief in Rome. RC gave way to PC and amongst those who gained from the transition were the New Totalitarians, who could be feminists, leftists or egalitarians. This universal piety of 'equality' seemed to infect almost every facet of western life, while its virtues were most enthusiastically propounded by Europe's untouchable elites as they enjoyed the Asymmetric Equality of their Élysées and *arrondissements*. Language was actually altered to suit the requirements of this new sanctimony, so that, for example, the word 'foreigner' virtually vanished from Irish journalistic usage. From the time of the first appearance of the meaningless term 'non-national' in *The Irish Times* in 1982 up to

254

2017, it was used 1,730 times, as if the people it described were citizens of nowhere, untouched by any formative identity, whereas they were in fact nationals of somewhere else, with a sense of national selfhood no less than that felt by the Irish.

The dogmas of equality seemed even to govern health policy, for across the EU from the 1980s onwards we were assured that AIDS threatened us all *equally*. This state-backed lie caused one reader to write to the *Daily Telegraph*: 'I am a maiden lady in her early eighties. I have just recently received a public health warning to desist from anal sex, advice which I do not think my personal habits have yet justified.'

Newspapers were now in the business of promoting the fictions of equality rather than discussing the uncomfortable realities of epidemiology. Thus the clarion headlines that a government report had revealed a dramatic increase in heterosexual AIDS in Ireland. Only by going through the report's fine print did I find that the increase was almost entirely confined to African immigrants. When I asked the press officer responsible why this had not been pointed out in the official press release, she replied, 'Are you mad?'

This conscious process of actually directing news reports towards a particular outcome was vital to the peace process, which was predicated upon ignoring inconvenient truths. The deliberately savage murder by the IRA of the informer Eamon Collins in 1999 did not even cause a minute's delay in the latest round of talks with Sinn Féin–IRA, whose leaders – unlike those of the constitutional parties – were even made welcome at the British prime minister's country home of Chequers. After armed robbers stole £26.5 million in cash from the Northern Bank in Belfast in December 2004, the media universally presented the theft as a mysterious deed, as if it had been conducted by Martians. I knew otherwise, and wrote a column declaring the IRA responsible. I filed early to give me time to deal with any legal problems. That afternoon, I got a phone call from a deputy editor, saying that the editor, Geraldine Kennedy, had pulled the column because Sinn Féin was denying any IRA involvement.

'So is Sinn Féin editing this fucking newspaper? Could you put me on to her, please?'

'I can't. She's gone.'

I rang Kennedy on her mobile phone. It was apparently turned off. I checked the Sinn Féin statement. It was not even a denial of the IRA's responsibility, but an assertion that Sinn Féin's position was that the IRA was unconnected with the robbery. This was surely a journalistic nadir in the history of *The Irish Times* for, within days, both Irish and British governments formally declared that the IRA had indeed been responsible. But that was not the bottom of the barrel of appeasement.

Some weeks later, a group of IRA men beat a man named Robert McCartney to death in a Belfast pub, cutting his throat and gouging out an eye. This barroom butchery metamorphosed into a full-scale IRA operation, with rioters being mobilised to prevent any police intervention, while squads of women, armed with sponges and disinfectant, removed all forensic evidence. Clearly, and not inaccurately, the Sinn Féin–IRA alliance felt it could get away with anything it wanted, and not be held to account.

As it happened, some days later, I penned a needlessly provocative column about the ruinous allowances being given to single mothers, which lured them into a lifetime of state dependency. I invented the term MOB – Mothers of Bastards – because it was both legally correct and eye-catching, and I also wanted a handy acronym. In my mind, I had played with Single mothers Absent Dads, SAD, and a few others. But finally, MOB is what I wrote and MOB was what I duly got.

On the day it appeared, it drew only a couple of telephone criticisms to *The Irish Times*. But once RTÉ got to work, the tumbril began to rumble, and Máirín McGrath on the *Irish Times* switch rang me to say that the phone lines were besieged by women callers, many of them clearly not having read the column, but responding to mangled versions of it on air. Without being asked by anyone, I immediately wrote a column of apology and retraction. But it made no difference to the lynch mob now loose in the media. That Thursday, the letters page was given over *in its entirety* to attacks on me. Almost every single columnist across the board then moved in for the kill, while the *Daily Mail* even sent two journalists to the doorstep of my unmarried sister and mother of two at her home in Cincinnati, Ohio.

This column sealed my status. To that entity which Eamon Dunphy has shrewdly dubbed 'Official Ireland', I was now – and for ever would be – an official outsider. This Official Ireland is a reincarnation of the Ireland of the 1950s, suffocating dissent and stifling genuine originality, while engaging in sanctimonious orgies of self-congratulation. I grasped the fullness of Official Ireland's anathema for me the following year when I learnt that *The Irish Times* was preparing a special supplement about the 1916 rebellion, but without inviting any contribution from me – even though I had been writing about this period for decades. This was rather like having a supplement about the economy without consulting the economics editor. Next, a deputy editor killed a column without taking the mandatory step of informing me. Again, a studied insult. After he put the phone down on me when I sought an explanation, I knew my days in *The Irish Times* were over.

I rang Tony O'Reilly, the owner of Irish News and Media, and was offered a job on the spot. I resigned from *The Irish Times*. I then received phone calls from the editor and the managing director pleading with me to change my mind. I was told that a recent but confidential readers' survey had revealed that subscribers believed that I was the journalist who most embodied the principles and values of the newspaper. However, this was all too late – and soon thereafter, I began to be airbrushed from the newspaper's chronicles. When it produced a special supplement for its 150th birthday, even though I had written 'An Irishman's Diary' for one-sixth of its entire lifespan and had used that column to engineer a revolution in Ireland's attitude to the Great War, my name was not mentioned once. Moreover, when the newspaper's online archive appeared, my original article about the Irish in the Great War in 1980 – which was the very foundation of the rediscovery of so much Irish history in the decades that followed – was excluded. Every other page of that issue was available online, including the front-page promo for the article, but the entire page containing it was missing. I had become an exemplar of a particularly Irish fate, the word for which has been borrowed by virtually every language in the world – 'boycott'.

Thirty-One

NEWSPAPER COLUMNS ARE generally distinguishable from the humble mayfly by the latter's greater wisdom and longevity, so I don't propose to revisit my output with the *Irish Independent* in any detail. However, one piece that I wrote during my time there has lodged approvingly in the internet, from which it revisits as regularly as Halley's Comet, and I cite it here as evidence that most of my output down the decades was not in the least controversial or adversarial.

And that was the summer; another gone. No other time of year begins with such infusions of melancholy as the one now upon us. The leaves are beginning to turn to crispy brown paper in the autumn sun. Soon they will be gone, and the empire of the early dusk and the long night begins.

There are consolations to be got from the roaring fire and the buttered scones and those cold, clear winter days when you can see a fence from 40 miles. But I know what each season means: another layer of one's life lived, another chapter concluded, another landmark passed. And I also know how quickly the past 10 or 20 years have passed. Those are the units we live by, and they are the merest gossamer standing between us and a return to the utter nothingness from which we emerged.

It was on days like these, 21 years ago, that I took my mother on the Shannon. The weather was kind, and each day the gallant old sun shone with a wan but gamey warmth. One evening I cooked lamb chops, and I gave her two. She was thrilled; a lady of modest habit, she had never before had two chops on her plate. And I felt guilty then that I had never before provided her with such an ordinary pleasure. During that trip, she seemed troubled; she had difficulty understanding simple things. I thought it was age. It wasn't: it was a brain tumour that was diagnosed over the coming weeks, and would kill her as winter deepened.

Death, when it finally came, was a merciful deliverance. But I was shocked by the terrible grief that followed and seemed to consume my entire life. I know in part what it was. Both my parents were now gone. Their six children now stood on the end of the bough. One by one, we too would fall. I knew that, of the six of us, one of us would probably go to five funerals, and one of us would go to none. Bereavement strikes so deep because it is not just separation but a foreshadowing. The knells are for everyman. The scythe scythes all.

Grief is a form of madness for which the only asylum is time. But it does not cure – merely acclimatises and habituates. I think about my parents every day of my life. I think about the love I didn't show, and all the good deeds that went undone. Guilt is an anvil upon whose unremitting iron we shape so much of our inner selves.

Yet I am oddly pleased about one thing that I did, that summer 21 years ago, the summer of the Italian World Cup, when Pavarotti's 'Nessun Dorma' was everywhere. Even now, I never hear those opening chords without thinking of 1990, of the last summer of my mother's life, and of the very last party for all her offspring. The sun shone throughout that long July evening, and every single one of her children and her grandchildren sat beneath the apple and pear trees in her garden, and drank wine and ate a vast Chinese take-away banquet of many courses. One of my nieces had a child's karaoke machine, and we sang songs well into the morning, not knowing that this was also a farewell to the family as a living unit. We had one further appointment, for my mother's funeral; the following

December, we buried her in an icefield of a cemetery that was as cold and hard and bitter as it had been many years before when we'd laid my father there when I was a boy.

There was never to be a full family moment together again. Families do not usually stay cohesive once the maternal hub has gone. The centre holds the parts, like the axle on a merry-go-round. For my mother's home was more than her home. It was the one place in common for her children. Nowhere else would quite do. And something strange happens when a mother dies: a core is gone from your life. You become a new and a lesser person. Dimensions are lacking. The obligations to think about that reassuring home-from-home, and to provide emotionally for someone else somewhere else, perished with her.

I have visited my mother's house just once in recent years, via a Google Earth satellite: but never again. The beautiful front garden in which she took such immense pride has been covered in tarmac and is now a car-port. In the back garden, the fruit trees beneath which we sang on that summer's evening, only yesterday but oh so long ago, have all been felled. Her home has been utterly rewritten as if she were never its author. The only human record that remains of it is in the minds of her children and grandchildren. We are like time capsules, our memories each bearing a defining freight that no one else will ever know or see, into the dark folds of deepest space.

The dying of the summer has always filled mortal man with dread, because it foreshadows our own end.

How many more autumns await each one of us? The months ebb, the bells toll and the leaves fall.

One issue which troubled me from the outset was inaccurate or misleading headlines over my columns; the format of 'An Irishman's Diary' meant that it was headline-free. The central problem was that subediting was done by unidentifiable casuals, upon whom no retribution could be wrought. Unaccountable decision-making is the thief of competence. In one column about the epidemic of suicide amongst young men, I declared that we could not possibly reintroduce the 'taboo' on suicide which had been the traditional social mechanism to limit its depredations. Sure enough, the headline declared, 'Time to re-introduce taboo on suicide', prompting an entire radio discussion on how awful Kevin Myers was to propose such a barbarous measure. Another headline declared that 'Africa has given the world nothing but AIDS'. In my column I had used the qualifier 'almost', pointing out that although this might make us feel uncomfortable, the truth was that the continent which has 15 per cent of the world's population was also home to 70 per cent of its AIDS cases.

The great Zambian economist Dambisa Moyo has pointed out that a trillion dollars in aid to Africa has seen that continent sliding into bankruptcy. By her calculations, between 1970 and 1998, the proportions of Africans dwelling in poverty rose from 11 per cent to 66 per cent. At independence, Ghana's per capita GDP was higher than South Korea's. Today, it is one-tenth of South Korea's, and falling – and Ghana is one of Africa's few 'success' stories. The population of every African country was – and still is – doubling every twenty years. Ethiopia's, for example, was 35 million in 1980. Shortly thereafter, it had a very African famine, during which its population rose, reaching 48 million by 1990. Today its population is 115 million and it is expected to reach 150 million by 2050. Britain's population in 1881 was the same as Ethiopia's in 1980, and it still has not doubled, despite the arrival of millions of immigrants. I thought that only a fool would *not* address this issue; as it turned out, only a fool *would* address it.

This affair led to a ringing personal endorsement from the great Mark Steyn. He is one of the most important observers of what is now perhaps the irreversible decline of the west, which has been maimed by what had originally been designed to protect its citizens – the welfare state. Since its foundation in Bismarck's Germany, state welfarism has mutated into a vast vote-buying auction between politicians, burdening central government with almost bottomless financial responsibilities for its citizenry. With the contraceptive pill and abortion on demand, thus freeing women from the reproductive servitude that is the mammalian norm, the nations of Europe have undergone what Steyn correctly calls 'deathbed demographics', as their populations have simply failed to replace themselves. Yet a modern state still needs willing hands to do the menial work, sweeping the streets and wiping the bottoms of the old and of the relatively few native babies that are born. Instead of the careful importation of limited and assimilable numbers, Europe opened the floodgates – the metaphor is intentional – and almost overnight, native, working-class communities across Europe were expected to adjust their ways to the needs of their guests; otherwise, the middle-class left-liberals, secure in their bourgeois ghettoes, swiftly termed them 'racist'. By such moral torpor, the peoples who had invented the modern world were now busily uninventing themselves. The native white populations of every single country in Europe, including Ireland, and also the USA, are not achieving the replacement levels of 2.1 children per woman, and wherever populations are rising, this is because of immigration. Any useful discussion of what is existentially perhaps the most important issue in European history has been killed at birth with the garrotte called 'racism'.

David McKittrick's majestic work *Lost Lives*, tabulating the dead of Northern Ireland's Troubles, led me to write a memoir of my time in Belfast. I did so in a frenzied fortnight, but with too little reflection. I inadvertently omitted some episodes of interest, including that episode of insane gunfire revelry which I have referred to in the Beirut chapters. I named the book *Watching the Door*. It was rejected by around twenty publishers, before being picked up by The Lilliput Press, and, after getting fine reviews, it was republished by Atlantic Books in London.

At a dinner with Atlantic's editors in Dublin, we were joined by Christopher Hitchens, and though we had not seen one another in two decades, we fell into one another's arms like soulmates who had made our separate journeys from the muddy groupthink of the lazy liberal left to individual libertarianism. He downed Chivas Regal whisky and smoked cigarettes with a hedonistic frenzy that suggested that a firing squad was waiting for him, which, figuratively, it was. We never lost touch until the laws of medicine finally supervened, as they were surely obliged to if they were to retain any authority over human affairs, and, with a dauntless grace, this gallantly dogmatic atheist went to meet his maker. I hope

Christopher was suitably chastened by the warm and Trinitarian welcome He gave him.

But long before that celestial encounter, I had received an email from a British Army officer I knew from my recent writings on Northern Ireland, asking me a simple question: did I know of any examples of guerrillas successfully changing sides during a war? The US Marine Corps, alongside whom he was serving, was hoping to recruit Sunnis who had been their enemies. Was this a practicable proposition? It was a remarkable vote of confidence that I could be entrusted with such headline-worthy information. I told him about 'The Broy Harriers', IRA men in the 1930s who had been recruited into the Garda Special Branch, to serve alongside their former enemies against their former friends. The outline I sent to him was used in part to create a structure that lay behind the successful surge of 2007, which freed vast amounts of Iraqi territory and people from the tyranny of al-Qaida. I am proud of my small role in this victory. This, however, was not the reason why the General Officer Commanding London, Major-General Sir Sebastian Roberts, invited me as his personal guest to a small lunch at St James's Palace; the invitation was extended merely as an expression of thanks for all the work I had done for Irish soldiers of the Crown in the past.

That I remained an enemy for some might have been one reason why others continued to support me. The depth of that enmity came to light when a reader told me to check my Wikipedia page. This declared that when I worked in Belfast I was a secret agent for the British Army and regularly raped little boys. The victims' families were intimidated into silence by British intelligence, which threatened them with murder, courtesy of British-controlled loyalist paramilitaries. This entire fable was a criminal libel, a term which means that such utterly baseless and evil lies might induce reasonable people to do violence to me. The legal advice I was given was that I could not possibly sue Wikipedia in Ireland, where it had no legal presence, and that seeking justice in the California courts would be the equivalent of embarking on a land war in Asia. Instead of suing, I wrote about the episode; that was my first personal experience of the Evil Black Hole of the internet, where there is no accountability, logic, law or restraint.

A new dawn had meanwhile arrived in Ireland, and I must say I greatly liked much of the Tiger era, not least because the success of the Irish confounded left-wing whingers, who preferred poverty, unemployment and despair as weapons to denounce the evils of capitalism. Yet, as history has repeatedly confirmed, the greatest wealth that the Irish possess is in that cliché 'social capital'. The qualities this resource implies – a spontaneous affability, an uncanny ability to communicate with strangers and a thirst for gaiety – had enabled the Irish to prosper in exile. Now, similarly liberated from the twin inhibitions of oppressive Catholicism and Iron Age Fenianism, the Irish at home were doing the same. This was exemplified most acutely by an entity that had once done so much to enforce those inhibitions, perhaps the most important civil institution in Ireland, the Gaelic Athletic Association. Its new-found maturity and generosity were reflective of Irish society as a whole, most significantly in its agreement to host Ireland's rugby international with England at Croke Park, where once armed servants of the Crown had killed fourteen players and spectators. No one in attendance will ever forget the thunderously respectful silence that greeted 'God Save the Queen', a thermonuclear noiselessness that erupted from the ground and engulfed the whole island. Alas, rugby did not remain at Croke Park. Had it done so, the entire economic and cultural balance of Dublin could have shifted a little away from the pampered southside to the deprived northside of the city. But that aside, Croke Park remains a worthy tribute to a fine man and a very great patriot, former GAA Director Liam Mulvihill.

Many Irish entrepreneurs were exhibiting comparable vision and flair. Emblematic of this was the purchase by some Irish business people of the great London hotels, the Savoy, the Connaught, the Berkeley and Claridge's, plus, as a nice little bonus, Battersea Power Station. There is, of course, a downside to all this, for what made such dazzling adventurism possible was Ireland's membership of the euro. This allowed banks to borrow money from German banks and then to lend it at criminally low interest rates, while a farcically negligent regulator was responsible for the oversight – in both contradictory senses of that word – of the crazier transactions that characterised the later stages of the Tiger years.

Our banking system was supervised not by a savage Cerberus, but a blind goldfish, and when collapse came, the goldfish was given early retirement on full pension. Yes, GUBU again.

However, so wedded were the Irish to what is in effect the Bundes-euro that, rather like the tolerance shown for the unsynchronised bus and train departures of past decades, there has been little serious complaint about its role in ruining us. The Irish taxpayer borrowed billions to reimburse the German banks for their vast losses on the Irish property market. Our national debt at the time of writing is about €200 billion, but of guilt or remorse amongst the euro elite there is not the slightest trace. At bottom, I think being 'good' Europeans was what distinguished us from the British, or rather the English, and, rather like Roman Catholicism in earlier dispensations, being loudly adherent to the Treaty of Rome and all its subsequent compacts remains a defining characteristic of the more immature and insecure expressions of Irishness.

But at least the Tiger proved that the Irish didn't just carry the hods anymore, and I choose as the personal embodiment of that transformation the former hod-carrier Seán Mulryan. His company, Ballymore Group, barely survived the ruthless EU-imposed austerity that followed the Tiger years. After a truly torrid decade, he is now one of the most important property developers in Britain, the owner of the largest land bank in London, the creator of the City Island development in the centre of the Thames and the author of a portfolio of wonderful buildings.

Just as hearteningly, a new openness had arrived in Ireland, as the photographer Spencer Tunick discovered when he sought to take some of his famous naked-crowd pictures. More than two thousand Irish people publicly queued in the open air to participate, nude and untroubled. At the start of this story, remember, professional models in Dublin refused to pose publicly in ladies' underwear, and nudists gathered in cloacal covens where their names were even more secret than their pudenda.

The blessing upon this new Ireland came with the visit of Queen Elizabeth II to Dublin, and, most particularly, to Islandbridge Park. Naturally, I was not invited to the ceremony there, but after discovering that little oversight, I asked Seán Murphy of the British Legion to get me a place on its delegation, which he did. The ceremony was superbly done, with the Army Number One Band under the baton of Colonel Mark Armstrong, an outstanding musician and patriot, as always outdoing itself. Then, as the two heads of state went to examine the Memorial Records which I had deconstructed all those decades before, Seán whispered, 'Come with me.'

He led me to the roped edge of the throng. Already there – by prior arrangement – were men of that terrorist tattooed band, the Ulster Defence Association, Maze-prison muscles rippling under their suits. The president talked briefly to them, with the queen standing slightly aloof, clutching her handbag as if she feared that their traditional habits might prevail over their recent house-training, and they would make a grab for it before high-tailing it back northwards.

As the two heads of state sauntered towards the exit, Mary McAleese suddenly spotted me.

She said, 'Kevin, is that you?' She turned to the queen. 'This is the journalist who kept the flame of this place alive for so many years. He fought the good fight, and like so many battles, it was worth fighting.'

The queen nodded smilingly at me, and I – according to the account in *The Irish Times* by that excellent journalist Mary Fitzgerald, upon which these few lines are based, for, not having been invited there in the first place, I was too nonplussed to register anything – apparently blurted out 'Your Majesty.'

The absurdity of decades of non-contact between the two states was finally exposed in Cork, where security arrangements were abandoned in the face of the irresistible exuberance of the welcome. The fishmonger Pat O'Connell became an international celebrity when the queen – herself a fivefold mother-in-law – erupted with laughter after he told her that the particularly ugly monkfish was called 'the mother-in-law of fish'.

So much of the cycle that I had sought was near to completion – but not all. A subject I returned to regularly was my desire for Ireland to be present once again at the Remembrance Sunday service at the Mall in London, at which we had always been present until that homunculus of depravity, Seán MacBride, decided otherwise. This absence had become a proudly negative badge of identity – England's Official Non-Friend, as

Olivia O'Leary has memorably put it – for England's first colony, which spoke English, used English common law, graced the pages of English literature with some of its finest writers, and which, through the decades of independence, had also cheerfully unloaded its surplus population (including the Myers family) into Britain's cities.

In 2011, I was greatly honoured to be asked to give the annual address on Remembrance Sunday in St Patrick's Cathedral, before President Higgins. I focused on the Second World War, out of respect for the few veterans whom I knew would be present. In addition to remembering some our own dead, name by name and deed by deed, I expressed keen approval of the men of the Defence Forces who had chosen to defend our neutrality. I also spoke of the German civilians killed in the Allied bombings of their cities, as well as honouring the memory of an Austrian Jew, who had pointedly assumed an Irish name – Michael O'Hara – to serve alongside Allied forces. Days before war's end, he was captured by Nazi forces, murdered and largely forgotten by the world until my address. For the first time ever in such a service, I named some of the Irish women killed in the war against the Third Reich. Sitting alongside me before I mounted the pulpit was the Tánaiste, Frances Fitzgerald. After the service ended, she came over and shook my hand and said: 'Thank you so much for mentioning the women.'

So I naturally assumed that in 2014, the centennial of the outbreak of the Great War, my opinions and knowledge of the Irish in the two world wars would be of some interest to RTÉ. But it was not so: the station's programme-makers did not invite me to discuss anything. In a comparable oversight, the government did not invite me to the official unveiling of the Commonwealth War Graves Commission Cross of Sacrifice at Glasnevin cemetery, which was erected to honour the men and women of the Crown who had been buried there without headstones or grave-markers – even though back in 1989 I had been the journalist who had first revealed this shameful lapidary denial. However, I invited myself, this time through the good offices of George McCullough, the Glasnevin Trust's chief executive.

A selection of my talks and articles on the Great War was published in October 2014, with Thomas Pakenham, Lord Longford, officiating.

This gave me the chance to revisit and dismantle myths that have achieved a factual status which, despite my best efforts, they retain to this day. The first concerns the landings from the *River Clyde* of the Royal Dublin Fusiliers and the Royal Munster Fusiliers in Gallipoli in 1915, which are widely proclaimed as examples of unparalleled Irish gallantry and bloodshed. In fact, a careful analysis shows far smaller casualties than were reported at the time, and what appears to have been a mutiny (or at least an intelligent refusal to obey suicidal orders) by hundreds of Irish soldiers who declined to leave the safety of the *River Clyde*. Another fiction concerned the attack by the 7th Leinsters on the Somme, on what the regimental history calls 'one of the darkest days in the history of the battalion'. As Michael Tierney had indicated all those years before, it was indeed a dark day, but this was because the men had refused to leave their trenches, and almost all their officers and NCOs had been killed in a futile attempt to make them do so. Once again, myth had trumped fact – and in both instances, despite my best efforts, still does.

London nonetheless remembered while Dublin forgot, and I was invited to a reception at Buckingham Palace to meet the queen. Rachel briefed me on how I should address her: 'Your Majesty', initially, and 'Ma'am' thereafter, to rhyme with 'spam'. I had been sent a security pass to enter the palace grounds, and outside my hotel, I got a Cockney taxi driver straight from central casting.

'Buckingham Palace, please, and put this pass on your windscreen to get you through security at the palace gates.'

'Blimey, guv, I been waiting all my bleedin' life for a fare like this.'

Proud as a victorious Roman Emperor returning from Germania festooned with laurels, he swept into the palace grounds past red-coated guardsmen and armed police officers. Guests were directed into a large reception area where waitresses were handing out glasses of champagne and mineral water, but, wanting to stay completely sober, I took only the latter. I happened by chance to be standing nearby when the door to the royal reception area was opened, so I was one of the first to shake hands with Her Majesty and His Royal Highness. Polite words were uttered, and I returned to the main reception area, as the other guests queued to shake the royal hands. A dozen waitresses were standing forlornly, holding trays of untaken champagne, so I rather gallantly chose to relieve as many as possible of their burdens. Soon, I had downed half a dozen glasses, and as the room refilled, I felt as triumphant as Hillary and Tenzing on top of Everest. I had met the queen and had not made a complete fool of myself. A hand touched my elbow. I turned smilingly.

'Her Majesty will be speaking to you in thirty seconds.'

Next moment, she was addressing me and some other guests nearby: 'Do you all know one another?'

'Them? Never set eyes on them before,' I declared affably. 'Know you better than I do them.'

'Really?' she said, a little puzzled.

'Yes, President McAleese introduced us at Islandbridge. You remember? Kevin Myers. Pleased to meet you … again! Ha ha!'

An inscrutable look had settled on her face. Not for the first time in her life, she was being addressed by a drunk.

'Not that you and I talked very much,' I chuckled, giving her, I seem to remember, a playful nudge. 'She did most of the talking; Mary's good at that. That was the first time I'd met her also. Are you enjoying yourself? I am. Very much. Fine place you have here. Lovely ceiling,' I finished, pointing, as if, unaided, she would have been unable to find it.

'It's wonderful that so many Irish people could be here,' she continued, perhaps a little desperately.

'Not at all, our pleasure …'

I paused, suddenly but acutely aware that I should now be using her secondary title, but for the life of me, I couldn't remember what it was. Over the queen's shoulder, I saw a waitress pouring a glass of Mumm champagne, and so, beaming triumphantly, I finished with a cordially vocative, 'Ah, Mumm.'

'Is that nice Cawk fishmonga here?' she asked, in tones that suggested the monkfish would be better company than me.

'Pat O'Connell? Could well be, Mumm, could well be. You two got on like a house on fire, didn't you, Mumm?'

'It has been a real pleasure meeting you.'

'Not as much for you as it has been for me, Mumm.'

And bathed in the warm glow of my proud smile, she moved off, while I continued to perform a hearty breaststroke through the royal vats of champagne.

Thirty-Two

IN FEBRUARY 2013, a month before the renewal of my contract with Independent News Media (INM), I wrote the following about the company's most important shareholder. 'The award of €150,000 damages to Denis O'Brien against *The Irish Daily Mail* is utterly absurd. For who takes seriously what any columnist says? ... Now, I'm not in the business of knocking a fellow columnist. Let me just say that Paul Drury had a bad day in the office (like many that I've had) when he wrote his column about Denis O'Brien. This alleged that the telecoms multimillionaire had manipulated RTÉ's Charlie Bird into giving favourable publicity to his relief efforts in Haiti in order to offset the forthcoming Moriarty report. Was that assertion correct? Answer: Not remotely.'

I continued: 'I've been a columnist for three decades. I know the difference that columns make: almost none ... Moreover, we columnists have to be allowed to be wrong in our judgements: he who lives in terror of error lives in fear of freedom.'

I went on to say that social media had totally changed the nature of public discourse. 'Convulsions pass through them like vast electric storms in the toxic methanous atmosphere of early earth. These rages usually emanate from cretins who think only with their twitching thumbs. No one remembers anything that is said during these tweeting-fits, any more than a wheelbarrow remembers what it has carried or a corkscrew recollects the vintage of a wine. This is the hysterical world so many people now inhabit: incontinent, frenzied, ephemeral and utterly amnesiac.

'Denis O'Brien is now effectively the proprietor of this newspaper. I presume that he wants it to be profitable. A modest word of advice. Timid newspapers do not sell. Newspapers whose columnists are scared of offending the powerful do not sell. Newspapers whose lawyers are hyper-intent on avoiding libel-action remain in unsold heaps on the news-stands. Denis O'Brien didn't just damage *The Irish Daily Mail*, a rival newspaper, with his libel action: he damaged journalism generally – and he is the biggest single employer of journalists in the country ... If we in the regulated press are further weakened by even more litigation, the victors will be the outlaws of the untamed range, beyond the reach of even Denis O'Brien.'

The column was not carried; I had no sense of how prescient it was. So many elements that were to end in my ruin were present – taking on the man who was effectively my boss and one of the most powerful men in Ireland – meanwhile sparing a fellow columnist in trouble any sanctimonious effusions, yet defending the freedom to be wrong and warning of the dangers of the social media. Only in one regard were my assessments inaccurate, when I said that social media were ephemeral and amnesiac. As I would discover, four years later, their memory is as geologically retentive as a quartz crystal.

Shortly thereafter, my career in INM over, I moved to the Irish edition of *The Sunday Times*. The asymmetric angers that had characterised Irish life for so long continued to fume and flourish, giving me much food for copy. For example, during the centenary of the 1916 Rising, we had a weird fusion of the old and the modern, as Official Ireland, far from questioning the morality of the rising, instead imposed a feminist agenda upon it, with President Higgins to the fore. 'Constance Markievicz and Margaret Skinnider did play a prominent combatant role at St Stephen's Green,' he proclaimed. 'Yet most of the ICA [Irish Citizens Army] women were not armed, and Margaret Skinnider had to cite the Proclamation to insist on her right to throw a grenade into the Shelbourne Hotel.'

I asked: 'Which part of the proclamation did Ms Skinnider, The Scrupulous Scot, use as a legal argument to justify throwing a high explosive fragmentation bomb into a crowded hotel? The bit about the Republic "guaranteeing religious and civil liberty, equal rights and equal opportunities to all its citizens" (even if the Skinnider grenade had just blown their tonsils through their eyeballs)? Or maybe the next line, "to pursue the happiness and the prosperity of the whole nation, and all its parts" (including those scattered on the floor of the Shelbourne lobby)? Or perhaps the next line, about "cherishing all the children of the nation equally" (even if we've just killed them)?'

I also observed that the president had praised the women insurgents without once mentioning local girls Louisa Nolan and Florence Williams, both awarded the Military Medal by the British War Office for their bravery under fire while tending to wounded soldiers. And why, I asked, had there been no mention of Dr Ella Webb of St John's Ambulance Brigade, who was decorated with the Silver Medal of the Order of St John of Jerusalem for repeatedly cycling through the gun battles to check on the wounded in the city's hospitals?

Things got no better as the grim pattern of commemoration repeated itself. Not a single politician attended the memorial services for the two unarmed police constables, O'Brien and Lahiff, murdered in cold blood by insurgents, one of whom was the self-styled countess and remorseless snob, Markievicz. (Four years later, a small memorial event to commemorate the 530 RIC men killed between 1916 and 1923 had to be cancelled largely because of opposition from the IRA army council's political front.) Nor did the failure to honour the memory of innocent and unarmed police constables murdered in 1916 cause any public upset, unlike the failure of the Abbey Theatre to commission enough women to write commemorative drama for the century. Yet the empirical truth was that it was impossible to name many successful women playwrights, not just in Ireland, but almost anywhere, including the commercial theatres in the West End or Broadway. I pointed out that Garry Hynes – perhaps the finest theatre director in Ireland over the past fifty years – who had loudly denounced the Abbey for its failure to select women playwrights, while the Abbey's artistic director between 1991 and 1994 had not main-staged a single work by a woman playwright. Moreover, of the thirty-six plays I was able to identify (during many hours of research) that she had directed in her entire career, just four had been written by women.

When the *Sunday Business Post* asked Garry Hynes to respond to these observations, she replied: 'Kevin Myers is like a child. You just want to slap him and send him from the table.'

What would the National Women's Council or Barnardo's et bloody al. have said if I had spoken about slapping Garry Hynes like that? The ensuing silence confirmed how the many state-sponsored single-issue advocacy groups had effectively coalesced into a multi-issue monolith of Political Correctness. This alliance was now wielding enormous political power and detested dissent, even as it was endlessly fragmenting. In this new order, Amnesty International, formerly a wonderful organisation for prisoners of conscience, was now campaigning for gay marriage and gay adoption rights, though perhaps not too loudly in Saudi Arabia or Gaza, where walls tend to fall terminally on homosexuals. What will Amnesty do when – as seems inevitable – a hyper-liberal secular state imprisons a Catholic for campaigning against gay adoption? Meanwhile, critics of this moral order were routinely denounced in the new official terminology that had replaced the anathemas of Catholicism: *xenophobia, hate-speech, misogyny, racism, Islamophobia.* A vast body of 'rights' had been created, but there was no matching corpus of obligations.

A strange silence now accompanied the transformations that were occurring in Irish life. Large numbers of medical graduates were leaving the profession, or the country, within a decade of graduating. The outcome was that by 2017, 38 per cent of our medical practitioners were foreign, as Generation X became Generation Ex. I analysed the results: this new Ireland had 261 doctors named Patrick, 335 named Mary, six called Maureen, and 791 named Mohammed (spelt in various ways). Three times more doctors were named after the prophet who had brought Islam to Arabia than the saint who had brought Christianity to Ireland. And this not in a Gulf desert state but in the wet Atlantic isle that had previously furnished half the world with doctors. This was the same land which had declared that homosexual marriage was equal to heterosexual marriage, but without bothering to define the deed which legally consummated the former, as the latter required. But what matter, if it made us *feel* better?

I strongly dislike the terms 'right' and 'left', for they serve only to confuse, especially in today's corrupted parlance, which terms anyone who wishes to peacefully and lawfully protect traditional notions of identity and marriage as 'far-right' – whereas you would have to be a masked rioter burning buildings and the people inside them to be termed 'far-left'. Even without the terminological bias now infusing journalism, this kind of language was hopelessly anachronistic. In medieval battle, the most loyal of the king's warriors stood on the right of the line, their hearts exposed to the right-handed sword thrust of the warriors opposite them. Such concepts were of limited usefulness in an era of social media and the web.

My own preference to the left-right decision is David Blundy's chosen alternatives to the spine, namely head or heart. The head rationally chooses outcomes, regardless of how good it makes one feel; the heart opts for policies that are emotionally rewarding, almost regardless of the long-term consequences. The gathering demographic catastrophe of Africa – which is almost certainly leading to the greatest famine in world history, with an ecological collapse in at least a dozen peri-tropical countries – is what results if you gorge your heart to excess.

I am not an ideologist, simply a utilitarian, pragmatic rationalist, for whom the only question about any policy is: *does it work for me?* This takes me to one of the last columns of my newspaper career, in 2017, after unbroken months of gruesome 1916 worship.

In September 1994, I was taken on a helicopter air-sea rescue training exercise out of Shannon. One of the crew was a woman. I was then middle-aged and she was young. Now I am old and she is dead.

There is no justice in how life distributes favours to some even as it withdraws them from others. And so it was that early last Tuesday morning Dara Fitzpatrick gave her life as she had spent it, in the doing of her duty to strangers, as did her colleagues, Mark Duffy, Paul Ormsby and Ciarán Smith. I did not know these three men, and their lives and their loss are no less significant than hers. I honour them as I honour her: heroes all of the Irish nation ...

During our long conversations all those years ago, she begged me not to make her a heroine, and I obliged her then. But post-mortem, I can say that she admitted that she was both fully aware –

and fearful – of the terrible dangers of her trade. She knew her crew would be flying a helicopter into raging westerlies, as windscreen wipers swiped in vain at a horizontal Niagara of water, with utter ink-black darkness beyond, and ink-black above and ink-black below, and with just the glow of the instrument-panel in front and the thud-thud of the rotors overhead to guide them through the howling, starless Atlantic night. Anything could go wrong: fuel-pipes, instruments, engines, the complex-gearing, the whirring blades overhead and, not least, human decision-making.

Hitting the sea at 100 mph would be like colliding with concrete. The only outcome would be death – and so it proved. She and her fellow crewmen have gone the way they would so often have feared, in the calm of a pre-operational briefing or the sleepless, ceiling-studying watches of a fretful night.

I can find no consolation in their loss save this. A nation which acknowledges its obligations to passing strangers has reached maturity, a metric that may be measured both by the final journey of the crew of Rescue 116 and the subsequent dedication of their colleagues, who have spent the ensuing days looking for their bodies. These men and women were – and are – prepared to sacrifice all that others might live. They have thus provided a clear, ethically superior corrective to that meretricious and reactionary moral order by which this state has so triumphantly celebrated those that did the very opposite.

Duffy and Smith, Ormsby and Fitzpatrick: a terrible duty is born. Over the years, I've interviewed many fine people, who have toiled for the starving in Africa or for Dublin's homeless, who landed on Normandy's iron shores or braved the fire-filled skies of Nazi Germany, all of them doing what they believed to be right, and solely for the benefit of others. But I have met none finer than Dara and her ilk who, in fog or gale, snow or hail, ply their lonely trade, unseen, unsung and uncelebrated, amid the wild night over the steep Atlantic stream, for those in peril on the sea.

When we pass from this world into either the extinction of a godless nihilism or the realm of heavenly perfection, in that final microsecond of change, the fearful, querulous soul might wonder: how was this life that I now leave? Was all duty done? Were people made better, wiser, happier by my fleeting mortal span? Shall the world grieve at my departure?

It was for comparable reasons of respect for duty done that over the decades I had sought full acknowledgement of our forgotten soldiers, and history was on my side. On 1 July 2016, a uniformed soldier of the Irish Defence Forces, Sergeant Gerry White, stood at the Cenotaph at Thiepval, along with comrades from the armies of the UK, Australia, Canada and New Zealand, to commemorate the centenary of the first day of the Battle of the Somme. Even the BBC was moved to observe that it was an extraordinarily Irish occasion. As I wrote that week:

Yesterday, did not representatives of the two Irelands come together on the bloodied pastures of Picardy? … Now I desperately want Theresa May to be the next British Prime Minister, with Theresa Villiers as her deputy. Add Arlene Foster and Mary Lou McDonald, and from such straws, the four women could shape enduring Hibernian bricks. Indeed, once markets have settled down, and the EU bullies realise that vindictiveness is a sure way to bring ruin on us all, some realistic optimism should return.

This acclamation of the four women, who would, I hope, help usher in an era of better relations within Ireland and the larger archipelago, was written by a man soon to be denounced as a misogynist. The following Remembrance Sunday, our ambassador in London did what had been seemingly impossible for so long: he once more laid a wreath for Ireland at the Cenotaph. Our lads were finally honoured and so it looked as if my life's work was done, in the gentle twilight of unspoken congratulation. Moreover, *Watching the Door* seemed set for something of a revival. A production company in Dublin had taken a film option on it and Michael Dobbs, the creator of the magnificent television series *House of Cards*, had appeared on BBC Radio 4 singing its praises, causing a pleasing surge in sales. By happy chance, I expected to meet him during the last weekend of July in Cork, where he, Rabbi Julia Neuberger and I were all to appear as part of a history festival.

The Wednesday before, my page editor on *The Sunday Times* suggested that I depart from the normal Irish focus of my work. Would I do a piece on the gender-pay differentials within the BBC? I preferred not to, as we have seen, but foolishly I said yes, and was promptly pushed from my sill into the unforgiving waves of a bitter and shoreless sea.

Thirty-Three

DRIVING BACK FROM west Cork that Sunday afternoon, I stopped at a service station, and as I filled my car's tank, a man alongside me turned to his little boy, and said: 'That there is Kevin Myers – he's very, very famous, and he's in big, big trouble.'

This was the first inkling of the global nature of my fate. After I resumed my journey, I turned on the radio to hear rapturously delivered news reports about how this depraved monster, who shared my name but almost none of my habits, was finally being brought to justice. Who was this anti-Semitic, racist, woman-hating thug? How was it that it was only now, on the last Sunday of July 2017, that this ogre was finally being exposed? At least a sense of proportion was in evidence: although North Korea had fired a ballistic missile over Guam the previous night, this vile beast was, quite rightly, the number one news item *around the world*.

I stayed that way, as over the coming days my fellow journalists lined up to heap fuel around my pyre, and on two grounds: one was anti-Semitism, the other misogyny, plus a fusion of the two, memorably encapsulated by the *Independent*'s mob-pleasing description of my 'toxic rant'. In this foam-flecked uproar, facts would have been like a fire extinguisher upon the ceaseless pleasures of the inferno. To be sure, I had long been a critic of extreme feminism, as has almost every woman I know: this does not make me a misogynist, a hater of women, as the foregoing pages testify. Moreover, in addition to being one of the few defenders of Israel in the Irish media, I had repeatedly written about the

Holocaust, I had with equal frequency written about the Irish who served in the war against the Third Reich. Indeed, it was my very knowledge about the Holocaust which was then distorted by a loose grouping of *Guardian*-connected journalists into making me a Holocaust denier. The foremost of these was Roy Greenslade, Professor of Journalism at London City University, and an unapologetic supporter of the Sinn Féin cause: for years, even while working for *The Sunday Times*, no less, he had been a pseudonymous columnist in the Sinn Féin-IRA publication *An Phoblacht*. Moreover, Greenslade is particularly well-respected in Ireland, and he is a close friend of Pat Doherty, a one-time member of the IRA's army council. He is also a regular guest on RTÉ programmes.

What follows was discovered by the Irish social media analytical company, VMGroup, whose splendid MD, Vivienne Mee, upon her own initiative, began to analyse the social media traffic against me. That Sunday, six separate accounts with links to media outlets alleged that I was an anti-Semite and/or a Holocaust denier. Three of these had strong links to the Guardian Media Group, both before and after this episode. The first to allege that I was 'a known Holocaust denier' was Tim Fenton, at 10.49 a.m. Dawn Foster, a writer and broadcaster for *The New York Times*, *The Washington Post*, Sky News, BBC, CNN and *The Guardian*, for which she had had 440 posted pieces, tweeted, 'They hired a Holocaust denier, then commissioned, edited & published an anti-semitic [*sic*] column, very tough on anti-semitism [*sic*].'

However, it was Greenslade who was by far the most powerful and influential of them. At 7.09 that Sunday evening he gloated, 'Kevin Myers adds anti-semitism [*sic*] to his anti-republicanism. Result? Sunday Times drops him. Good.' At 7.37 he added, 'It took the Irish Independent eight years to remove Kevin Myers's article on being a holocaust [*sic*] denier from its website.'

Where in the name of God had all these terrible, life-destroying Holocaust-denying fictions come from? Well, in 2009, there had been talk of the EU copying Austrian and French laws that made it illegal to deny the Holocaust, or that six million Jews had died in it. Since I detest the notion of historical facts being guarded by the criminal law, I had written a column in the *Irish Independent* opposing any such proposal.

Its headline ran: 'I'm a Holocaust denier'. As with the inflammatory headline over the BBC column, it was written by a subeditor. Columnists do not write the headlines over their pieces and are frequently enraged at the parodies of what they had written, not least because these so often serve as a corrupting lens through which readers will view what follows. Admittedly, in the article I said that I was a 'Holocaust denier', but only in this very particular sense: possibly the majority of the victims of the Final Solution were not killed in the death camps such as Auschwitz, Treblinka and Sobibór – where of course millions were stripped, gassed and immolated – but were shot in vast numbers or uncountably worked to death in factories beneath the Harz Mountains. In 1941 *alone*, as German forces poured murderously across Eastern Europe, Wehrmacht and SS soldiers, often aided by local auxiliaries, shot over one million Jews, and some 2.6 million Soviet Jews were slaughtered without going near a camp.

Die Endlösung was industrialised only in its later phases, and from first to last millions of Jews who dwelt east of the Nazi–Soviet 1939 line of partition were individually murdered by thousands of Gentiles, who if they survived the war, mostly went unpunished. The Holocaust as it is widely understood began in early 1942 and depended on trains. Russia's railway gauge is 5 foot, 1,520 mm; that of Poland, home of the main extermination centres, was the Stephenson Standard, namely 4 foot 8½, 1,435 mm. Although much of Poland lay within the Russian empire in the 1840s when the Warsaw–Vienna rail link was constructed, the Polish patriot and industrialist Henryk Łubieński chose a gauge that was compatible with the Stephenson Standard used by Prussia and the Habsburg Empire, rather than that of Russia. A century later, because of that act of metric subversion, it became logistically impossible to transport Soviet Jews by rail to the Polish death camps.

So, from June 1941, many thousands of German soldiers and special police, aided by local Gentiles, became the pioneer, mass-executioners of the Final Solution, while the now forgotten Romanians slaughtered at least 200,000 Jews, without using gas or furnaces at all. Thus the word 'Holocaust' – *burnt entirely in one fire* – does not in any sense communicate the all-encompassing and very personal evil of the Third

Reich and its local accomplices. Indeed, it actually *conceals* what should be an unbearable burden of guilt for tens of thousands of Axis soldiers. This was the central purpose of that column, and back then, *absolutely nobody* complained about it. Not merely were its assertions irreproachable, but some had been gained from a primary source. My history teacher at school, Mr Orton, had told me about the two incompatible gauges, and he had reason to know. Born and raised Herbert Oppenheim to a Jewish family in Vienna, he and his mother escaped before the Gestapo got them: the rest of his family, without exception, vanished up Łubieński's railway to Poland, never to return.

But now, in 2017, eight years after my article appeared, someone found it on the internet and used its headline to 'prove' that I was the opposite of what I actually was. Furthermore, my assertion that the death toll for the Final Solution could not possibly have been *precisely* six million Jews was also isolated as if to confirm the Holocaust-denying lie, whereas I believe that if you include the hundreds of thousands of Jews killed fighting the Nazis – the most decorated ethnic group within the Soviet forces – the Jewish death toll would be well *over* six million. (The magnificent American historian Timothy Snyder, who is highly respected in Israel, puts the *Endlösung* figure at 5.5 million, making him a criminal according to Austrian and French laws.) That is the background story to the malevolent confection that I was a Holocaust denier, and it was this confection that was then tweeted by the initial cluster of online journalists and then re-tweeted and Facebooked and re-Facebooked around the world, with the global mob-hatred thereafter growing exponentially.

This was anti-Semitism at its most disingenuously opportunistic, for it was debasing the lives and deaths of millions of Jews. Post-mortem, they had now become weapons of untruth, to be used not against a genuine Holocaust denier but against one who had spent decades helping to educate the Irish people about the ultimate evils of the Third Reich. Moreover, I had often written about the Irish men and women who had died fighting it, and these included an uncle after whom I have the honour to be named: my mother's brother Captain Kevin Teevan, Royal Army Medical Corps, an Irish Catholic who volunteered to fight the

Third Reich and left his young bones in Africa. My work on this subject was one reason why I was chosen in 2011 (two years after the publication of that column) to make the Remembrance Sunday address in St Patrick's Cathedral before President Higgins – hardly a duty to be given to a Holocaust denier. Furthermore, I had for many years been the foremost defender of Israel in the Irish media – and now the very opposite of what I was and am (and by God will remain) was being promulgated as 'fact' in gathering surges of hyper-hatred through the sewers of social media. These falsehoods have had perhaps irreversible effects on my reputation, for, like barnacle larvae, they have established homes in the minds of London's liberal elite, and upon this metropolitan hull they cling to this day.

Having been advised by the very best counsel, including my lifelong friend and solicitor Dermot Fullam, not to sue all my defamers, for litigation is both astonishingly costly and psychologically ruinous, I chose the conciliatory route with *The Guardian*. I sent its readers' editor, Paul Chadwick, over a dozen of my articles attesting to the irrefutable nature of the Nazis' genocidal ambitions.

'A word-search through the *Irish Times* archive would have shown your reporters that I have written about the Final Solution some twenty times and the Holocaust around fifty times,' I told him. 'Other articles by me on this subject have appeared in *The Sunday Telegraph*, the *Irish Independent*, the *Belfast Telegraph* and *The British Army Review*. The former editor of *The Guardian*, Alan Rusbridger, even asked me to join the staff of your newspaper in part because of my writings on the Holocaust … [and] far from being an anti-Semite, I am regarded with much respect by the Jewish community in Ireland, which is no doubt why several years ago the Jewish Women's Association invited me to be their guest speaker at their annual lunch, an honour I eagerly accepted. Presumably, this is also the reason why the Jewish Representative Council came out unequivocally in my support during the recent controversy … I am proud to think that I have done more to educate the Irish people about the abominations of the Holocaust than any other Irish journalist.'

He replied: 'I agree that the simple description of you as a "Holocaust denier" is not accurate because you are not a Holocaust denier in the usual sense of that term. Your writings indicate that you deny on etymological grounds that "holocaust" is the appropriate word for the Nazis' attempt to exterminate the Jews. You do not deny that the Nazis made such an attempt.'

Yet, despite this admission of my complete innocence, Chadwick refused to take down the lies that I was a Holocaust denier, and when I last checked, they were still in place (albeit with a footnote – for the few who follow such minutiae – saying that I denied these allegations).

In the meantime, J.K. Rowling (with 13 million followers) and Chelsea Clinton (with 2.4 million followers) had joined in the global fray of tweets as west became east and east became west and the fevered cycle of hatred resumed. Meanwhile, various enemies had dug up four columns from long before which were now being recycled as if they were examples of my recent journalism. Mothers of Bastards was one. So too was the inaccurately inflammatory headline, 'Africa has given the world nothing but AIDS', which I didn't write. Another was an even older column, a satire based on an Engels essay about the Irish, in which the word 'Travellers' replaced his original term 'Irish', but with the Engels explanation removed, so what was meant to be satire (rather like Swift's proposal to eat Irish babies) was transformed into an apparent statement of real opinion. But by far the worst was that I was a Holocaust denier.

It was only later that week that I heard that RTÉ's Audrey Carville on Monday's edition of *Morning Ireland* had begun her interview with an Englishman named Gideon Falter, who, to his credit, makes it his business to expose anti-Semitism, by describing me as the author of an article that denied the Holocaust. As we have seen, this was an utter falsehood. He was then goaded into making increasingly inflammatory attacks on me. *Morning Ireland* could have interviewed almost any Irish Jew, who would have declared that I was *not* an anti-Semite. Maurice Cohen of the Jewish Representative Council later that morning issued a statement proclaiming that the allegations that I was an anti-Semite were a gross distortion of the factual record, asserting that my many articles on the Holocaust had played a vital role in educating Irish people about its true horrors. 'More than any other Irish journalist, he has written facts about the Holocaust that would not have otherwise been known by an Irish audience.'

However, true to form, the *Guardian's* report of the Council's statement the next day did not even mention its rejection of the description of me as a Holocaust denier, or its praise for my work in revealing some of the abominable truths of the Final Solution. Meanwhile, in their frenzied pursuit of me, journalists from other newspapers then contacted Alan Shatter, formerly Minister for Justice and Defence, and in both offices amongst the finest the state has ever seen, urging him, as a Jew, to denounce me. He steadfastly refused. His career had been shamefully ended by an earlier lynch-mob; and as both a Jew and a gentleman, he was not going to assist another mob to do the same to me. Other members of Fine Gael showed no such reticence. Thus the new Taoiseach, Leo Varadkar, presumably in response to the shameless falsehoods that had been promulgated on RTÉ, denounced the article – and thereby, of course, its author – as misogynistic and anti-Semitic. He even congratulated *The Sunday Times* for its prompt action – namely, instant dismissal and public vilification without anything like due process. Never before in the history of the state had any taoiseach so uncompromisingly sided with a multinational against an Irish citizen. His words were later echoed elsewhere, with the uncanny fidelity of an agreed policy, by the Tánaiste, Frances Fitzgerald. The last time she and I had met, we had exchanged kisses, and the previous occasion – at St Patrick's Cathedral – as we have seen, she had thanked me for honouring the Irishwomen who had given their lives in the war against Nazism. Soon afterwards, the former leader of the Labour Party, Joan Burton, whose inspired leadership had brought her party close to its deathbed, similarly denounced me for my misogyny and anti-Semitism. However, as with Fitzgerald, the last time I had met Burton was at a Remembrance Sunday service, where we had exchanged kisses. This cannot be said of the National Women's Council, which, quite unkissed, soon added its own heroic denunciations of me.

At 6 a.m. on Tuesday, after my second sleepless night, I accepted an invitation from Mary O'Hagan, a producer with Seán O'Rourke's radio programme on RTÉ. I was almost hallucinating with fatigue as I drove to RTÉ and I felt then and later that the interview was a mess. But some people have said that the authenticity of my regret for offending Claudia Winkleman and Vanessa Feltz was unmistakable (though, of course, my original article had been trying to compliment them, and I note with gratitude that the former has apparently never said a word about the whole sorry affair). Seán asked me about those in the editorial line of command who should have spotted my blunders, and I replied that enough misery had been caused already: these people had mortgages to pay and debts to cover, and nothing would be gained by bringing ruin on them as well as on me.

'I am the captain of my soul and the author of my own misfortunes,' I managed to improvise from Henley's lines. As I drove home, my phone repeatedly rang with calls of congratulation: it was over.

It wasn't. It still isn't.

I am reminded of one of the wartime broadcasts that the recently captured P.G. Wodehouse made on German radio. He said, 'Young men often ask me, "How did you manage to get interned?" My advice to them is as follows: stay just where you are and you'll find you may leave the rest to the Germans.'

It's pretty much the same with a lynch mob. You really don't have to do very much; and soon you'll be profoundly impressed by the sheer imagination, vituperation and venom its members are able to summon to the task. I can say this with some certainty, for that week alone, INM titles had fourteen columns attacking me, and *The Irish Times* nine. However, I trust their authors' pride in their heroic contributions to 21st-century journalism will not in any way be diminished by my confession that I have not managed to read them all. However, it would be churlish of me to deny that Fintan O'Toole's twin attacks on me over the space of four days were amongst the two most successful personalised attacks in Irish journalism of recent decades, as well as being the most imaginative. His columns had long since become catwalks in which he displayed his moral superiority and flaunted the silken sheen of his sanctimony. Since my personal egg-timer was now running low on sand, I usually found that I had better things to do with my remaining granules than endure the pious ejaculations of his endless self-encomia.

His first attack basically asserted that I was a bully and a coward. 'The joy of his career choice is that there are so many groups to afflict,' he proclaimed unctuously. 'All you have to do is to ensure that your targets are people with less power than a well-paid male star columnist. You can take your pick of who to pick on: women, Africans, poor people, Travellers.'

Naturally, he did not provide any specific examples, but just listed some lazy and unsubstantiated generalisations that were already filling the internet. He continued: 'Let's not kid ourselves, Myers would still be in his pulpit if he had stuck to straight misogyny. The keynotes of his column were on familiar themes – that women are to blame for the discrimination they suffer because they work less hard than men, are less charismatic and driven and have the bad taste to have babies.'

This was grotesque. My column was about some of the best-paid people in Britain, none of whom were in any sense victims of discrimination, in the course of which I deplored the absurd, licence-subsidised salaries being paid to men such as Gary Lineker, Chris Evans, Graham Norton and Jeremy Vine, whom I even called 'a jackanapes on steroids'. I used no such language about any of the women. I then added: 'Naturally, the woman-presenters demanding "equality" with the top-paid men are not demanding the same for the Jamaican waitress in the BBC canteen.'

That final line went to the very heart of the issue – and it was certainly not gender-equality. Four days later, O'Toole was back on the job again, though he had never attacked Gerry Adams with such ferocity twice over in under a week, though many would agree that the crimes of the Sinn Féin leader are perhaps marginally greater than mine. This time, O'Toole declared that I had said that a successful woman must be a 'monstrous harridan', a term I have *never* used.

This is what I had written: 'Of course, in their usual, pitifully imitative way, Irish tabloids have tried to create a similar controversy here. That's impossible, because of the ubiquity of Miriam O'Callaghan and Claire Byrne across the airwaves.'

O'Toole's version runs as follows: 'Myers tells women to forget equality and man up – but then complains about the ubiquity of Miriam O'Callaghan and Claire Byrne on the airwaves.'

This is journalistic ventriloquism at its most nastily inventive. I do not intend a full exegesis of this sentence, but let me begin by saying that I don't tell just *women* to forget equality, I tell everyone. No metric exists that will confirm the moral or intellectual equality of any two human beings, and this applies as much to O'Toole, who at one stage was holding down two jobs, one lecturing at Princeton in the US, the other as the *Irish Times* literary editor in Dublin, as it does to the Jamaican tea-lady. I have held these opinions for over a score of years: they can be denounced as wrong, stupid and ill-informed, but cannot be held as proof of my 'misogyny'.

I have never in my life used the term 'man up', and for good reason: women are the bravest people on the planet. No man who had ever endured the bloody and agonising eruptions of childbirth would ever have sex again. Also, I did not 'complain' about the ubiquity of Byrne and O'Callaghan, but about the pathetic attempts by Irish tabloids to replicate the BBC scandal in Ireland. Finally, I went one stage further about RTÉ's women, which O'Toole (I wonder why?) did not quote: 'But it's Marian Finucane that lays bare the self-pitying falsehoods of the BBC women: in 2009, her contract awarded her €520,000 for just two radio programmes a week, even allowing her a long summer break. ... So how was her agent able to negotiate such a deal?'

It was of course the negotiating skills of Finucane's agent – as with the two BBC women – which really explained her high income. That *The Irish Times* allowed O'Toole to falsify my criticism of the tabloids into a criticism of the women broadcasters is a true measure of how far its standards have fallen in recent decades, matched by its circulation, which plummeted from 117,000 in 2006 to 57,000 at the time of writing.

As for the implication that I am a coward who has only picked on the weak and the vulnerable, this comes well from a journalist who after a dozen years of silence about me then chose to attack me only when the lynch mob had already tied me to the stake. But I suppose he had a point about my cowardice. For it is certainly a hallmark of a coward to repeatedly drive through the besieging army around Sarajevo alone and under fire, to walk Beirut's bloody streets after nightfall to deliver copy, and to return to that city after surviving a mock execution. Moreover, it was I who had revealed Martin McGuinness' role in the murder of Patsy Gillespie, who accused Gerry Adams of being responsible for the death of Jean McConville, who had actually *caused* the Smithwick Tribunal into garda collusion with the IRA to come into existence, who was the first to blame the IRA for the Northern Bank robbery. And, finally, it was I who had so severely criticised my newspaper's proprietor Denis O'Brien for suing *The Irish Daily Mail* that the *Irish Independent* had not merely refused to carry my column, but soon thereafter discontinued my employment.

Meanwhile, O'Toole's primary employer (he had several), *The Irish Times*, even at its most inventive, could not possibly repeat the Holocaust-denier lies, because most of my many articles on the subject had been published in its pages. (Indeed, it could of course have used its own archives to prove that I was not such a creature. It did not.) Instead, it concentrated on the allegations of misogyny, which had now become 'facts'. One of the nine attacks on me in its pages was by Kathy Sheridan, headlined: 'The Battle with Myers' hateful views goes back a long way.'

Now, Sheridan declared that I 'denigrated women as dull, mediocre, workshy wasters and shriekers and men as the pitiful victims of feminazi justice'. Newspaper columnists often resort to hyperbolic paraphrasing of other journalists' work, to intensify some innate absurdity they wish to criticise. These words of hers were not of that variety, for they were false in every regard – but how could any ordinary reader, unaware of what I had actually written, have guessed that *The Irish Times* would permit such defamatory fabrications? Not merely had I never said that women were 'dull', 'workshy', 'mediocre', 'wasters' or 'shriekers', or any synonyms thereof, in that column or any other, I simply do not think like that. Indeed, had anyone been able to find a genuine example of such lazy, sexist abuse from me, anywhere, at any time, it would surely have been triumphantly revealed as proof of my misogyny. This did not happen, because no one could make known that which did not exist. In particular, I have *never* used the term 'feminazi': for this was *me* she was talking about, the man who had written more about the Third Reich than any other journalist in the history of *The Irish Times*. I know far too much about the Final Solution to compare its titanic barbarism with anything ever sought, achieved or intended by even the most lunatic of feminists. Though she said much more, let us leave it there: overall, her column was so inept and inaccurate that one of her *Irish Times* colleagues emailed me, strongly urging me to sue. I declined.

Meanwhile, my chums in *The Guardian* were not letting up, and in an interview with Vanessa Feltz, once again called me a Holocaust denier. Its own files would have revealed the opposite. Sixteen years before, in 2001, it had reported the recent discovery of evidence that proved that Francis Stuart was an anti-Semite, which would have destroyed his libel case against me, as reported earlier in these pages. *The Guardian* continued: 'Kevin Myers said he was bitterly disappointed that newspapers were forced to pay out to "this dreadful imposter … It's disgusting that we had to pay out such a sum to a man who obviously held deeply anti-Semitic views and worshipped Hitler … The award to this man was a grotesque miscarriage of justice. What's even more disturbing is to think about all those who defended this Jew-hater and how they exalted him for so long in Ireland."'

That was in the *Guardian*'s own files, which they could have used, as I have done to write these words; and that truthful report of 2001 was written by the same *Guardian* journalist who in 2017 managed not to mention the central truth that the Jewish Representative Council had completely rejected the baseless allegation that I was a Holocaust denier. *The Guardian* also solicited a denunciation of me from Denis MacShane, the former British Labour MP who had been imprisoned for fraudulently claiming parliamentary expenses. This preposterous buffoon knew nothing about me apart from the lies of the social media and whatever else his colourful imagination, so adept at fiddling money from the taxpayer, was capable of conjuring from the ether.

By this time, the normal journalistic appetite for empirical facts should surely have demanded an investigation into how such gross falsehoods had gained international traction, especially since the truth was so readily available. Yet the only journalistic investigation was an internal one within *The Sunday Times,* which must have revealed the emails to me, with which I began this account. These clearly indicated that, from the outset, *The Sunday Times* staff members were aware that

I had mentioned the religion of the two women (though, I repeat, as a compliment, albeit a profoundly foolish one). No public action was taken against anyone in the chain of command, and certainly not against Frank Fitzgibbon, the editor of the Irish edition of the newspaper, which the following Sunday carried an abjectly virulent attack on me, as if Fitzgibbon had been innocent of all responsibility. And after that first Sunday, I never heard from him again.

Meanwhile, my reputation was being systematically destroyed across the world, not merely contemporaneously, but retrospectively also, as the production company that had taken a film option on *Watching the Door* dropped the project. Television programmes looking back on the Troubles now studiously ignored my own perceptions of them, even though I had been a witness to some of its earliest horrors. The destruction of my life had entered the fourth dimension. Not merely was my future being undone; so too was my past.

Thirty-Four

THE NEXT STAGE of the saga proved to be a parable of our times. The political and journalistic classes that had united to destroy me gathered to demand the freedom of Ibrahim Halawa, an Irishman who had been arrested in Egypt after addressing a Muslim Brotherhood rally protesting against the regime in Cairo. He was no doubt a young, innocent abroad, who may not have known that the Brotherhood is one of the most anti-Semitic organisations in existence. In time the Irish government would spend some €2 million on diplomatic moves to secure his release, concluding with the government jet being sent to bring him home. This was the same government that had assisted in my destruction.

But two other forces were at work on my side, both of them employing truth as a weapon. A listener to *Morning Ireland*'s defamations about me, Karl Martin (whom I had at that point never met), had formally protested to RTÉ about the description of me as a Holocaust denier, based solely on his extensive knowledge of my work. RTÉ rejected his objection out of hand. He then took his complaint to the external investigative process, run by the Broadcasting Authority of Ireland. This body agreed with him, declaring that *Morning Ireland* had not dealt fairly with me and had misrepresented my views in a way likely to mislead listeners. But instead of accepting this finding, RTÉ in effect rejected it, issuing a statement that *it was surprised and disappointed with this finding* (my italics) and was considering its response.

This was unprecedented. RTÉ had never, so far as I am aware, rebutted a finding by the Broadcasting Authority. From the outset of this sorry affair, lawyers had warned me against suing the many outlets that had defamed me: actions for libel are often costly and bloody encounters, wherein the plaintiff might well be more ruinously defamed in court by the defending counsel than in the original offence. Such allegations were legally privileged, thus feeding newspapers with their headlines and the pack with their raw meat. Furthermore, a new 'jury' had come into existence, beyond the bounds of the court and the reach of the law, namely, social media. In this lawless sanctuary tweeters could filter and distort the evidence, no matter how outlandishly, solely in order to defame a plaintiff further, and this time the plaintiff would be me.

Despite these certainties, my legal advice now shifted radically. In rejecting the findings of a statutory body, RTÉ had gone too far; now I must sue. But I was given a stark warning. If I lost, the minimum cost to me would be a quarter of a million euro, perhaps rising to over a million, with two million as a possibility and ruin to follow. Nonetheless, I chose to sue; and for two years, I never had a single night's sleep as the horrors of failure faithfully woke me each morning at two, and I would spend the night gazing at the ceiling and worrying what misery I was about to inflict on Rachel. I lost most of the hair on my head, and what remained turned white, while those who had so foully defamed me personally stood to lose nothing – their sleep, their savings or their homes, never mind their hair.

The second process based on truth was represented by the Jews of Ireland, who remained my most loyal supporters. The Jewish Historical Society invited me to chair an international panel discussing the centenary of the Balfour Declaration, during which I (naturally) named every single Irish soldier killed in the liberation of Beersheba and Gaza. The media were told about this. Not one news outlet reported it; the fiction that I was an anti-Semite was quite simply now an Official Truth. I was warmly welcomed to the Holocaust Memorial Day service, and later I gave a lecture about our civilisation's debt to the Jewish people in the Jewish Museum in Dublin before its largest audience ever. This, too, was unreported. The Israeli ambassador, Ze'ev Boker, attended the talk and some weeks later treated me to a hugely enjoyable afternoon-long lunch. Later I was a guest at the embassy's celebrations marking Israel's seventieth birthday. Ze'ev also invited me to a small farewell party in his house before he left for a new appointment in the US. I shall always be grateful for his support and that of Deborah Briscoe, Maurice Cohen, Quentin and Louise Crivon, Yanky and Mona Fachler, David Goldberg, Jonathan Hoffman, Estelle and Seton Menton, Aida Phelops, Alan Shatter, Seth and Nora Tillman, Trevor White and many other Jews whose names might not be mentioned here but are forever recorded in the sacred Hebraic ledger of common decency.

Meanwhile, two women, Professor Eda Sagarra and Penny Perrick (who is Jewish), each sent me a €1,000 cheque to pay for a court action to defend my good name, and these are now framed on my kitchen wall. Many others stood by me, but there are too many to list. The former British military attaché Colonel John Wilson was so appalled at the global idiocy that the moment it erupted he had flown over from England to be with Rachel and me. But officially in Ireland I was *dead*. All government invitations to commemorations for Great War anniversaries ceased, while someone actually went to the trouble of going into the official database to delete my name from the guestlist for the National Day of Commemoration to which I had been invited for over twenty years, and which had been created partly in response to my campaign to honour the Irish dead of the Great War (see page 19). Moreover, the abysmal divisions resulting from a single inept column, in their own strange way, mirrored those that had occurred over Brexit and Trump. Plain people took my side, and though there was not a single formal complaint about me to the Press Ombudsman's Office, there were sixteen complaints about the way I had been treated by *The Sunday Times*.

I was walking near the Botanic Gardens with Eldad Beck, an Israeli journalist who had come to Ireland to report on this curious story of how Ireland's most pro-Israel journalist was being denounced as an anti-Semite by a mob whose usual emanations were anti-Israel. Curious soon got curiouser, as we encountered a Leopold Bloom-like character standing outside a barber's shop, who, on seeing me, and in a very thick Dublin accent, proudly introduced himself as Arthur McGuinness, Dublin's only Jewish barber.

'Kevin Myers is our best friend, and the only supporter in the media that Israel has. Anyway, I thought he was complimenting the old dolls! We're a trading people: that's what we've always been. Look at me – a barber's shop here, and I sell second-hand furniture round the back!'

Eldad murmured to me: 'Either Mossad set this up, or you did.'

While we were talking, passers-by came over to shake me by the hand and wish me well. I have never received a single word of abuse from the public, only words of sympathy, accompanied by much mourning over the death of free speech, slain by the despotism of political correctness, in full view of a compliant and even exultant media. In this new political order, the internet has become the Unter den Linden of our new Reich: Facebook's sunless boulevards echo to the stamp of marching feet, while beneath them faecal hatred can be heard sloshing through Twitter's stinking sewers. Silent submission rules: for cowardice has always been the most vital social currency in all despotisms, since it is the base metal from which tyrannies can machine-stamp the coinage of obedience, timidity, suppression or exile.

The double-standards now rampant through the Irish media became spectacularly evident sometime later when Dr Ali Selim of the Islamic Cultural Centre appeared on RTÉ television. 'I am not an advocate of female genital mutilation,' he proclaimed, 'but I am advocate of female circumcision. We see female circumcision in the same way as we see male circumcision. It might be needed by one person and not another, and it has to be done by a doctor and practised in a safe environment ... Cosmetic surgeries, if needed, should not be confused with female genital mutilation.'

Far from this abominable aspiration – *cosmetic surgery to a little girl's genitals?* – causing feminist uproar, there was instead a thunderous silence from the National Council of Women, that august body which had so roundly denounced me for observations that were milk and water in comparison. Naturally, Fintan O'Toole managed to find mitigating uncertainty where there had actually been crystal clarity, referring to Selim's 'highly ambivalent remarks about female genital mutilation'. But there was nothing remotely ambivalent about Selim's declaration that he was 'an advocate of female circumcision'. Nor was there about the original stance of the Islamic Cultural Centre where Selim worked, which initially had said that 'female circumcision must be recommended and defined by a professional medical doctor' (a declaration it later withdrew). No media or political denunciations followed this double-endorsement of this abomination, which was now not even just a theoretical threat: official estimates were that at least 5,000 females in Ireland had by then undergone genital mutilation – though clearly, these irreversible horrors were as nothing compared to a few clumsy words from Kevin Myers. And the elegant but extraordinary coincidence to all this was that one of the poems that had so moved and angered me in 1991, when I had written an enthusiastic column about the poet Mary O'Donnell, had been about female genital mutilation. Another poem in that same collection had been about the gorge of Babi Yar in the Ukraine, where in September 1941, German troops shot nearly 34,000 Jews over just two days. This had been my very point in that 'Holocaust-denying' column: the Germans had started the extermination of Europe's Jews well before Auschwitz had begun its own programme of mass-murder by gas.

But facts and proportionality were now irrelevant, and it soon transpired that my initial belief that the hysteria over my column would have dissipated by 2018, the centenary of the end of the Great War, was hopelessly naïve. An internet lynching is not bound by the usual temporal limitations of human affairs but exists in another dimension that knows neither amnesia, kindness nor exhaustion. I was now almost totally excluded from all media discussions on Ireland and the Great War, especially on RTÉ, where there could be no doubt that I had introduced the topic into Irish life. However, the admirable Donal Croghan of Kilkenny County Council invited me to the unveiling of the city's splendid new war memorial, and afterwards the local Army commander, Major General Kieran Brennan, asked me to the barracks for tea – unsurprisingly, for the Defence Forces have individually been amongst my stoutest friends.

But that was it. The only mention of me in *The Irish Times* in connection with the Great War was a sneering reference to a category of self-evidently loathsome people described as 'the likes of Kevin Myers'. Nor was I included on the government guestlist for the Armistice Day ceremony at Glasnevin Cemetery starting at 8 a.m. However, after my lovely and ever-loyal Rachel tweeted angrily about my exclusion, and literally at the last minute for acceptances to be accepted, at 4.00 p.m., on Friday, 9 November, I received an email inviting me to the ceremony.

As dawn rose at Glasnevin that Remembrance Sunday, droves of people came up to thank me for my work over the years. I left early, because I wanted to be at Islandbridge by 11 a.m., for the British Legion ceremony. However, as I walked towards my car, I found its exit blocked by two platoons of soldiers doing a last-minute practice. Their commanding officer saw me and came over to introduce himself.

'Are you leaving already? We wouldn't be here but for you.'

'I was hoping to get to Islandbridge. My car's over there ...'

'You go and get it. I'll clear the way for you.'

He moved his soldiers then radioed ahead to allow me through the roadblocks surrounding the cemetery. The story was much the same at the three venues where I spent the rest of the day: Islandbridge, St Patrick's Cathedral and the British Military Cemetery at Grangegorman. Strangers shook my hand and told me about their family members who had served in the two wars. Now, finally, they could speak of them in public, largely because of my efforts. Nor was this embrace confined to Dublin: later that month, William Shawcross, the historian son of the great Nuremberg prosecutor of the Nazi war criminals, invited me to London for the annual Anglo-Israeli dinner, where I was warmly welcomed, most particularly by the historian Lord Bew and Dean Godson, one of the most eminent Jews of London.

Normal service was resumed shortly thereafter, when the French government made the *Irish Times* journalist Ronan McGreevy a Chevalier des Arts et des Lettres for his work on the Irish and the Great War. His first article on the subject had appeared in 2014, thirty-four years after my inaugural piece and three years after President McAleese had, while speaking to Queen Elizabeth, credited me with keeping alive the memory of the Irish dead. The *Irish Times* report on McGreevy's award made no mention of my efforts down the decades. Several people whom I know – including the former Taoiseach and later EU ambassador to Washington, John Bruton – wrote to the letters' page of *The Irish Times*, pointing out who had actually been responsible for the reclaiming of that part of our history. None of these letters were published. For a former Taoiseach and senior EU diplomat to protest so publicly over a matter unrelated to his own career is almost unprecedented, but quite without a precedent of any kind is a newspaper's decision to conceal that protest.

For I was still *persona non grata* in the Dublin goldfish bowl. While meeting my steadfastly loyal literary agent, Jonathan Williams, at the Royal Marine Hotel Dún Laoghaire, three former *Irish Times* journalists emerged from the hotel's Hardy Bar. I rose and greeted them, identifying myself, as a matter of courtesy. All three glided by me, each gently flicking away my outstretched hand. At a public function when I introduced myself to a woman of distinction in the public service, her face instantly turned hard and set, and her handshake was as tentative as if I had asked her to caress my liver. On another occasion, I was attending a book launch in Dublin, where some academics, all of whom I knew, simply turned their backs on me, while others pretended not to see me, their eyes sliding sightlessly past my unwelcome form.

But the real Ireland remained warm and welcoming – for that very same evening, I went to Kevin Street Garda Station, for a talk about the RIC and DMP men who had served in the Great War. No less than twenty gardaí, from superintendent down, came over to shake my hand and congratulate me on my work. These were the patriots who had chosen to serve the state and the Irish people, and they were not going to be influenced by the passing vapidities of the mob.

In November 2019, I was called to a meeting of my counsel and RTÉ's at the Four Courts. In preparation for this, and feeling that there must be something missing in our case, I contacted the hero of this episode, Karl Martin, and asked him to send me RTÉ's correspondence. He did so. The conclusion of the letter to him from RTÉ began thus (allegedly quoting me):

'I'm a Holocaust denier.'
These are Mr Myers' own words. He may have qualified his headline statements by then writing that there was certainly genocide waged against the Jews by the Nazis in what he describes

as 'one of the most satanic operations in world history'. But if he is being described around the world as a 'Holocaust denier', it is only because he described himself as such. We will not therefore be apologising to Mr Myers.

It is hard to imagine an utterance that is more replete with oxymoronic arrogance and idiotic hubris than that: the very quintessence of licence-subsidised RTÉ-ology. I passed it to my legal team.

My personal strategy at this point was that any settlement in my favour must include an undertaking by RTÉ to include it in the main news of the day. Thinking that the Four Courts meeting was the opening round of several such encounters, and would accordingly be brief, I put just €2 in the parking meter. But when my splendid team turned up – my solicitor Eamonn Denieffe (Dermot Fullam having retired) and my barristers Declan Doyle SC and Jennifer Goode – their air of confidence was unmistakable. Resolution was at hand – but so too, I felt, were the car-clampers. So distracted was I at this trivial prospect that I completely forgot to suggest that any settlement must involve a guarantee that RTÉ News' main bulletins would report the outcome. Without these stipulations, RTÉ agreed to meet our financial demands, on two conditions: the terms would be confidential, and they would choose the timing of the announcement.

Ludicrously, I was nearly as relieved to find my car had not been clamped as I was at the settlement. But once I got home, I realised I (and I alone) had made a grave mistake, and contacted my legal team: had we reserved a veto on the timing of the announcement? We had not. I immediately knew that RTÉ would make it on the Friday morning ten days hence, when local government elections were taking place and when newspaper comment-columns for Saturday and Sunday would already be full.

I was right. *Morning Ireland* broadcast an apology shortly before 9 a.m. on the Friday. It was, however, read with real sincerity by Brian Dobson, a broadcaster of great gravitas and unimpeachable integrity. It ran:

On July 31st 2017, *Morning Ireland* introduced an item that suggested that Kevin Myers was a Holocaust denier. This was untrue and defamatory of Mr Myers' character. *Morning Ireland* acknowledges that Mr Myers has for over three decades repeatedly testified to the scale and wickedness of Hitler's Final Solution. *Morning Ireland* acknowledges the damage done to Mr Myers' reputation. We regret this and unreservedly apologise.

But the moment the recorded apology was over, *Morning Ireland* went live to Audrey Carville, the broadcaster who had been responsible for the original Holocaust-denial defamation, and who was now chirpily promoting that evening's *Late Late Show*. This was less likely to have been accidental but instead was serving as her on-air redemption, even though her words that Monday morning had done me grave damage, as well as costing the station a small fortune. Sure enough, *RTÉ News*, which in 2017 had repeatedly revelled in my personal ordeal and later that year – almost joyously – announced the station's rejection of the Broadcasting Authority's finding in my favour, never mentioned either the settlement or a parallel statement from my solicitors in any of its bulletins.

Similarly, the independent broadcasting outlets, including TV3, Newstalk and Today FM, stayed silent on my victory. The various radio magazine programmes, which for a month had trampled all over me, never whispered a word about my legal triumph. Even more incredibly, *The Irish Times*, for which I had written most of my pieces on the Holocaust, and which had then played a significant part in the destruction of my good name in 2017, also ignored the settlement. The same outlets then managed to overlook a jubilant statement from my friends in the British Legion in Ireland, hailing my legal success.

The settlement would have been newsworthy anyway, but what should have made it the headline story that it never became was RTÉ's financial position: this was so dire that the station had had to mount a fire-sale of its art collection *that very same week*. This netted RTÉ some €150,000, every penny of which, and far more, would now be squandered on settling my case. Not one newspaper connected the two events or joined the dots to see that RTÉ had preferred to lose money in their ideological quest against me than tell the truth. Whereas, from the outset, I would have settled for an apology and a retraction, without damages. RTÉ's aversion to the truth was shared by *The Guardian*, to which Eamonn, my solicitor, had sent a statement detailing my complete victory, of which not a word was printed.

Other journalists proved to be less reserved, as three more (but only three) now gallantly emerged to proclaim my innocence in public: Eoghan Harris and Niamh Horan in *The Sunday Independent* and Lionel Shriver in *The Spectator*, to join the few who had already done so: Ruth Dudley Edwards, Mary Kenny and Ben Lowry. But from the massed ranks of my former colleagues in the two islands, silence. There are of course different kinds of silence, and for different reasons: around the same time as my destruction, a quasi-Nazi lie in *The Daily Telegraph* asserted that only three national banks in the world were not controlled by the Rothschild family. The *Telegraph* took down the falsehood, and while it and its author were forgotten, the social media hounds and newspaper-pack that had burned me alive never uttered a word of complaint. And then, not long afterwards, the *Irish Times* journalist Kitty Holland responded to the UK election outcome with the following tweet, 'It's a great result for Zionism. Monsters are roaring their delight.' She subsequently deleted the tweet, and then tweeted an apology three days' later: 'Last Friday morning, in the aftermath of the UK elections, I posted a tweet on this account which resulted in a great deal of upset. I apologise sincerely for the hurt caused,' but she did *not* apologise for having made the clear equivalence between Zionists and monsters, which makes the apology almost meaningless. Result: nothing. No comeback, no frenzy, no lynching, and her position in the newspaper remained unchanged.

Amazed at the silence of *The Irish Times* over my victory, I wrote a joint letter to the newspaper's Board and its Trust to enable both bodies to consider what I have reported here.

'*The Irish Times*' energetic role in my public lynching in July/August 2017 violated the newspaper's historic obligations towards objectivity and fairness,' I wrote, before informing him of the newspaper's subsequent failure to report RTÉ's recent settlement with me: 'This was a clear breach of *The Irish Times*' obligation to inform its readers of matters of national interest. Though RTÉ's self-inflicted economic tribulations are properly a matter of public concern, the station nonetheless gratuitously and recklessly brought this case on itself, resulting in further grave financial losses. This made my case a major news story – yet incredibly, no *Irish Times* journalist even enquired of me as to how much the settlement had cost the station. Moreover, since RTÉ News similarly *never* reported the outcome, most Irish people remain ignorant of it today. This is a scandalous violation of the news-responsibilities of both media outlets.'

I finished with these words: 'I do not need to tell you of the great and noble traditions embodied within the newspaper and which the Trust and the Board are charged with protecting. This letter is written in the hope that some public restitution of the reputations of both myself and of the newspaper you have the honour to serve is still possible.'

Perhaps the letter got lost in the Christmas post, because neither body favoured me with an acknowledgement, never mind the detailed reply that traditional courtesy demanded. Whatever the reason, now I knew that the moral core of the newspaper whose newsroom I had first entered that wet February morning in 1979, and whose values had enriched the Irish nation like no other force in its history and for which I had felt such infuriated love for so long, was now no more.

Meanwhile Official Ireland was now white-water rafting into a terrifying future on currents that had been unleashed by the endless propitiation of the IRA, by the Anglophobia that was legitimised by the disdainful, often racist media coverage of Brexit, and by the many fictions that had run through the decade of centenaries. All these served to sanitise republican atrocities of the past, not just of a century before, but of more recent decades also. Skilfully mastering these currents were the helmsmen of the IRA army council, their objective now to direct the anger of ordinary people, so many of whom had been crushed by austerity, against the political and administrative classes whose incomes and pensions had largely remained intact through the recession. Fortunately, not even Sinn Féin's leaders had grasped the degree to which they had captured the popular imagination of the Republic's electorate, for had they done so and doubled the number of candidates standing in the general election of 2020, they would probably have triumphed. Sinn Féin would then have been able to form a government without coalition partners, and both An Garda Síochána and the Republic's Defence Forces would have been ultimately answerable to a political party which has *never* severed its links to the IRA's army council. They could then have had unhindered access to the cornucopia of the state's intelligence files. As it was, Sinn Féin emerged as the largest party in the island of Ireland, and any hope that they might at least have buried their sordid war in the moral sewer to which it belonged was soon rebutted by their leader Mary Lou McDonald, who declared that had she been old enough when it was underway, she too would have enlisted in the ranks of the IRA to do her gallant bit.

Incredibly, Leo Varadkar, the medical doctor and Fine Gael leader whose ineptitude, hubris and vacuous posturing had helped to more than halve his party's representation in the Dáil from seventy-six seats in 2011 to thirty-five in 2020, was then rescued from the garbage-heap of history by the timely arrival of the COVID-19 virus. This allowed him another four months of unelected and almost presidential governance over an economically battered and epidemiologically bewildered people, and with almost nightly television broadcasts to burnish his reputation, plus the promise of a few hours a week of clinical work, his approval ratings accordingly soared. It is an ill-wind indeed, even when bearing a plague.

So it could fairly be said that my journalistic career had ended in almost complete failure, yet a few modest truths still proclaimed themselves within that qualifier, *almost.* The most important was that ordinary people (and of course Rachel, my life and my love, and our two families) have sided with me throughout this horror show, as most particularly have the Jews of Ireland, alongside an unwavering band of friends whose smallness in number is inversely proportionate to their decency, courage and moral worth. The second is that only moral nonentities join a lynching: the larger the mob, and mine was huge, the more contemptible are its members and the tinier are their scruples. The third truth is that even as the smoke lingers from the fires which destroyed my reputation, the more discerning quills of history are being sharpened. It is not me they will damn, but those who held the burning tapers to the kindling at my feet and whose fervent bellows fanned the flames into an inferno. It is the heretic that makes the fire, not he who burns in it, and that is how this sorry affair will ultimately be remembered. Moreover, as the viral pandemic that had rescued Varadkar's reputation now spreads vast personal tragedy and economic ruin across the world during the second half of 2020, I finally understand how the vanity of ambition and the folly of pride are less than the dust from which we came and to which we shall unfailingly return. And in my personal twilight, I also know that I have won my battle, my long, long battle, and public remembrance in Ireland can never be the same again. So, try as it has and try as it might, and try again as it surely will, Official Ireland can never take that away from me.

We *will* remember them.